# Raise Your Voices

# Raise Your Voices

## *Inquiry, Discussion, and Literacy Learning*

Edited by
Thomas M. McCann
Andrew Bouque
Dawn Forde
Elizabeth A. Kahn
Carolyn C. Walter

ROWMAN & LITTLEFIELD
Lanham • Boulder • New York • London

Published by Rowman & Littlefield
An imprint of The Rowman & Littlefield Publishing Group, Inc.
4501 Forbes Boulevard, Suite 200, Lanham, Maryland 20706
www.rowman.com

Unit A, Whitacre Mews, 26-34 Stannary Street, London SE11 4AB

British Library Cataloguing in Publication Information Available

**Library of Congress Cataloging-in-Publication Data**

Names: McCann, Thomas M., author.
Title: Raise your voices : inquiry, discussion, and literacy learning / edited by Thomas M. McCann, Andrew Bouque, Dawn Forde, Elizabeth A. Kahn, Carolyn C. Walter.
Description: Lanham : Rowman & Littlefield, an imprint of The Rowman & Littlefield Publishing Group, Inc., [2019] | Includes bibliographical references.
Identifiers: LCCN 2018032744 (print) | LCCN 2018039167 (ebook) | ISBN 9781475844306 (electronic) | ISBN 9781475844283 (cloth : alk. paper) | ISBN 9781475844290 (pbk. : alk. paper)
Subjects: LCSH: Language arts (Secondary) | Interaction analysis in education. | Inquiry-based learning.
Classification: LCC LB1631 (ebook) | LCC LB1631 .R23 2019 (print) | DDC 428.0071/2—dc23
LC record available at https://lccn.loc.gov/2018032744

Printed in the United States of America

# Contents

# Foreword

Discussion is a foundational medium through which we are able to externalize inner explorations and hopefully expand our explorations through dialogic interactions with others (Haroutunian-Gordon, 2009). Discussion remains foundational across contexts—family life, peer social networks, community settings, and certainly in schools. In the context of schooling, there is substantive research documenting how rare it is to find routine instantiations of rich dialogic discussion (Applebee, Langer, Nystrand, & Gamoran, 2003; Nystrand, 1997). This important volume takes up that challenge in several important ways.

First, the authors are deeply entrenched in both theory and practice. They demonstrate clearly that decontextualized theory is insufficient to inform practice. Teaching is a complex intellective endeavor, much like medicine, that requires adaptive expertise (Hatano & Inagaki, 1986) in taking foundational empirically established theory in multiple domains and translating such foundational knowledges to be responsive to the ubiquitous diversity of classrooms and other sites of practice. This diversity presents itself along multiple dimensions: individual personality differences among students, differences in skill sets and dispositions, differences in linguistic repertoires, differences in the cultural contexts of students' lives outside of schools or official sites of practice, and differences across disciplines being taught (Lee, 2007). Then there are contextual differences in terms of school climate and accountability expectations at multiple levels (Cohen, Spillane, & Peurach, 2018). The chapters in this volume situate both foundational principles for designing, orchestrating, and following up on discussions and the practical multidimensional decisions that teachers must make in such work. Each chapter is replete with examples from real classrooms or other settings to illustrate and ground foundational principles for discussions.

Across the chapters, the range of problems with which teachers must wrestle are addressed. The chapters tackle the intersections across reading, writing, speaking, reasoning, and interestingly listening by all parties. The complexities of hearing what others are saying present real dilemmas for teachers and students, these participants in discussions who may enter the dialogue situated differentially with regard to power. These issues around critical listening and dispositions to wrestle with complexity are essential for preparing students for participation in democratic debate (Gutman, 1999; Hess, 2009). Such issues are also addressed thoughtfully in these chapters. The chapters also consider a range of learners—English language learners and diverse learners with special needs—as well as sites of learning including digital medium and prisons. It is precisely the breadth and depth of tackling this multidimensional space around designing, coordinating, and following up on discussion that signal the importance of this volume. Too often calls for promoting discussion fall back on simplistic conceptions of the work and assume that particular techniques are sufficient in themselves. The real-world examples provided across chapters illustrate the complexities that arise in discussion that require multidimensional breadth and depth of knowledge on the part of those who seek to design rich discussions.

What is not always made explicit is the influence of the research Dr. George Hillocks Jr. conducted on teaching literary response and writing in both narrative and argument genres (Hillocks, 1971, 1986, 1989, 1995, 1999, 2005, 2007, 2016; Hillocks & Ludlow, 1984; Smith & Hillocks, 1988). A number of the authors, including me, were directly trained by Professor Hillocks, who passed away in 2014, and others were indirectly influenced by his work through their professional networks. Hillocks led one of the most important teacher training programs in the country, the master of arts in teaching (MAT) program at the University of Chicago. Hillocks's MAT program was deeply consequential for several reasons. MAT students taught by him would work under his tutelage on theory and then plan lessons based on foundational theories to implement at Ray School, a Chicago Public School down the street from the university. As they sought to actually teach lessons, all members of the cohort were present along with Hillocks, after which they would return to the university to deconstruct what had happened. This practice—unusual in teacher-education programs where quite often there are disconnects between what teacher-education students learn in their university classes and what they experience in isolated student teaching practicums—socialized a professional disposition to engage in continuous formal study and to be reflective on one's practice. From this work evolved a network of researchers and teacher researchers who continue to collaborate and engage in professional reflection through a listserv that has been maintained since 2003. Across the chapters in this book, there is attention to how to prepare students to make judgments about constructs and themes they will meet in formal texts to follow through what Hillocks called gateway activities: what is entailed in supporting students in constructing arguments, or what is entailed in planning for the interrogation of generative questions or in planning the sequencing of texts. In many ways, this volume is a testament to the power of Hillocks's breadth and depth of foundational research, rooted in theory and practice.

Carol D. Lee, PhD
Edwina S. Tarry Professor of Education and Social Policy
Northwestern University

## REFERENCES

Applebee, A. N., Langer, J. A., Nystrand, M., & Gamoran, A. (2003). Discussion-based approaches to developing understanding: Classroom instruction and student performance in middle and high school English. *American Educational Research Journal, 40*(3), 685–730.

Cohen, D. K., Spillane, J. P., & Peurach, D. J. (2018). The dilemmas of educational reform. *Educational Researcher, 47*(3), 204–212.

Gutman, A. (1999). *Democratic education*. Princeton, NJ: Princeton University Press.

Haroutunian-Gordon, S. (2009). *Learning to teach through discussion: The art of turning the soul*. New Haven, CT: Yale University Press.

Hatano, G., & Inagaki, K. (1986). Two courses of expertise. In H. W. Stevenson, H. Azuma, & K. Hakuta (Eds.), *Child development and education in Japan*. New York: Freeman.

Hess, D. E. (2009). *Controversy in the classroom: The democratic power of discussion*. New York: Routledge.

Hillocks, G., Jr. (1971). *Observing and writing*. Urbana, IL: National Council of Teachers of English.

Hillocks, G., Jr. (1986). *Research on written composition: New directions for teaching*. Urbana, IL: National Conference on Research in English/ERIC Clearinghouse on Reading and Communication Skills.

Hillocks, G., Jr. (1989). Literary texts in classrooms. In P. W. Jackson & S. Haroutunian-Gordon (Eds.), *From Socrates to software: The teacher as text and the text as teacher*. Chicago: National Society for the Study of Education.

Hillocks, G., Jr. (1995). *Teaching writing as reflective practice*. New York: Teachers College Press.

Hillocks, G., Jr. (1999). *Ways of thinking, ways of teaching*. New York: Teachers College Press.

Hillocks, G., Jr. (2005). Preface: What have I tried to teach my students. In T. McCann, L. Johannessen, E. Kahn, P. Smagorinsky, & M. Smith (Eds.), *Reflective teaching, reflective learning* (pp. xxii–xxvii). Portsmouth, NH: Heinemann.

Hillocks, G., Jr. (2007). *Narrative writing: Learning a new model for teaching*. Portsmouth, NH: Heinemann.

Hillocks, G., Jr. (2016). The territory of literature. *English Education, 48*(22), 109–126.

Hillocks, G., Jr., & Ludlow, L. (1984). A taxonomy of skills in reading and interpreting fiction. *American Educational Research Journal, 21*, 7–24.

Lee, C. D. (2007). *Culture, literacy and learning: Taking bloom in the midst of the whirlwind*. New York: Teachers College Press.

Nystrand, M. (1997). *Opening dialogue: Understanding the dynamics of language and learning in the English classroom*. New York: Teachers College Press.

Smith, M., & Hillocks, G., Jr. (1988). Sensible sequencing: Developing knowledge about literature text by text. *English Journal* (October), 44–49.

# Acknowledgments

We, and many high school students, are fortunate to know several teachers who engage learners every day in extensive discussions about substantive matters. These discussions not only support literacy learning but also immerse students in the essentially democratic and inclusive processes of collaborative problem solving. We are grateful that a number of these teachers have accepted our invitation to share insights about their classroom practices in the chapters of this book.

We could not have conceived of a book like this one without the influence of George Hillocks Jr. and Martin Nystrand. Hillocks taught us that *inquiry* was the process that most supported adolescents in learning to write coherent, elaborated compositions and to read complex texts critically. In Hillocks's view, inquiry necessarily involves students working together to explore areas of doubt and to construct meaning by closely observing objects and behaviors and carefully examining data. Hillocks taught us how to plan strategically so that students could sustain dialogue over time and enjoy the experiences of community and discovery. Nystrand helped us to distinguish the types of discourse in the classroom—the differences between *recitation* and *authentic discussion* and the differences between the teacher-dominated talk and the learner-involved dialogue. Nystrand helped us to recognize the teacher's moves that advance dialogue and the teacher's stances that discourage dialogue.

The contributors to this book are only a small sample of the many valued friends and colleagues who have influenced our thinking about classroom discourse and literacy learning. We are grateful to our old friends Larry R. Johannessen, Peter Smagorinsky, Michael W. Smith, and Joseph Flanagan for helping to shape our thinking about teaching English language arts. We owe a debt to our university colleagues Lara Crowley, Michael Day, John V.

Knapp, Brad Peters, Judith Pokorny, Kathleen Renk, and Jessica Reyman for their influence on how we think about teaching and teacher preparation and for their support for our research endeavors. We also thank school leaders from Adlai E. Stevenson High School for their support for our efforts to engage students daily in meaningful dialogue: Dr. Eric Twaddle, Dr. Gwen Zimmerman, and Troy Gobble.

We appreciate that our students and teaching colleagues at several schools have shaped our thinking about classroom discourse, including students and teachers at Maine East High School, the University of Chicago Laboratory Schools, York Community High School, James B. Conant High School, West Chicago High School, and Adlai E. Stevenson High School. We are indebted also to our teacher-education students at Northern Illinois University for their insights into the kinds of issues and forums that encourage adolescents to deliberate with each other about consequential matters.

We are very grateful to Carol D. Lee for her insightful and generous foreword. As usual, Carol is especially supportive of classroom teachers who follow inclusive inquiry practices to advance the language learning and critical thinking of all students. We also thank editors Sarah Jubar and Emily Tuttle from Rowman & Littlefield. We are grateful for their appreciation of the merits of the project and for their attentive work in advancing the book from initial conception to finished product. We appreciate also the contributions of the many hands of the editorial and production staff at Rowman & Littlefield for their careful attention to the refinement of a collection of diverse voices.

# Introduction

This is a book about classroom discussion. We understand that discussions often extend beyond the classroom, especially into digital platforms. But we are mostly concerned with the discussions that engage learners in the class-room, even when those discussions continue in the halls of the school and online. We might call these discussions *curriculum conversations* or *instructional conversations*, as we think about the many ways that students learn from talking to each other.

Early in our teaching careers, we witnessed some impressive instances of dialogue in other teachers' classrooms, when learners contributed eagerly to lively exchanges. In most instances, these were explorations about interpretations and evaluations of specific works of literature. We understood from our teacher-preparation courses that discussion was a good thing—and perhaps an essential element in literacy learning—but we also knew that we had difficulty in realizing the kind of classroom dialogue that we admired.

We certainly came prepared for class with lists of questions and often provided the questions to students to "guide" their reading and to ready them for discussion. Of course, these "discussions" seldom transcended above recitations of recall about the details from a text. Certainly the problem might have been in the questions we asked, but we judge that our failures were more complicated than that.

Even when we posed interpretive questions, we had specific answers in mind. We confess to having attempted, through our sequence of questions, to lead students down a path to our own understanding about a text. When few students contributed or the room fell uncomfortably quiet, we felt a need to jump in and answer our own questions. Despite our many failed attempts at some sort of classroom dialogue, we knew that discussion could be much better. After all, we had seen wonderful exchanges in the classrooms of other teachers, and we wanted our classrooms to be more like these. We needed to learn much about how to foster sustained, meaningful dialogue.

Over the years, we have sought—through our reading, observations, data collection and analysis, interviews, conversations with peers, and reflection—to learn how to make discussions exhilarating for our students and powerful experiences for their literacy learning. Drawing from the contributions of many experienced teachers we admire, we share in this book what we have learned about planning, initiating, sustaining, extending, and assessing lively and productive oral discourse in our classrooms.

We hope that the chapters in this collection support classroom teachers in their own efforts to cultivate learning environments where students are eager to talk to each other as part of the program of literacy learning. The contributors to this collection share classroom vignettes and insights about practice in many contexts. All of the contributors are currently or have been classroom teachers, and each emphasizes a different element that is part of the complex of classroom conversation. We expect that readers can find areas of emphasis and classroom contexts that resonate and that will serve teachers in their efforts to promote dialogue.

While this collection offers many distinct voices and widely varied teaching situations, all of the contributors honor the following principles about authentic discussion, whether or not they refer to these principles overtly:

1. *Discussion is different from recitation.* While recitation has a place for affirming facts and assessing students' recall, *authentic discussions* engage learners in a variety of other procedures beyond recall—for example, summary, synthesis, analysis, and argument—that are important "moves" for literacy learning. We define *authentic discussion* after Nystrand (1997) as discussion about questions that do not have pre-specified answers.
2. *Discussion supports literacy learning.* As Britton (1983) famously noted, "Reading and writing float on a sea of talk" (p. 11). Our work with language begins with talking, and it is possible to design conversational experiences that will immerse learners in the kind of intellectual moves that support reading and writing development.
3. *Inquiry drives discussion, and discussion is an integral part of inquiry.* Inquiry introduces areas of doubt, and learners can navigate through these areas by grappling with their peers about the questions and problems that represent the line of inquiry. We don't direct students to turn to a peer and discuss the first topic that comes to mind; with attention to students' interests, we introduce substantive problems that invite a series of connected conversations among peers.
4. *Everyone should feel included, valued, and comfortable in discussions.* It is unlikely that learners will participate willingly in discus-

sions if they feel incompetent or disrespected. In classrooms that are supportive and safe, students enjoy interacting with their peers and generally have a positive experience with their learning.

5. *Learners can participate in discussion in a variety of ways.* We are all different. Some students will be the first to join the conversation, while others hold back until they have heard what others have said. Students "participate" by listening critically to others, by indicating both subtly and explicitly their reactions, and by contributing vocally when they can (Schultz, 2009).

6. *The focus for discussion should be matters of some consequence to learners.* We know that students participate eagerly in discussions when they are tackling problems of some significance to them. In fact, when students harbor strong feelings about a problem or concern, it is hard to keep them from talking.

7. *Discussions should not be rare and isolated experiences but should connect and build on each other as supports for inquiry.* Any productive conversation supports literacy learning; but when discussions build on each other over a series of days or weeks, students are exploring the depth and breadth of a problem, allowing for synthesis and analysis of several related texts. These experiences are part of critical thinking.

8. *Discussions can take a variety of forms and, ideally, extend beyond the classroom.* We think of "discussions" primarily as spoken language events, but we also "discuss" in our writing, both in print and online. The discussions that begin online can continue in the classroom, and the classroom discussions can extend online.

9. *Productive discussions seldom occur by chance.* We have perhaps all experienced "teachable moments," when opportunities for discussion present themselves. More often, teachers plan carefully for productive discussions that support target learning outcomes, connect across several class meetings, and engage all learners.

10. *Teachers and students can learn how to engage in authentic discussion through reflection on practice and through renewed efforts to make discussions as authentic and meaningful as possible.* While conversation seems intuitive, the facilitation of discussions is a learned skill for teachers, and participation in discussions is a learned skill for students. Teachers and students benefit from conscious attempts to look at what they have said and reflect on ways to make discussions better—that is, more inclusive, more purposeful, more civil, and more productive.

Not only do we want the users of this book to access the sample learning activities and the recommended strategies for promoting discussion, but also we want teachers to witness what happens during discussion to reveal how, through extensive oral interchanges, students immerse themselves in many literacy and critical-thinking procedures that serve learners in their development as readers and writers. In other words, we are confident that the contributors to this book will show the reader how to plan, prompt, sustain, and evaluate substantive classroom conversations, and will reveal why such conversations are important.

We have organized the several contributions under four categories.

First, we want to establish what authentic looks like in practice and show how it is possible to avoid turning a potentially vibrant line of inquiry into transmission, indoctrination, or recitation. In this first part, "Inviting Conversations," we demonstrate some basic functions of discussion to support writing development and the critical reading of complex texts.

A second part, "Reflecting on Practice to Foster Engagement and Learning," offers examples of how teachers are able to connect a series of discussions into a coherent line of inquiry. This second part includes attention to the potential for the use of digital means to support and extend discussion, and invites the reader to consider ways to assess how students are working together and to judge the efficacy of the discussion activities to advance learning toward significant literacy goals.

In a third part of the book, "Expanding Conversations," contributors report on ways in which they have included all learners in discussions. The chapters show how it is possible to bring English learners into the conversation and how to draw on the stores of knowledge and special talents of differently abled adolescents to enrich discussions. Our contributors also recognize that there are many ways to contribute to discussion, and the learners who seem least inclined to speak in front of a whole class of peers can demonstrate in a variety of ways how they react to the contributions of others and can advance their own ideas in both subtle and graphic ways.

The last part, "Including Everyone in Conversations," acknowledges that teachers have to learn how to be facilitators of discussions, and students have to learn how to be productive and civil participants in small-group and large-group deliberations. The contributors in this part share ways for teachers to look closely at their own practices and ways for learners to become aware of how they talk to each other and how that talk positions them to write extensively, logically, and coherently, and to read challenging texts critically.

*Part I*

# Inviting Conversations

Anyone who has sat through a literature class in college probably expected that at some point the members of the class would engage in discussion. In other large enrollment classes that featured lectures by a prominent professor, there might have also been "discussion sections" to provide opportunities for students to talk about the content of the lectures. These formats imply that the interchanges among students support learning somehow, whether or not the teacher had thoroughly formulated a rationale for the discussions. The chapters that follow in this section not only reveal the instructional value of discussions but also show learners engaged in discussions and illustrate the processes at work as students talk to each other about substantive issues.

If teachers value discussion as essential to learning in the classroom—and they should—then they need to attend to two important considerations: (1) an understanding of the ways that authentic discussions support learning to write elaborated compositions, to read complex texts critically, and to refine skills in public speaking and active listening; and (2) a recognition of the substantial skills needed to plan and facilitate sustained discussions.

It is not enough to accept blindly anyone's claim that discussions will support reading and writing; a teacher needs to understand how learners construct understanding and develop language proficiencies through their frequent interchanges with peers. The teacher's understanding of the theory behind practice will guide decision-making—both in planning for sustained inquiry and in making moment-to-moment decisions as discussions develop in the classroom.

The contributors to part I and throughout the book see learning as a socially situated process of co-constructing meaning. In American classrooms, a view of learning as the transmission of knowledge still dominates. A more progressive alternative, perhaps, is a view of learning as independent and chance discovery. We see a third option, as Gordon Wells (1999) describes: "Classrooms should become communities of inquiry in which the curriculum is seen as being created emergently in the many modes of conversation through which the teacher and students dialogically make sense of topics of individual and social significance, through action, knowledge building and reflection" (p. 98).

In this conception of an inquiry- and dialogue-based environment for learning, students and teachers engage together in problem solving, whether the problem concerns the interpretation and assessment of complex texts, the evaluation of social policy questions, or other matters that invite definition, analysis, or argument. In these active situations, learners have access to the tools they need, such as texts and other "artifacts," and most importantly, they have frequent opportunities to discuss with each other as an essential element in inquiry.

The chapters that follow begin by defining *authentic discussion* and distinguishing it from *recitation*. While discussions would seem to be intuitive and "natural," any teacher can recall times when discussions seemed impossible to initiate or quickly fell flat. Authentic discussions seldom occur by chance, and they can quickly descend into unintended recitations or indoctrination.

We know that the quality of classroom discourse matters. In fact, we judge that teachers who want to advance the literacy skills of their students need to engage learners frequently in authentic discussions. This apparently simple action to advance learning also invites teachers to reflect deeply about their practice and to take steps to refine their approach to fostering genuine dialogue that immerses learners in critical thought and civil exchanges with peers.

One classroom teacher observed to us that when students write in high school, they might produce five or six elaborated compositions per semester. Students may have developed these compositions through two or three drafts, yet the opportunities that these compositions present for students to engage in procedures for critical thinking and language use are limited when contrasted with classroom situations in which students engage daily in extensive interchanges that immerse them in various procedures—arguing, defining, comparing/contrasting, interpreting, judging, explaining, and so on. As the contributors to part I offer, practice is necessary for students to rely on "inner speech" to construct meaning, to recognize the expectations of audiences, and to command procedures for complex language use. Daily classroom interchanges in service of inquiry offer these opportunities for practice.

Chapter 1 reviews some discussion basics—what discussion is, how it emerges, how it can descend into recitation, and how teachers can stay true to discussion as a tool for inquiry. Chapter 2 illustrates how learners who engage in discussions practice the intellectual moves that are necessary for elaborated writing. Chapter 3 offers several examples of students discussing literature and illustrates how teachers can scaffold discussions to invite deeper and deeper explorations of complex texts. Chapter 4 explains how daily oral interchanges immerse students in a variety of public speaking experiences that move learners well beyond the conventional and limited public speaking experiences in a typical high school speech class. Together, these chapters deliver the basics for authentic discussion in the service of writing logically, reading critically, and speaking and listening skillfully.

## REFERENCE

Wells, G. (1999). *Dialogic inquiry: Towards a sociocultural practice and theory of education.* New York: Cambridge University Press.

*Chapter One*

# Inquiry and Discussion

## Thomas M. McCann

While almost any discussion in an English language arts class will be a positive learning experience, discussions are most powerful in advancing literacy learning when they are planned and purposeful. Discussions are most powerful when they are *authentic* and when they are integral to *inquiries* into matters of consequence to adolescents.

## WHAT ARE *AUTHENTIC* DISCUSSIONS?

Martin Nystrand coined the phrase *authentic discussion* in his influential *Opening Dialogue*. Nystrand distinguishes *authentic discussion* from *recitation* by noting that during authentic discussions, learners grapple with questions that do not have pre-specified answers. Recitations are common and perhaps pervasive elements in schools.

Imagine that students have read Jack London's "To Build a Fire," and the teacher has conscientiously prepared for class with a list of questions, perhaps ones that the students were encouraged to use to guide their reading. We might hear questions such as these:

- Who is the narrator of the story?
- What is the narrative point of view?
- Why does the central character take this dangerous journey?
- How is the dog useful to the man during his journey?
- How does the man know how terribly cold it is?
- What event makes the journey more treacherous?

We might categorize these questions as literal level items. In most cases we can point to a detail in the text to answer the question. Certainly the teacher knows *the answer* for each of the questions. But the teacher might also ask these questions:

- Why would the man begin the journey when it is obvious that he will be in grave danger?
- What do you think the author would expect us to recognize about humans' relationship to nature?
- Why do you think the author has partnered the man with a dog?

These questions might lead to authentic discussion, or they might continue the recitation. Much depends on the word *pre-specified* in Nystrand's definition.

We can well imagine classroom exchanges based on the questions above. First, a teacher might want to get a general sense of who in the class has actually read the story and can recall some basic elements. The recitation might serve as a kind of review of basic narrative elements, such as point of view, setting, conflict, and plot. But some questions are speculative. If asked in a dialogic spirit, the apparently interpretive questions might invite students to venture an analysis. Imagine an interchange among students developing like this:

Nacho: I think London probably thought that nature is too powerful and unpredictable for us to control. The man thought he was so tough that he could overcome anything, and he thought he was real smart and had everything planned. He didn't count on thick snow hiding some thin ice and open water. When he got wet by coming into contact with a basic element of nature—you know, water—his life was in danger.

Sara: That's good, the way you put it—basic element of nature. Then he needed another basic element—fire—but he couldn't make the fire. He wasn't in control of this element of nature.

Robert: It seemed like the dog was better prepared to survive the forces of nature than the man was. The man thought he was so smart that he was better than the dog, but the dog knew instinctively when there was danger and how to survive. He wasn't going to let the guy catch him for his own advantage. The guy was going to cut the dog open to warm his hands.

Liam: And the guy was too stupid to see the branch full of snow hanging over him. That's what put the fire out. Nature ends up being more powerful.

This exchange appears *authentic* in that students are sharing their analyses, and they are building on each other's ideas. You wouldn't want to point to the response from one student alone and say, "That's the *correct* answer." In fact, the combination of all of the responses (and more that would follow) would be a rich discussion of implications of the story.

Of course, such interchanges are only possible when the teacher poses a question or frames an interpretive problem in a way that suggests that the teacher is not fishing for a specific answer. Nystrand calls this invitation to open responses making a "dialogic bid." The teacher could also ask apparently interpretive questions but signal that she already has an answer in mind and it is the students' task to figure out the interpretation that the teacher endorses. Usually from their experience with a teacher, students know whether a teacher is prompting recitation or inviting discussion.

Facilitating recitation is relatively easy, although finding many respondents is often difficult. In fact, the teacher's edition of a literature anthology will offer lists of questions and provide the answers. The teacher then poses the questions (*initiates*), students answer (*respond*), and the teacher assesses the responses (*evaluates*). This is the common I-R-E pattern that dominates in schools. It is always easy to bring recitations to closure because all of the questions have been answered to the teacher's satisfaction, even if she had to answer some of them herself.

But the facilitation of *authentic discussion* is more demanding. Discussion requires much preparation, commitment, and discipline. Find below three brief classroom vignettes that show teachers who appear to be fostering inquiry and authentic discussion but miss opportunities. After reading these contrasting scenes, consider a view of a classroom where students engage in genuine inquiry and engage in authentic discussion.

## DESCENT INTO RECITATION

To see how easily inquiry and discussion can descend into recitation, let's visit Mr. Corby's tenth-grade class. The students have been reading *To Kill a Mockingbird*, and Mr. Corby wants to prepare the students to look critically at the behavior of Sheriff Tate and Atticus toward the end of the novel. Imitating the methodology of psychologist Lawrence Kohlberg, Mr. Corby offers the students a scenario that poses an ethical challenge. He expects that as they discuss, the students will express a standard by which they can judge Tate and Atticus. On a screen at the front of the room, Mr. Corby projected the following scenario and asked a student to read it aloud:

> Imagine that you live in a small town. One evening as you are sitting in your car, waiting for your friend to emerge from the Lil Napoleon Quik Mart, you see two men scuffling at the corner of the street. You are at a safe distance, and neither man can see you in your car. You are close enough to recognize both men as familiar residents of the town.

You suddenly realize that the fight has become deadly, as one man plunges a knife into the chest of the other man, who falls dead on the pavement. The killer runs away, taking the knife with him. You could provide a definitive identification of the killer. What will you do? Why?

Mr. Corby: What will you do in this situation? And why would you take the action that you do?

Stephanie: I think I have to call the police right away. You have to consider the family of the deceased.

Benjamin: I don't know. I am not sure that the guy didn't see me. I have to think about my own safety. If he could kill this other guy, he could kill you.

Leonard: If they were fighting, it could be self-defense. You never know. It is not up to me to decide that the guy who ran away was guilty.

Mr. Corby: But wait a minute. Are you saying that because you don't know the circumstances of the assault and death, you are *not* going to call the police?

Leonard: I don't know. Maybe he was just trying to protect himself. Let someone else figure it out.

Mr. Corby: You're kidding me. You're not going to call the cops right away?

Leonard: I feel bad, but I don't know what is going to happen to me if I report this as a crime. I've got to protect myself. I wouldn't say anything because what if the police can't find the guy and he comes after me?

Dorian: I would report it so that he could get caught. You never know if the guy could hurt someone else in the town, including me. So it's like self-preservation if you turn him in.

Kevin: I would tell if the police *asked* me. I would feel guilty if the killer killed again.

Benjamin: It's not your business anyway. The killer could find out you told and he could come after you.

Mr. Corby: What are you worried about?

Benjamin: If I was going to die for telling, then I would keep quiet. It's a small town and they could find out who told.

Mr. Corby: So, for your own safety, you would keep quiet? Isn't there a legal obligation to report the crime to the police?

Dorian: I would report it to the police so he wouldn't kill anyone again, and so the family knows who did it. If it was someone I know, I would want to know why that person did it, so I might hesitate to call the police until I found out about the circumstances.

Stephanie: You would want to know that person was punished.

Greg: I would tell the police because I would want that person to be punished. I would want to help the family of the dead person and get the killer off the street. You are the one who saw him. You have the information, so you have a responsibility.

Stephanie: You have to give back to society in order to receive. I would turn him in to the police.

Ellen: I would feel guilty if I knew and didn't report what I knew to the family.

Sarah: Feeling guilty can give you a lot of emotional problems.

Benjamin: I didn't know if he was defending himself or not. You don't know who started the fight. I would still report it to the police because he could go ahead and kill someone else.

Leonard: If it was an accident, you could try to help the person or encourage him to turn himself in.

Mr. Corby: An accident? How could it be an accident?

Leonard: You never know. You saw it from a distance.

Mr. Corby: Yeah, but . . .

Stephanie: I would tell the police who was involved. That's the right thing to do.

Mr. Corby: Well, a lot of you said you would turn in the killer right away. What tells us that it's the right thing?

Stephanie: Morals.

Ellen: Common sense.

Greg: Society.

Stephanie: Our education. Ignorant people do ignorant things.

Mr. Corby: So, we agree—that as a witness to a crime, you have to report what you saw to the police.

In the vignette above, did you notice how Mr. Corby got more and more uncomfortable as the conversation progressed? Certainly the discussion is better than most that you are likely to see in a tenth-grade class, but Mr. Corby felt he was losing control because the students weren't all saying what he wanted them to say. He expected that the students would voice a legal and ethical principle that if you witnessed a crime, you had an obligation to report it, especially if it were a serious crime. But some students persisted in reporting that they would hesitate to report the crime—because they wanted to protect themselves or because they had some doubts about the circumstances for the crime. With the observations moving away from Mr. Corby's plans, he interrogates students to edge them toward his preconceived conclusion. In fact, in the end, he reports a consensus that isn't actually consensus.

In reflecting after class, Mr. Corby noted that he wasn't satisfied with the discussion. He admitted that when students didn't conclude in the way he had anticipated, he felt obligated to steer them toward the "correct" conclusion. The alternative, and a time-consuming one, would be to trust in the inquiry process: while Benjamin and Leonard report that they would hesitate to report the crime, Stephanie, Greg, and Ellen insist that there is an obligation, on many grounds, to report the crime. If the exchange is genuine inquiry, these discussants should be allowed to engage with each other to negotiate a principle that would direct behavior. This collision of adverse opinions puts everyone in a position to support conclusions and consider the alternatives offered by other speakers. That's part of inquiry. The process, as much as the final conclusion, is important.

As Mr. Corby, a teacher of many years, reflected on his lesson, he noted that it was as if he could not help himself. Over many years of observations of other teachers and a few years of his own teaching, he came to expect a certain script—with the teacher posing questions and evaluating responses.

A new inquiry-based view would mean that the point is not the answer by itself but the dynamic process of grappling with problems and practicing procedures such as analysis, argument, summary, and synthesis. Mr. Corby was reflective enough to recognize when the inquiry was slipping away, but he needed to have the means to bring the discussion back to its initial authenticity.

## INDOCTRINATION IN THE GUISE OF INQUIRY

Another danger is that a teacher can begin discussion as an open exploration of ideas, such as themes that emerge from literature, and then direct students down a specific path. The following vignette features a teacher facilitating a whole-class discussion about a scene from *A Raisin in the Sun*.

Mr. Bryan: My next question refers to Mr. Lindner in the second act, scene 3. Lindner says this to Walter: "But you've got to admit that a man, right or wrong, has the right to want to have the neighborhood he lives in a certain kind of way." Is there any truth to what Mr. Lindner says? I mean, do we have a right to say who we want to associate with?

Sharon: He is trying to buy them out so they don't move into his neighborhood. He says they are nice, hardworking people, so there is no reason to try to keep them out. I think it is against the law.

Mr. Bryan: So, you judge that although he is being very polite and all, he is wrong and unjust in trying to buy out the Youngers.

Aaron: Well, he hasn't exactly broken the law. He is trying to buy the house from them. He didn't refuse to sell.

Mr. Bryan: Okay. Technically, he hasn't broken the law. But does his claim to having a right to exclude the Youngers make any sense? I mean, isn't he looking for a means to exclude certain people from the neighborhood?

Aaron: It sounds terrible, but he is doing what most of us do. If we are honest, we all exclude people in some way. Lindner sounds like a polite bad guy, but he is doing what we all do to some extent.

Mr. Bryan: You think we all exclude people? Is that a *right*, like Lindner claims?

Aaron: There are certain things that the law says you have to do, but you can decide who your friends are and who you will let into your home.

Mr. Bryan: But who you let into your home, isn't that different? You don't own the whole neighborhood.

Aaron: I know there are laws that say you can't keep people out of a neighborhood, but we have a right to restrict people in a lot of ways.

Mr. Bryan: If we are going to be a humane community, and I think Hansberry would agree with me on this, we can't decide some people are worthy of inclusion and others aren't.

In this instance, by interrogating some students and paraphrasing the responses of other students, Mr. Bryan was revealing what he endorsed as a correct answer. Although we might all condemn the character Lindner from the play, a genuine inquiry into his character and what Lorraine Hansberry expected us to notice about his character would allow for an authentic dialogue about him.

The discouraging part of the exchange is that students note quickly that the teacher sides with some speakers and seeks to alter the opinion of others. Students recognize a kind of unfairness and disingenuousness to the teacher's actions: what began seemingly as inquiry became a kind of indoctrination. When students witness this, it is difficult thereafter to engage them again in discussion as part of a process of inquiry. In a sense, a trust has been broken.

## MISSED OPPORTUNITIES

As part of research into what happens during classroom discussion (McCann, Kahn, & Walter, 2018), I had an opportunity to observe in an English class where students were discussing a controversy about teaching the concept of white privilege in a social studies class in another school. All but two students in the class identified as African American, and the teacher was white.

The discussion sequence included a forum in which the students assumed the roles of members of the community in order to imagine the arguments from several perspectives. On the third day of the sequence, after the students had heard the competing views, I observed the large-group discussion. Below is a composite of the discussion in order to highlight a missed opportunity for pursuing inquiry beyond the teacher's initial intention.

Ms. Widerhaken: So, to come back to the question from the case, should teachers still be allowed to teach the concept of white privilege at their school?

Silvia: It is also about where you come from. People see how you look and judge what you are all about. A lot of times, it is not just black people and that white people aren't that saggy, most of the time. If you are saggy, then it is likely they come from the hood. White people who do come from the hood, they are saggy just like us. But you have white people who come of advantage, from the top white class. The white people that come from the hood, they are saggy just like us.

Ms. Widerhaken: That resembles a little bit of what I was saying before. But are you supporting what Shawna said, it is on us to make a different choice?

Silvia: After, though, you know, perhaps the next generation is worse than us. People of our generation now, it is like they don't need to work for anything. They can just do whatever they want. If you have to go to work every day, they will be like "*no.*" You got to have to work every day. If you don't, you are not going to get paid. Children are not going to get stuff like that. Then children are going to see that. They are going to be worse than him. They are going to go on like that. That is just how it is. Everyone needs to put the work in because they want so much. They got big dreams. Then they need to put the work in if you want to amount to something and have people respect you.

Ms. Widerhaken: To bring this back to the original question, it seems to me what you were saying is there are so many more issues out there that need to be dealt with, that cannot just be about this.

Stephen: I will go on with what Michael said before. I don't believe they should be judged by who you appear to be, on the image. You could be dressed like a thug and be smart. You can also dress smartly and be a thug. People should not be judged by those images and what others see in us.

Claudine: I want to go on with what Michael said about if we were to dress differently, we might be judged differently. We used to live in Alabama, where my family was raised or whatever you want. They were raised in a little bit more poverty. So there was this white guy who had lived across the street from us. He dressed all slummy. But we had left our house and he broke in at Christmastime. We found out that he had stolen everything because he thought we had it so good. Because we dressed better than he did.

Ms. Widerhaken: Your neighbor broke into your house and stole your gifts?

Claudine: The guy came across the street, and we weren't in the house because the security thing that we had on the door, like anyone that came up, you could see who it was, so it was him who had done it. I think that, except for a best friend, we are still going to be judged by looks. You know.

Ms. Widerhaken: So, you think we ought to be teaching about white privilege in school so that students learn how to put themselves in someone else's place?

Claudine: That's kind of it, but it doesn't really matter.

Sam: Who cares? They can teach white privilege or not.

Ms. Widerhaken: Why don't you think it matters?

Claudine: I am not speaking for Sam, but I know we are taught about that at an early age. We know all that stuff about white privilege. That's nothing new to us.

Sam: Some black guy gets choked to death in New York for selling loose cigarettes on a street corner. Then a white guy shoots nine people in a church in South Carolina and the police arrest him without a scratch. How does that happen? That's what I want to talk about.

Ms. Widerhaken: I see what you mean. But if we were going to advise the school board at Millikan High School, what would you suggest?

Silvia: Yeah, that's all right. They can teach about privilege. I guess some people don't already know about it. Some people need to learn, even if some people in the community get irritated.

The critical moment in the exchange above is when Sam refers to the contrast between the arrest of Eric Garner and the arrest of Dylann Roof. Sam notes, "That's what I want to talk about." To this point, the class had already been having a rich conversation about perception, profiling, and potential, but Sam's observation raised the level of seriousness. Ms. Widerhaken, an optimistic and supportive teacher, sought to move students toward positive problem solving, and she hoped to keep learners "on task." But this seems to be a missed opportunity to expand the inquiry and discuss matters that students recognized as more consequential than the question of whether or not to teach students about white privilege as part of the social studies curriculum.

In the moment in the classroom, it is sometimes hard to recognize a need to open the discussion to another and perhaps more significant aspect of the problem at hand and to allow for a digression from the planned agenda. As teachers who hope to engage students in discussion at each class meeting, we have to remind ourselves to be prepared to expect these possibilities and to embrace the potential for expanding the discussion. It seems almost tragic when an opportunity is lost to raise the level of significance in the inquiry and discussion for the sake of staying true to the lesson plan as originally designed.

If Ms. Widerhaken had allowed for the expansion of the question of teaching white privilege to include the ultimate privilege of remaining alive after having committed a horrible crime while others are killed for trivial or unsubstantiated offenses, the students would have much to say, they would have been eager to read related matter, and they would have written elaborated analyses.

## A GLIMPSE OF AN AUTHENTIC DISCUSSION

As reported elsewhere (McCann, Johannessen, Kahn, & Flanagan, 2006), a reliable means for starting classroom conversations and for practicing the facilitation of discussions is to introduce a set of problem-based scenarios. There's no need to reproduce an entire set of scenarios here, but this chapter offers one sample scenario and a composite of the kind of discussion that a scenario inspires.

Problem-based scenarios work to prompt discussions if the questions they raise do not require special knowledge and are genuinely debatable, suggesting that all students have something to contribute. A general rule is to focus on problems that resonate with adolescents, with a narrative set in a school. In this example, the scenario centers on a question of justice. An immediate learning goal would be for the students to define the concept of justice as part of preparation for thinking critically about literature that explores issues about justice, which could include texts that range from Walter Dean Myers's *Monster* to Shakespeare's *King Lear*. One scenario presents this problem:

> During World Geography class, as Mr. Strata lectured, Harlan Fleming noisily wadded up a sheet of notebook paper into a ball and sailed it across the room and into the wastebasket next to the teacher's desk. The wad of paper rattled around the metal wastebasket before falling to the bottom.
>
> Mr. Strata stopped his lecture and filled out a disciplinary referral form about Harlan. Harlan protested: "You never said we couldn't throw paper away during class." Mr. Strata responded, "You should know by now what kind of behavior is appropriate for class." Harlan went immediately to the Dean's Office where he was assigned a three-day in-school suspension. After Harlan's departure, Mr. Strata told the class, "From now on, if anyone throws a wad of paper across the room, he or she will be sent to the Dean's Office and will probably be suspended." Were the actions of Mr. Strata and the dean just? Explain.

It is preferable for students to discuss scenarios like this first in small groups. This step allows everyone to contribute and prepares students to generate criteria for defining and to identify support to illustrate the rules they derive. In the large-group discussion, the exchange might proceed along the lines of the following composite.

Mr. McGreal: What did you decide about Mr. Strata and the dean?

Carlos: First, we judged that the punishment is way too much for what he did. I know that he made some noise that was disruptive, but that was just a moment, no big deal. I mean, come on, a three-day suspension for that? I think that the teacher was just pissed at the kid for some other reason.

Auggie: We agreed (*looking around to partners for affirmation*). Maybe the kid needs to be corrected or something, but there is no need for that punishment. That's just stupid. I mean, if they want Harlan to learn not to throw wads of paper across the room, you could just talk to him about it.

Lisbeth: Unless this was like the fifth time he did it, after the teacher warned him several times.

Franco: We don't know that. So this is like a severe punishment for something minor.

Mr. McGreal: I have the impression that you don't think Harlan deserves any punishment at all. Is that right? And how did you decide that?

Auggie: I can see some kind of punishment, like taking him out of class and saying not to do that again. I mean, he did disrupt the class.

Mr. McGreal: But Harlan says that Mr. Strata never told the class that they couldn't throw away paper during class. Does that matter?

Melissa: I know what he is saying, like a teacher can't have some secret rules like no gum-chewing or no phones out or something, and then punish you for violating the rule. Throwing away a wad of paper during class is no big deal, but he threw it across the room and it made some noise. The teacher thought it was disruptive. I can see some small punishment but not a suspension. That is way too much.

Franco: I agree with Melissa. I think our group said about the same thing. There might be some small punishment. I'm not sure what that would be. Even if the teacher didn't say *specifically* that you can't do something, you should know. I mean, even when a teacher doesn't say *specifically* that I can't get up in class and open the window or something, I know, because I have been in school for a long time and I just know that you don't just get up and walk around during class, like when the teacher is talking. It is common courtesy.

Mr. McGreal: Let me sort this out. So we are saying as a class that as part of *justice*, you can't have secret rules, but some rules we should just know because they are common sense or something? Is that right?

Gary: You're asking *us*? Then, yeah, those should be the rules.

Mr. McGreal: What are they, then?

Gary: You can't punish people for breaking some secret rules. You have to tell everyone what the rules are.

Franco: And you don't have to say all the time what the rules are. There are some rules that you should just *know*.

Many teachers have been part of countless discussions like this one. When learners see the scenario, they recognize the situation because they have often seen questionable punishments for students in school. The scenario presents a problem that all the students can feel confident they know something about and can contribute an opinion about.

Guided by the intention to have the students generate criteria for defining an abstract concept, the teacher poses the authentic question to initiate discussion, asks follow-up questions to seek details and clarification, invites several participants, and reports apparent consensus for the students to evaluate. The teacher is not interrogating students to say what he deems a correct answer; he remains open to possibilities.

With discussions about such scenarios, it becomes easy to predict what students are likely to say. At the same time, students occasionally offer surprising insights or express criteria in new ways. Several classes who discuss the same scenario are likely to derive more or less the same rules, but the path toward their conclusions can vary widely. For all of the variation, a common experience is that students try out ideas, offer rationales, refine their wording, attend to variations, and test out tentative conclusions against new situations.

In other words, the students have worked on procedures for defining and can transfer these procedures to their writing and to their reading of narratives in which the question of justice remains ambiguous. Such experiences honor students for having the competence to make decisions and implicitly underscore the value of collaboration and deliberation in forming judgments.

## CONCLUDING THOUGHTS: THE PLEASURES OF
## INTERACTING WITH PEERS

In the introduction to this volume, the editors have noted the substantial scholarship that documents that students attain higher scores on measures of reading and writing achievement when they have frequent opportunities to talk to each other. Nystrand (1997) points to the positive correlation: the more students engage in authentic discussion, the higher achievement in reading and writing.

We have seen similar evidence over three decades (e.g., Applebee & Langer, 2013; Applebee, Langer, Nystrand, & Gamoran, 2003; Graham & Perin, 2007; Hattie, 2009; and Hillocks, 1984, 1986, 2005; Nystrand, 2006). In fact, if you work in a school where reading and writing achievement lags, you can offer a solution: provide frequent opportunities for students to interact, especially in connection with reading and writing. That's the simple plan, and the contributors to this volume offer the finer points about executing the plan.

But strong performance on measures of reading and writing achievement is just part of the story. We also know that students will be much more satisfied in school when they have frequent opportunities to interact with peers, especially when they are talking about matters that they find consequential. Despite reports that many of today's adolescents often experience their interactions online, especially via their smartphones (Sales, 2016; Turkle, 2015; Twenge, 2017), students in high school English classes still prefer talking to peers to completing quiet seatwork or listening to the teacher drone on. And obviously, achievement and satisfaction are connected: learners are more likely to engage and persist with elaborated writing and complex texts when they are satisfied with the related conversations that make these literacy efforts seem important.

In order to appreciate the characteristic experience of students in a typical high school, let's take an imaginary bus ride. Let's suppose that your school district has sponsored your entire department to participate in a potentially life-changing professional development experience being held at a university located a five-hour bus ride away. When you get on the bus, you probably look for a friend to sit next to, until you discover that the trip organizer has assigned seats according to some undisclosed plan.

When the bus gets moving, several conversations begin. Some are about politics, which only angers and frustrates you. You hear conversations about yoga, cribbage, and lacrosse, none of which interest you. One of the trip organizers calls everyone's attention and suggests that everyone on the bus talk about a recent popular motion picture. You have seen the film and offer your assessment of it to the traveler next to you.

Your new conversational partner launches into a long analysis that includes commentary about camera angles, set design, costumes, soundtrack decisions, special effects, casting, and writing. In fact, when you try to add a few observations, your partner corrects you and generally makes you feel like an incompetent movie-viewer. As the ride continues and the subject changes, the conversational partner impresses you as the foremost authority about everything, reducing your role to the listener who nods in agreement as expected.

Although a lunch break allows you to get off the bus for a short break, you can't wait for the ride to be over and to reach the university as soon as possible. The journey seems interminable, and you only hope to endure until you reach your destination. If you don't think this is the way that teenagers feel at school every day, you don't know teens.

To extend the analogy a bit, imagine the ride home. Things have changed. You can choose to sit wherever you want, and you sit next to one of your friends on the staff. You naturally engage in a conversation about subjects of common interest—music, your current reading, family, travel plans, and so forth. The frequent exchanges between the two of you affirm that you both know much about the subjects that you chose to talk about. The conversation is so pleasant that you seldom look out of the bus window, and space and time evaporate. In fact, your total absorption in the extended conversation might be considered a "flow" experience, making the return trip seem at least half the distance and half the time as the departure trip.

If this analogy for the classroom and the dialogue in the classroom makes sense to you, it wouldn't take much to reproduce the conditions that distinguish that return trip. It would mean that students often get the chance to talk to the people they like and with whom they feel comfortable. Over time, with attention to building a sense of community in the classroom, everyone would feel comfortable in talking to everyone else. It would mean that the students' choices for the subjects of their conversations are often honored. It would mean that the conversations about areas of doubt that the class could explore together would generally affirm that everyone knew something and was sufficiently competent to contribute.

Over time, as students had many chances to talk to many classmates, a feeling of community would emerge. These factors set up the conditions for learning and for enjoying the experience of learning. Of course, to sustain these conditions, a teacher would have to be committed to inquiry and dialogue, disciplined enough to monitor the discussions to ensure they are authentic and that everyone is respectfully included, and strategic enough to link conversation over days and weeks as dialogue supports writing and includes attention to a variety of texts.

Long ago, in describing the practices in a middle school demonstration center, George Hillocks (1967) encouraged discussions as part of the processes of inquiry that led to students' discoveries:

> Fifth and last, the discovery method generates and preserves the *excitement* in learning that is every student's *right*. When a student himself has an insight into the importance of word order or the meaning of a story, that insight is far more meaningful and exciting than the same insight delivered by the teacher as information. The method has a certain excitement for the teacher as well—on those days when the class discovers what the teacher's preconceptions may have kept him from seeing. (p. 34)

The italics in the quote are the author's. Interestingly, Hillocks characterizes the experience of discovery as a *right*, not the exception and the privilege of the few. As we have all probably experienced, the opportunities for rich face-to-face conversations with our peers give us pleasure, and the discoveries that these conversations engender spark *excitement*. When inquiry is genuine and the discussion is authentic, students discover much and experience the excitement of working with peers and learning rich concepts and procedures.

## REFERENCES

Applebee, A. N., & Langer, J. A. (2013). *Writing instruction that works: Proven methods for middle and high school classrooms*. New York: Teachers College Press.

Applebee, A. N., Langer, J. A., Nystrand, M., & Gamoran, A. (2003). Discussion-based approaches to developing understanding: Classroom instruction and student performance in middle and high school English. *American Educational Research Journal, 40*(3), 685–730.

Britton, J. (1983). Writing and the story of the world. In B. M. Kroll & C. G. Wells (Eds.), *Explorations in the development of writing: Theory, research, and practice* (pp. 3–30). New York: Wiley.

Graham, S., & Perin, D. (2007). What we know, what we still need to know: Teaching adolescents to write. *Scientific Studies of Reading, 1532-799X, 11*(4), 313–335.

Hattie, J. (2009). *Visible learning: A synthesis of over 800 meta-analyses relating to achievement*. New York: Routledge.

Hillocks, G., Jr. (1967). The art of noble hypocrisy: Discovery in the classroom. In *Euclid in retrospect: 1967 conference bulletin*. Washington, DC: U.S. Department of Health, Education and Welfare, Department of Education.

Hillocks, G., Jr. (1984). What works in teaching composition: A meta-analysis of experimental treatment studies. *American Journal of Education, 93*(1), 133–170.

Hillocks, G., Jr. (1986). *Research on written composition: New directions for teaching*. Urbana, IL: National Conference on Research in English/ERIC Clearinghouse on Reading and Communication Skills.

Hillocks, G., Jr. (2005). The focus on form vs. content in teaching writing. *Research in the Teaching of English, 40*(2), 238–248.

Kohlberg, L. (1981). *Essays on moral development*. San Francisco: Harper & Row.

McCann, T. M., Johannessen, L. R., Kahn, E. A., & Flanagan, J. M. (2006). *Talking in class: Using discussion to enhance teaching and learning*. Urbana, IL: NCTE.

McCann, T. M., Kahn, E., & Walter, C. (2018). *Discussion pathways to literacy learning*. Urbana, IL: NCTE.

Nystrand, M. (1997). *Opening dialogue: Understanding the dynamics of language and learning in the English classroom.* New York: Teachers College Press.

Nystrand, M. (2006). Research on the role of classroom discourse as it affects reading comprehension. *Research in the Teaching of English, 40*, 4(May), 392–412.

Sales, N. J. (2016). *American girls: Social media and the secret lives of teenagers.* New York: Knopf.

Turkle, S. (2015). *Reclaiming conversation: The power of talk in a digital age.* New York: Penguin.

Twenge, J. M. (2017). *iGen: Why today's super-connected kids are growing up less rebellious, more tolerant, less happy—and completely unprepared for adulthood—and what that means for the rest of us.* New York: Penguin.

*Chapter Two*

# Authentic Discussion and Writing

## Elizabeth A. Kahn

A considerable body of research reveals that frequent participation in authentic, dialogic discussion significantly enhances students' growth in writing (Applebee, Langer, Nystrand, & Gamoran, 2003; Hattie, 2009, 2018; Langer, 2001). But too often in English language arts instruction, speaking and writing are seen as two distinct strands rather than two interwoven and complementary ones.

Hattie's research synthesizing the results of eighty thousand studies of classroom instruction found that out of 250 different influences on student achievement, authentic discussion is among the most significant teaching/instructional strategies "with the potential to considerably accelerate student achievement" (2018, n.p.). Authentic discussion is a potentially stronger influence on achievement than other methods frequently used in teaching writing, such as direct instruction, teaching outlining strategies, individualized instruction, and using technology (Hattie, 2009, 2018). In short, research suggests that students learn to write by talking as well as by writing.

Surveys of secondary students reveal that they prefer discussion (whole class or small group) to other modes of instruction. However, teachers frequently lament that although they would like to engage classes in authentic discussion, students aren't necessarily willing to participate, despite their reported preference for discussion. In fact, teachers often describe the process of trying to engage students in discussion as "it's like pulling teeth." Observational studies of secondary English language arts classes confirm that authentic, dialogic discussion is rare (Applebee et al., 2003).

Though it is rare, there are English language arts teachers who make authentic, dialogic discussion a frequent activity in their classrooms (McCann, Kahn, & Walter, 2018). So what methods work to successfully engage students in authentic discussion? How can teachers promote authentic discussion in their classrooms? And how does engaging in authentic discussion help students become better writers?

This chapter focuses on how teachers can design instruction that will engage students in authentic, dialogic discussion and how, through engaging in authentic discussion, students learn strategies and procedures that enhance the effectiveness of their writing. This chapter primarily emphasizes the role of authentic discussion in teaching argument writing—writing that involves taking a position, making claims, supporting claims with evidence, explaining reasoning, and anticipating and responding to opposing arguments and opposing evidence. However, similar principles can be applied in using authentic discussion in teaching other types of writing as well.

## ENGAGING STUDENTS IN AUTHENTIC, DIALOGIC DISCUSSION

To understand the role of authentic discussion in teaching writing, it helps first to look closely at what takes place when students engage in authentic discussion. The following excerpt provides an example of a class engaged in authentic discussion. This excerpt takes place as students are examining "The Case of Restorative Justice" (see textbox 2.1).

### Textbox 2.1. The Case of Restorative Justice

Gina Garza walked into history class, and as she walked by Tim Tarzanski's desk, she screamed, "I hate you. I hate you! You're a *liar!*"

Tim was startled and snapped back, "What's your problem? You're crazy!"

The history teacher, Bruce Bruno, clearly perturbed and uneasy, sent Gina and Tim to the assistant principal's office.

The assistant principal, Sara Sweet, talked to both Gina and Tim. Gina said that Tim had posted on social media that "Gina Garza loves illegal aliens who are criminals, murderers, and drug dealers." Gina said it was a lie and explained that in class discussion she had expressed her opinion that undocumented immigrants who have spent almost their whole lives in the United States should be granted citizenship. She said that she thinks Tim is mad at her because she didn't want to go to the school dance with him.

As a result of Tim's post about her, she reported getting bullied on social media and being subjected to negative, insulting comments from some students during school. She said that some of the comments on social media called her abusive and offensive names and some were scary threats, such as, "We're going to get you!" and "Better watch your back." As a result of these comments, Gina was experiencing anxiety in school. Ms. Sweet asked Gina if she wanted to bring in the local police and possibly file charges. She said if Gina did not choose to involve the police then the school would deal with the situation using the new restorative justice system of discipline. Gina said she did not want to involve the police.

The next day Tim and Gina met with a student and faculty panel convened to facilitate restorative justice. Tim was very apologetic and said he was sorry. He said he meant it as a joke but admitted that maybe he had "gone too far." Tim agreed to the panel's suggestion that to "make things right" he would write a letter of apology to Gina, post an apology admitting he had made false statements about Gina on his social media account, and write a research paper on the negative effects of internet bullying. Gina agreed that this would be a fair outcome given Tim's actions.

The next week Gina's father called the assistant principal. He was quite upset. He reported that one of Tim's friends had confided to Gina that when Tim was out with his friends over the weekend he was bragging that he had "gotten off easy." He was laughing about how he had "really gotten" Gina and that she deserved it. Tim told his friends that he was scared when the police were mentioned but that in the end it all ended up being "no big deal."

Gina's father said that originally Gina had not told him about the threats she received and that he had just now learned about everything that happened. He said Gina's plans to attend the school's Valentine's Dance were ruined because she felt uncomfortable going. He complained that Tim had only received "a little slap on the wrist" for something that could have easily resulted in serious harm. He argued that a harsher punishment should have been given, and if this had happened in the past, it would have resulted in a week's suspension from school. He said that her parents should have been consulted because Gina is a minor and shouldn't have been making decisions on her own about whether to involve the police.

Mr. Garza and Gina now want Tim suspended for a couple of days because he was not sincere in his apologies. Tim's parents disagree, contending that Tim fulfilled everything he was required to do, so it is unfair to complain and change the terms of the agreement at this point. Tim's mother says that Tim's use of social media was outside of school and off school property, so actually the school is infringing on Tim's free speech rights and really doesn't have grounds for taking any action against him in the first place.

Mr. Garza argues that this restorative justice system makes discipline at the school a ridiculous joke and that students will feel they can do anything they want because the consequences are so lenient. He calls for the school to discontinue it.

## WHAT IS RESTORATIVE JUSTICE?

According to school principal Stanley Bullock,

> Restorative justice is a fundamental change in how we respond to rule violations and misbehavior. The usual response to bad behavior is punishment, such as detentions, suspensions, or removal of privileges. When you have a punitive system, the automatic response is to deny responsibility because you know you'll get punished. How is that helpful?
>
> With a restorative justice system, you are encouraged to admit what you did because you know there's going to be a restorative process to make things right. And one of the biggest benefits is that using restorative practices keeps kids in school. They aren't thrown out for disrupting class or violating minor rules like students in punitive systems frequently are.

Restorative justice addresses disciplinary problems in a cooperative and constructive way. If a student violates the rules and a restorative justice system is in place, the student is given the chance to come forward and make things right. He or she meets with a mediator or group of mediators and the affected parties to work it out.

To facilitate the process, the mediator asks nonjudgmental, restorative questions such as, What happened? How did it happen? What can we do to make it right? Through the discussions, they all gain a better understanding of what happened, why it happened, and how the damage can be fixed. "They'll talk about what can be done to repair the harm," says Principal Bullock. "They'll come up with a plan. The plan might be writing a letter of apology, returning or paying for the replacement of stolen items, doing community service, or writing a research report on the effects of a misbehavior such as bullying, internet harassment, or racial slurs. Hopefully the relationship will be stronger. It's really all about relationships—building and repairing them."

Principal Bullock reports that detentions and suspensions have decreased significantly since the new policy went into effect.

## STUDENT SPEECH RIGHTS OUTSIDE OF SCHOOL

The law says that in general students have the right to freedom of expression unless it infringes on the rights of others, threatens school safety, or interferes with the ability of a school to deliver its educational services and processes. When student expression infringes in these ways, schools can take action. These guidelines apply to off-campus online expression as well as traditional speech.

## CRITICISM OF RESTORATIVE JUSTICE SYSTEMS

Tim and Gina's history teacher, Mr. Bruno, is not a fan of the restorative justice system. He says it is a reaction against "zero tolerance" policies. Mr. Bruno says, "Some have described restorative justice as a 'softer approach.' I don't necessarily like zero tolerance policies, but this is too soft. You have to have consequences. You would drive one hundred miles per hour if you knew that all the cops would do was ask you to apologize and write a paper explaining why it is bad to drive one hundred miles per hour."

Mr. Bruno also wonders how this system will prepare students for the real world where "there aren't talking circles and mediation sessions; you have to pay fines or go to jail if you break the law. It's a punitive system in the real world." According to Mr. Bruno, many of the other teachers in the school agree with him.

## A MEETING OF THE MINDS

District superintendent Raquel Rich has organized a meeting to determine whether the restorative justice system was applied appropriately in this case. She has asked all of the parties involved to attend the meeting and present their viewpoints. The questions for the meeting are, "Do you agree with the way this case was handled by the school authorities? Why or why not? Be prepared to support your viewpoint with specific evidence."

## ROLES FOR THE SUPERINTENDENT'S MEETING

Tim Tarzanski: *Agrees* with the way the case was handled
Gina Garza: Even though she originally agreed, now *disagrees* with the way the case was handled
Assistant principal Sara Sweet: *Agrees*
Principal Stanley Bullock: *Agrees*

Gina Garza's father: *Disagrees*
History teacher Bruce Bruno: *Disagrees*

## QUESTIONS TO CONSIDER

* Was the outcome or consequences that Tim received fair and just? Why or why not?
* Was Gina treated appropriately in the process? Why or why not?
* Is a restorative justice system better than punishments such as detentions, suspensions, and removal of privileges? Why or why not?
* What are the potential benefits of each of the two approaches to discipline?
* What possible problems are there with punishments such as detentions, suspensions, and removal of privileges?
* What possible problems are there with a restorative justice system?
* What other possible actions do you think the mediation panel could have come up with for Tim to make things right? Are there any that would be better than what they decided? Why or why not?
* Should the school modify or discontinue the restorative justice system? Explain your viewpoint.

## WRITING TO ARGUE YOUR POSITION

The superintendent has asked that you write a letter to members of the board of education arguing your position on whether you agree with the way this case was handled by school authorities and whether the restorative justice system should be continued.

* Since this is a complex case, it will take at least a few pages to address all the important issues involved.
* The board of education is not yet aware of the details of the case, so you will need to begin by *providing a summary of the situation and of the different viewpoints.*
* You will need to *state your position/viewpoint* and *provide extensive evidence to convince others.*
* You will also need to *explain the claims and evidence raised by those who disagree with you* and to respond by *arguing against their claims and evidence.*

Ms. La Vega: So, Zach, you are saying that Tim got off too easily?

Zach: Yes, definitely. He did something that could have really been bad for her [Gina]. What he wrote about her on social media. She could have been hurt. There were threats.

Ms. La Vega: So why was it too easy?

Jordan: He just had to write a paper on bullying.

Jessie: And write a letter of apology and tell everyone he lied in his post.

Eduardo: The problem is that he was laughing at Gina. He even said he got off easy, bragging about it. So Tim was actually lying when he said he was really sorry about what he did. And the fact that he was laughing at what happened makes it even worse. I think he should have been suspended and then he would be sorry for what he did and learn his lesson. It says that the panel is "nonjudgmental," but they need to be saying, "You did something wrong, really bad!"

Marin: I don't agree that he should have been suspended. He could still be laughing even if he got suspended. But I do think that he should have to go back to the student and faculty panel. I think he should be reported to the panel that he wasn't honest in his apology. They should take further action.

Eduardo: Yeah, like suspend him!

Jon: I think he did his punishment, what he was required to do, so you can't go back now and say now you're suspended.

Ms. La Vega: Jon, you're saying he should not be "punished" any more?

Jon: Right, I mean, he did the time. I mean if you get a ticket and you pay it. You don't get another ticket if you laugh about it or say you got off easy. It's done.

Chaniqua: But the idea of restorative justice is different. It's not, here is a punishment. It's about what the article says; like it's about "making things right." The article says, "It's really all about relationships—building and repairing them." Not just doing a punishment. How does a suspension make things right or repair relationships? He definitely needs to be brought back to the panel and explain to Gina how he can be bragging and laughing. I don't think he'll be so tough in front of the panel.

Eduardo: I think it makes things right when people get what's coming to them, like a suspension for what he did, or having to deal with the police.

Ms. La Vega: What other concerns or responses do you have?

Monique: I'm going to say maybe he shouldn't be punished at all because he did it outside of school.

The excerpt is an authentic, dialogic discussion because students are involved in inquiry about a question that does not have a "right" answer or a simple solution: whether the actions Tim was required to take to redress the harm to Gina were appropriate or too lenient and whether the school authorities acted appropriately. Ms. La Vega does not push students to a predetermined answer or a particular viewpoint but instead uses uptake to encourage students to clarify their viewpoints and explain their thinking. It is also an authentic discussion because students—not the teacher—are doing most of the talking and are responding to each other, not only to the teacher.

## WHAT KINDS OF ACTIVITIES GENERATE AUTHENTIC DISCUSSION?

So as research suggests, igniting authentic discussion is not easy. What happened in this situation to promote authentic discussion? The activities involving "The Case of Restorative Justice" generate authentic discussion for several reasons:

- The case "translates" an abstract concept (restorative justice) into events involving specific people, relationships, and emotions that students can relate to.
- The case is complex and debatable with no simple answers or solutions.
- The information is accessible to students.
- Students have different opinions about the case.
- The activities involve students in examining and in trying to understand various points of view.
- The case involves significant, enduring issues and questions about justice, punishment, atonement for wrongdoing, reparations, and so forth.

Teachers can develop similar cases by creating their own narratives or by using actual published articles about problems, dilemmas, or controversies in the news (McCann, Kahn, & Walter, 2018).

Before this discussion took place, students participated in a sequence of activities that began with their reading the case (textbox 2.1). Next, students were divided into small groups with each group given a character from the list "Roles for the Superintendent's Meeting." Each small group discussed the case from the perspective of "their character" and planned what they would say—playing the role of that character—in the superintendent's meeting. The groups addressed the set of questions about the case. The next day students participated in a simulated superintendent's meeting in which each character presented his or her position and evidence and then the students— in their roles—had a chance to respond to what others said. The class sustained this authentic discussion for around thirty minutes.

On the third day, in a whole-class discussion, students came out of their roles and provided their own viewpoints on the case. The excerpt above is from this whole-class discussion. Students engaged in the discussion for about thirty to forty minutes, examining whether restorative justice policies lead to more or to less student misbehavior, whether Gina's parents should have been notified earlier and had a part in the decision-making, whether restorative justice policies will prepare students for the real world, whether restorative justice policies are fairer and more effective than zero tolerance policies, and so forth.

## AUTHENTIC DISCUSSION AND THE WRITING PROCESS

Students tend to struggle in writing effective arguments. They typically write strings of claims and subclaims, providing little or no specific supporting evidence (Hillocks, 2002). This pattern tends to occur not only when they are given a topic and required to supply evidence from their own knowledge but also when they are given evidence they can draw from in making and supporting claims. Their writing is often underdeveloped and suggests they see their job as simply stating their opinions, rather than as convincing an audience that may be skeptical or critical. They rarely acknowledge or address counterarguments or counterevidence or see themselves as joining or participating in a larger conversation (Graff, 2009).

Participation in authentic discussion helps address these weaknesses in argument writing. After the discussion sequence involving "The Case of Restorative Justice," students each began drafting a letter to the board of education—the writing that is described in textbox 2.1. Textbox 2.2 shows a typical excerpt of the students' writing.

## Textbox 2.2. Excerpt from Student Writing about the Restorative Justice Case

Some people are saying that Tim got off too easy because Gina heard that he was laughing about everything and didn't seem to be sorry that he had posted lies about her on social media. She was also really shaken up by the comments and threats she was getting. I agree that it is wrong for Tim to be laughing about what happened after he said that he was sorry and apologized. But he did what the panel and Gina agreed to, which was a letter of apology, a statement on social media that he lied about Gina, and a research paper on bullying. It doesn't mean there is something wrong with the restorative justice system. Some people are saying he should have been suspended and that would be harder on him and then he wouldn't be laughing, but he could have been suspended and still have been laughing about what happened and making fun of Gina. I do think that the panel should bring him back in to discuss the fact that he was laughing about everything. He needs to have more discussion with the panel and Gina about showing that he is truly sorry.

It doesn't mean the restorative justice system doesn't work or should be ended because if Tim were suspended instead of having restorative justice, there wouldn't even be a process for him admitting he was wrong and trying to make things right with Gina. He would probably just be saying the suspension wasn't fair and the principal doesn't like him. As the principal, Stanley Bullock, says, "The usual response to bad behavior is punishment, such as detentions, suspensions, or removal of privileges. When you have a punitive system, the automatic response is to deny responsibility because you know you'll get punished. How is that helpful?" The restorative justice system means there is the possibility that Tim and Gina can repair their relationship.

The excerpt illustrates how the discussion helps students in writing. In the excerpt, the student draws from claims and evidence in the discussion, addressing the claim that the discipline was too lenient and therefore ineffective. The paragraph counters this claim by providing an elaborated explanation of why a supposedly harsher punishment such as suspension would not result in a better outcome and references evidence from the case. Other students—taking a different position in their written responses—argue that the restorative justice system is seen as a joke and will lead to an outbreak of student misbehavior. Some also draw evidence from the testimony of the history teacher, Mr. Bruno, arguing that the restorative justice system will not prepare students for what they will encounter in the "real world" beyond the school.

As the discussion excerpt illustrates, when students engage in authentic discussion about a case like this one, they practice making claims, providing supporting evidence, explaining reasoning, and anticipating and addressing opposing arguments—essential strategies for writing effective arguments. Through discussion they directly engage with an audience that questions and critiques what they say.

As a result of immediate feedback from others, students get a firsthand sense of what they need to do to develop an argument to convince a questioning audience that may have a different perspective or viewpoint. Therefore, when they are developing a written argument, they are more likely to think of themselves as entering a conversation in which they need to address what others think about their argument and what will be convincing to them. As Graff (2009) argues, "It is what others are saying that motivates our writing and gives it a reason for being" (p. 8).

## OTHER ACTIVITIES FOR GENERATING AUTHENTIC DISCUSSION FOR WRITING

"The Thomas Jefferson Controversy" (textbox 2.3) is a shorter case that is based on discoveries about Thomas Jefferson being the father of children with Sally Hemings, one of his slaves. It is a controversy that has ignited and continues to generate discussion and a range of differing viewpoints. As students discuss whether this information about Jefferson should be included in a middle school history textbook, they focus on issues of whether it is always right to tell the truth, who should determine what is included in the study of history, what makes someone qualified or unqualified to be a revered leader of our country, and what is appropriate knowledge for different age groups.

### Textbox 2.3. The Thomas Jefferson Controversy

Thomas Jefferson, a spokesman for democracy, an American founding father, the principal author of the Declaration of Independence, and the third president of the United States, was also a slaveholder. As a result of a 1998 DNA study, researchers concluded that there is a "high probability" that Jefferson fathered at least one child of his slave Sally Hemings. Most historians maintain that evidence shows that Jefferson maintained a long sexual relationship with Hemings and fathered six children with her, four of whom survived to adulthood. The children were born after Jefferson's wife died. Jefferson freed the surviving children when they turned twenty-one.

A history textbook for middle school has added information about Jefferson's relationship with Hemings. Some parents object to the school purchasing this textbook. They argue there is no reason to include this information and that it would disillusion young students about our noble founding fathers and the greatness of our country's origins. They assert that this sordid speculation is more appropriate for students in college than young adolescents just learning about US history. Young students should focus on the positive contributions of a person like Thomas Jefferson. Others support the textbook, arguing that it is important to know the truth about our founding fathers and other aspects of American history even if it is negative or offensive. What is your viewpoint? Should this textbook and the information about Thomas Jefferson's relationship with Sally Hemings be included in a middle school history textbook? Would it be better simply to omit information about Hemings and focus on the contributions of Jefferson as a founding father, such as writing the Declaration of Independence, serving as the third president, introducing legislation that eventually laid the groundwork for free public education, and founding the University of Virginia?

The Thomas Jefferson Controversy generates different viewpoints and arguments in class discussion that can then be followed up with having students each write a composition to convince others of their positions about whether this information about Jefferson should be included in a middle school textbook. Since there are multiple viewpoints generated in the discussion, students have a reason to write—to convince others of their viewpoints through using evidence and reasoning (Graff, 2009).

Another strategy for promoting authentic discussion is to have students debate interpretations of a text or image. Using children's stories is a good way to introduce this kind of activity. Children's stories work well because (1) readings of the text showing images of each page are available online and can be projected in the classroom; (2) they are short; and (3) students can return to the text and illustrations for "close reading" and evidence. For a story such as Dr. Seuss's *Horton Hatches an Egg*, students can be divided into small groups with each group given a different interpretation of the story. The following are possible interpretations to distribute to the groups (groups do not see the interpretations others have received):

- The point of the story is that people should fight back when others take advantage of them rather than allow themselves to be exploited.
- The story is preaching the value of being faithful and dependable and condemns those who are irresponsible, have no sense of duty, and don't keep their word.
- The story promotes the idea that fathers should be just as involved in child rearing and caring for children as mothers are. Fathers are actually better at child care.
- The point of the story is that some children would be better off being taken from their birth parents and raised by adoptive parents or foster parents.
- The true significance of the story is that it reveals Seuss's sexism, and as a result, that his books should not be read to children. Seuss rarely includes any female characters in his stories, and in this one in which he does, women are portrayed as lazy, scheming, manipulative, and selfish.

Each small group discusses whether it agrees or disagrees with the interpretation and marshals the evidence for its position. In a whole-class discussion, each group explains the interpretation it was given and presents its viewpoint on the validity of the interpretation. After groups have presented their interpretations, the discussion is opened for students to react to the various interpretations, arguing which they think is best based on evidence from the story. As a follow-up, students write compositions in defense of their own interpretations.

## AUTHENTIC DISCUSSION AND PEER RESPONSE

Once students have created drafts of their writing, teachers can design small-group discussions in which students read each other's drafts and provide feedback to help writers improve their work. Students can provide feedback to each other, identifying where they have provided a context/summary appropriate for the audience, where they have supported claims with compelling evidence, where they have addressed counterarguments or counterevidence, and what may be confusing or need more development. This kind of authentic discussion also helps students develop as writers.

## CONCLUDING THOUGHTS

The composition in textbox 2.4 was written after Richard's class engaged in discussion of a case involving the causes and effects of marginalization. The case describes a third-grade teacher, Ms. Rita Buk, who is concerned because four students in her class are outsiders. She has not been able successfully to bridge the divide between these four students and the rest of the class. The high school students examined information about Ms. Buk's class, including photographs of the classroom; an explanation of some of Ms. Buk's teaching methods, such as her use of reading groups and a "traffic light monitoring system" for publicly documenting appropriate and inappropriate behavior; a sample set of lesson plans; and a detailed report card and discipline data for each of the four students who are outsiders in the class. The case also included a list of specific articles relevant to the issue of marginalized students from *Educational Leadership*, the *New York Times*, *Psychology Today*, NPR, and so forth.

Students engaged in a series of discussions similar to those in the restorative justice case. Students played roles of a school social worker, a playground and cafeteria supervisor, an English language learner coordinator, a gifted/talented coordinator, a principal, and Ms. Buk. The discussions focused on analyzing the causes, effects, and possible solutions for the problems of the four marginalized students in Ms. Buk's classroom. After participating in the series of discussions, students wrote letters making recommendations for Ms. Buk, explaining what she should change to help one of the four students.

---

### Textbox 2.4. Student Composition

Dear Ms. Buk,

Throughout the past few meetings, we have been discussing the fates of four of the children in your class. I have taken up a special interest in Rafael Hummel, a student who emigrated from a rural part of Germany that speaks Alemannic. Because of this, Rafael may feel like an outsider as his culture differs so much from all the other students. Therefore, in order to improve Rafael's situation in your classroom community, he needs to be able to challenge and express himself in ways not inhibited by the language barrier to allow others around him to better understand his culture while allowing himself to learn and excel in other classes.

Academically, Rafael Hummel's intelligence is still relatively unknown as he is never able to fully challenge himself in areas outside of English. From Rafael's report card, we can assume he is an extremely talented individual, and fairly smart with As in music and art, and a placement in the eighty-second percentile for math. However, his grades and performance in his other classes are all directly influenced by his lack of English. He has poor grades in all of the classes that directly require knowledge of English and American culture, and even in classes that don't need these, Rafael is excused from class more than half the time to attend English as a second language (ESL) classes. While this effort to get him to learn English is beneficial, I believe time should not be taken out of classes that do not require English, such as math and science, to attend ESL classes. This will allow Rafael to be challenged in these classes, which according to the *Psychology Today* article, is second of the "7 Secrets of a Happy Brain," where people should be engaging their strengths. Naturally, a happier individual with more emotional strength is more likely to engage in social interaction with others, and hopefully, Rafael would feel less of an outcast, even if he doesn't know English at a fluent level.

On the same topic of social interaction, Rafael should be given help to express himself in a manner more easily understood by other students, such as an electronic translator, so he can explain his culture to those around him. Currently, it appears Rafael is the victim of some bullying due to his drastically different culture. On the report card, Mr. Panzee reported that "some of the children at his table complained about his lunches." Rafael, who normally brought lunches that reflected his culture, was bullied into not bringing anything anymore, removing an opportunity to tell others about his culture as the other kids did not understand it. With an electronic translator, Rafael would be able to better explain his culture and his lunches. Other examples have shown that being able to explain their culture has made students feel more at home. Sidra, a Pakistani immigrant, stated that being able to tell others of her culture has made her "feel more comfortable and welcome" (*Educational Leadership*). As Rafael's culture differs so greatly, being able to explain it will both help his classmates understand him and help him feel more comfortable around them. This may also make him more willing to learn American culture and English.

Finally, less emphasis should be put on Rafael's ability to use English and more on his ability to express his emotions through more universal means. Studies have shown that the ability to prioritize emotions is the "activator of all knowledge, understanding, and applied skills" (*Psychology Today*). Through facial expressions and actions such as laughing, Rafael can further learn and challenge himself. Furthermore, the article uses the word *activator*, which implies that prior to this expression of emotions, none or few of these skills were in use. However, in Rafael's case, he is unable to control his emotions to a point where his other skills become activated. During recess, Rafael had lost his temper with some of the other kids due to a lack of mutual understanding. If Rafael had been better able to express his lack of understanding and the other kids were better able to explain the game, Rafael would not have lost his temper. The classroom should emphasize communicating with gestures and expressions rather than English.

> Unfortunately, Rafael Hummel is more or less of an outcast, so allowing him to express himself and explain his culture while allowing him to challenge himself academically can help improve his position socially.
>
> Richard Shu

Engaging students in authentic discussion is central in teaching them to write effective arguments. Through authentic discussion, they gain an understanding of different perspectives and issues that are significant. They gain an understanding of what others think about their argument (Graff, 2009). This understanding gives them a reason for writing—to convince others who may disagree with them. They encounter different interpretations of evidence. They practice making claims, providing evidence, explaining their reasoning, and addressing counterarguments and counterevidence.

Other activities are also important in teaching writing. Students may benefit from activities that guide them in planning and organizing their ideas, analyzing models, using effective transitions, and revising their writing. But without engaging students in authentic discussion—a process that helps them generate all the "stuff" to put into their writing—these other instructional activities will most likely not be as effective. Although this chapter has illustrated the role of authentic discussion in teaching argument writing, teachers can use similar principles and strategies in designing discussion-based activities for teaching other types of writing as well.

## REFERENCES

Applebee, A. N., Langer, J. A., Nystrand, M., & Gamoran, A. (2003). Discussion-based approaches to developing understanding: Classroom instruction and student performance in middle and high school English. *American Educational Research Journal, 40*(3), 685–730.

Graff, G. (2009). The unbearable pointlessness of literature writing assignments. *Common Review, 8*(2), 6–12.

Hattie, J. (2009). *Visible learning: A synthesis of over 800 meta-analyses relating to achievement.* New York: Routledge.

Hattie, J. (2018). *Visible learning plus.* Thousand Oaks, CA: Corwin. http://visiblelearning-plus.com.

Hillocks, G., Jr. (2002). *The testing trap: How state writing assessments control learning.* New York: Teachers College Press.

Langer, J. A. (2001). Beating the odds: Teaching middle and high school students to read and write well. *American Educational Research Journal, 38*(4), 837–880.

McCann, T. M., Kahn, E., & Walter, C. (2018). *Discussion pathways to literacy learning.* Urbana, IL: NCTE.

*Chapter Three*

# Discussion and Literature

## Carolyn C. Walter

The study of literature is not a closed book. Of course, if there were "just one right answer," it would be, but we need look no further than many of today's classrooms where students explore the same text through multiple critical lenses to see that this is not the case. If these multiple perspectives yield insights grounded in evidence from the text, the interchanges among peers broaden the understanding for all readers.

Similarly, the various life experiences that readers bring to a text will also contribute different perspectives. Consider the following exchange by two freshmen students reading Jamaica Kincaid's *Annie John*.

Jonas: The relationship that Annie John and Gwen have is just so weird; it's not natural.

Margaret Jean: If you think that, then you don't know girls!

Or consider the reflections of an experienced teacher who commented on how her sympathies shifted from Holden to his parents over the years as she moved from reading *The Catcher in the Rye* as a teenager to reading it as a beginning teacher in her twenties and finally reading it as the parent of a teenager.

Educators can let go of the "one right answer" mentality, honoring students' genuine exploration and engagement with the texts they teach. All teachers can follow the advice given in a postobservation conference to a relatively new teacher: "Once in a while, ask a question about the reading to which you do not have a ready answer. See what the students come up with. This is where the magic can happen."

Although the possibilities that emerge through discussions that invite varying perspectives seem both necessary and beneficial for all, building a classroom of shared exploration and discovery does not happen with the flick of a switch. It must be established with thought and commitment over time.

Strategies outlined in this chapter begin with low-threshold options requiring basic reading skills and inviting total participation and move to more extended and student-directed discussion activities. Teachers can scaffold these strategies within one unit or over the course of a semester, adjusting them as necessary for student abilities and curricular goals, so that students have increasing opportunities to practice the conversational turns of a discussion community where all voices are expected, valued, and heard.

## JOINING THE CONVERSATION

Inviting, even requiring, participation from the outset of class discussion with a dialogic bid—that is, a question or a problem for which there is no "one right answer"—helps not only to set the tone for class discussion but also to loosen students' thoughts and tongues for further discussion. After all, they've already spoken once, why not again?

### Try Titles

One low-stress dialogic bid involves teachers asking students to create and report without further comment titles of their own creation for scenes or acts of plays. Or if the chapters of novels being read do not have titles, teachers can ask all students to create and report their own. Here's a partial list of possible titles for chapter 8 of *The Great Gatsby*:

Alex: "The Swimming Pool"
Kisha: "Not Letting Go"
Ben: "Colossal Accidents"
Joe: "You're Worth the Whole Damn Bunch Put Together"
Opal: "Corruption and the Incorruptible Dream"
Sally Jo: "The Truth?"
Juan: "What Nick Knows"

While some students' titles reflect more complex, inferential readings of chapter events, others are more literal offerings of setting, such as "The Swimming Pool," or lines of direct text language such as, "You're Worth the Whole Damn Bunch Put Together" or "Colossal Accidents." Any of these suggestions will provide a useful springboard for the teacher to note and use as a place to begin more substantive discussion after the initial reporting. In the discussion below, Mrs. P chose to begin with Alex's title contribution, in part to recognize the contribution of a student who did not contribute to discussion frequently and in part to foster exploration of setting on a deeper level.

> Mrs. P: "The Swimming Pool" is an interesting choice. Of course, it is the setting for the important final scene of murder and suicide, but what else makes it interesting? What else do we know about Gatsby and his pool? About private swimming pools in general?
>
> Ari: This was the first time Gatsby had used the pool, and Nick says it was a little cool for swimming.
>
> Seth: This shows that the pool wasn't for Gatsby. Swimming pools, especially at this time, were a sign of luxury. I think it is important that Gatsby was killed in a luxury item that was part of a luxury package that he thought might bring Daisy to him. He didn't want it for tanning or exercise. He wanted it to bring him Daisy.
>
> Opal: Maybe Gatsby's time for getting Daisy has passed just as the summer has if it's cool and turning to fall.
>
> Kisha: This was the first time Gatsby was relaxing. He wasn't swimming laps. He was floating around on a raft.
>
> Mrs. P: So, was Gatsby just enjoying himself?
>
> Kisha: No, he was just wasting time. Gatsby wasn't giving up on Daisy. He wasn't leaving town. He says on page 161, "I suppose Daisy'll call too."
>
> Juan: He left himself open as a floating target in the hope Daisy would call. Of course, he didn't know about Wilson.
>
> Mrs. P: Interesting. What might this suggest?

Mrs. P begins the conversation by acknowledging the title's importance to setting and significant events, but her follow-up questions ask students to reflect further and delve deeper. Ari extends the importance of the setting with key details from the text. The next two students elaborate on what those details might mean within the larger context of the novel before Kisha's observations take a turn, with Juan offering an interesting new avenue for exploration. Mrs. P's follow-up question keeps the conversational discourse open to several possibilities such as Gatsby's single-minded obsession and its consequences or Gatsby's vulnerabilities or characters' mistaken understandings.

## An Important Word or Phrase

Sometimes the teacher or students will read whole passages or sections of text aloud in class. Or students may follow the text while listening to an audio recording. If any of these are the case, there are opportunities for turning passive listeners into engaged ones. Imagine students who are reading Zora Neale Hurston's *Their Eyes Were Watching God* and listening to the section of chapter 5 regarding Joe Starks's selection by acclamation as the town's mayor at a gathering where Janie as his wife is also asked to say a few words. After the part where Joe declines for Janie, saying that a woman's place is in the home, students might be directed to listen carefully to the subsequent passage describing the couple's actions and Janie's reaction as they head home. The teacher might ask all students as they are listening to note or underline a specific word or short phrase that stands out to them.

As they did with the title activity, students would report their selections to their classmates in a round-robin manner without further comment. Undoubtedly, there will be some repetition, but these will reaffirm students' readings and may suggest avenues for discussion. Responses from students might include these offerings:

Sunil: "strode"
Preyea: "made"
Walter: "down the road behind him"
Maya: "without giving her a chance"
Jesse: "feeling cold"
Miguel: "unconscious of her thoughts"
Dorthea: "made her face laugh"
Charday: "took the bloom off things"
Kamila: "invested"
Alfredo: "thought and planned out loud"

Again, there is no "right" answer, only a dialogic bid. In following up, the teacher may ask various students why their word or phrase seemed so powerful or may open the question to the whole class for response. The teacher may refer to a word or phrase that was offered multiple times: "'Made' or 'Made her face laugh' was mentioned four times. If something is *made*, what does that suggest? What might it say about Janie and her relationship with Joe?" In their explanations, students will be dealing with diction and word choice but in an inductive and less intimidating way than if they were responding to "How does Hurston use diction in this passage to convey meaning?"

Or students may divide and list their choices into "Joe words" and "Janie words." Looking at self-generated groupings, students will be creating word banks to inductively facilitate both inferences and generalizations about character when they are asked what the grouped words have in common and what these words might suggest about Joe's and Janie's characters at this point in the novel.

## EXTENDED STUDENT DISCUSSION

As students become more comfortable contributing in class and as they see their contributions valued, teachers may utilize other strategies that allow for more extended participation and development of reading and writing skills.

### Unpacking a Significant Passage

Descriptive reading, a close analysis activity demonstrated at a National Council of Teachers of English (NCTE) conference session by Carol Friedman and Tamara Jaffe-Notier, provides a strategy for further opening up self-directed discussion and discovery for students. As a whole class, one student or the teacher reads a relatively short passage of text aloud. Then, in a second reading of the same text, the teacher or a student begins rereading the passage, stopping to comment on a small portion of text (no more than two lines or to a hard stop) that seems significant before passing the reading off to the next reader to employ any one of the following options:

- The reader may continue to read as much as two lines of text or to a hard stop of punctuation.
- The reader may read as little as one additional word or phrase before commenting.
- The reader may go back to anything already read to comment further or to elaborate upon something already said.
- The reader may pass but only once during any class period.

This whole-class activity progresses with one student passing off reading/commenting to the next around the room. Thus, a progressing discussion of text from the *Their Eyes Were Watching God* passage might look like this, with the options students are employing articulated in brackets for clarification:

> Javier (*begins reading passage*): "Janie made her face laugh." If something is "made," it's artificial. This shows that this isn't natural for Janie.
>
> Nina (*continues reading*): "after a short pause, but it wasn't too easy." This is proof that Janie doesn't want to laugh. It's not easy for her to do. It's not automatic.

Sam (*continues reading*): "She had never thought of making a speech, and didn't know if she cared to make one at all." Janie doesn't seem to know what she wants. She can't even imagine possibilities like speech making. She's led a sheltered life without a lot of options.

Maya (*adds to last comment without reading further*): I'd like to add to that. Nanny made all the decisions for Janie like marrying Logan and Logan made all the decisions on the farm.

Colin (*further reflection building upon Javier's earlier reading and comment*): I want to go back to the line Javier read with "made." "Made" can also mean forced like "you made me do this." Janie is forcing herself to be the perfect wife for Joe. She forced herself to respond the way Joe would want.

Dorthea (*continuing with the text*): "It must have been the way Joe spoke out without giving her a chance to say anything one way or another that took the bloom off things." Janie seems to want an opportunity to speak. Maybe to know what she wants? Maybe just to have an opinion and not just be Joe's trophy wife.

Michala (*further comment on text without reading further*): I'd like to continue with this part of what Dorthea read. *Bloom* is an important word here that we've seen before. Janie wants a romantic relationship like the pear tree in bloom, and she thought she would get it with Joe, but "the bloom" is "off." She is not getting something in this relationship.

Beatrice (*additional comment of elaboration*): I'd like to continue with "bloom" too. Does Janie need to develop herself further, to "bloom"?

Although teachers may model this activity by beginning the first comment, with repeated class practice, students may initiate the process as it becomes an entirely student-based discovery approach to text, proceeding without any teacher input or initiation. Participating in this strategy, students choose the ways in which they wish to contribute to the ongoing conversation with the text and with their classmates—everyone takes a turn. There are opportunities for *uptake*, when Colin goes back to Javier's earlier comment on "made"; for *summary*, when Dorthea mentions Janie's desire for opportunity; and for *elaboration* and *extension*, when Beatrice further explores "bloom." These procedures are built-in features of the strategy.

## Genuine Questions and Controversy

"So, is Mr. Antolini gay?" asks Paul upon entering Mr. May's class after reading chapter 24 of *The Catcher in the Rye*. Rather than respond with his opinion or answer, Mr. May scraps his lesson plan and throws down a challenge: "Let's find out. Those who think that Mr. Antolini has made a pass at Holden, select a seat on this side of the room. Those who don't, take a seat on the opposite side. Take a few minutes to look through the chapter and underline evidence that would support your view."

After being given preparation time and a specific focus, a discussion might proceed like this:

Mr. May: Well, Paul, start us out. Since you've chosen to sit on the side supporting Mr. Antolini's making a pass at Holden, what makes you think so? Remember, arguments are stronger with references to the text.

Paul: Holden thinks so, and he was there. He also seems to have some experience. On page 192, he says, "I could hardly get my pants on I was so damn nervous. I know more damn perverts, at schools and all, than anybody you ever met, and they're always being perverty when *I'm* around."

Mr. May: Does the other side have a response?

Georgio: Mr. Antolini is married! If he's gay, he wouldn't he married to a woman.

Mathias: So, that doesn't mean anything. Some gay men marry women, especially at this time. His wife is older and rich. They don't have any kids, and she doesn't seem all that attractive with her hair curlers and all. Mr. Antolini does say that he's "admiring" Holden on page 192 as he's petting him.

Marcel: Since you brought that up, let's look on page 192. Holden says that Mr. Antolini was "sort of petting or patting me on the goddamn head." Holden isn't sure what is happening. He's been asleep and got up suddenly, and he's barely had any sleep for days.

Solange: Yes, and there's a difference between "petting" and "patting." *Petting* is something you do to a cat or dog to show affection. *Patting* seems a little more like "It'll be alright, reassuring like."

Latrice: My parents do that all the time. They go into our rooms after we're asleep just to make sure we're covered and maybe give a pat on the head as a small sign of affection. I think Mr. Antolini is being fatherly.

Marcel: Mr. Antolini gives Holden a lot of advice throughout the chapter. That's something a father would do.

Paul: Mr. Antolini was drinking a lot.

Mr. May: Can you tell me more about how that relates to your opinion?

Paul: Maybe his inhibitions were down; maybe he was making a pass.

Solange: Or maybe he was acting more like a caring father rather than a caring teacher because his inhibitions were down.

As an example of classroom debate that arose organically from a genuine question and sense of ambiguity, this topic for discussion worked well and lasted for the entire period. Was the original lesson plan covered? Not in the way it was planned, but notice what students were doing: making claims about the text and supporting them with specific evidence, listening to each other and utilizing uptake, elaboration, and counterargument as in the interpretations of what Mr. Antolini's excessive drinking might have meant.

Students were practicing many of the skills that Mr. May's original plan would have featured but in a more organic and engaged way. Mr. May acts as a facilitator at one point, asking for clarification regarding the drinking evidence, but he lets the discussion/debate proceed without undo interference. Were some insights missed? Perhaps, but much was accomplished by the students in a genuine way.

Teachers can look for these opportunities when they arise, but they can also build them into the curriculum by noting places within the reading where genuine ambiguities or differences of opinion may arise. Is Miriam a psychological manifestation or a real ghost in Truman Capote's short story "Miriam"? In his final encounter with Walton, is the Creature of *Frankenstein* a true monster? A true human? Is Martha in *The Things They Carried* a lesbian? In *Of Mice and Men*'s final scene, was George right to kill Lennie? In any event, teachers need to stay attuned to students' real questions arising from the texts.

To help students practice creating reasons and support for their opinions, another option is a forced ranking or list. At the end of a novel or play, students might be given a list of all the major characters within the text and simply asked to rank them from number 1 (most) to number 7 (least) admirable, with no ties in rankings allowed. Examining and then discussing various rankings at either end can yield spirited discussions that will require the support of reasons and evidence from the text in order to hold weight: why rank this character most admirable or more admirable than your number 2 choice? Other ranking options might include "Who has the most power?" or "Who is the most changed?"

## STUDENT-RUN DISCUSSION

Socratic seminars and fishbowls are well-known and well-used options for promoting extended discussion within the classroom. Of course, the most successful of these will also require advanced preparation on the part of both students and the teacher. These strategies do not happen magically. Another strategy that requires planning but yields high rates of involved discussion is "speed discussions."

"Speed discussion" is a term coined by students after they were first introduced to a discussion activity presented in the book *Project CRISS: Creating Independence through Student-Owned Strategies* because they equated these mini, one-on-one discussions with "speed dating." Similar to this precursor to online matchups, speed discussions introduce students to an array of ideas with the opportunity to explore ones that appeal to them in further detail later on.

The teacher begins by collecting an array of materials generated by students: every student submits a genuine question about the reading or every student submits a short passage from the reading that seems significant. These items may be elicited at the beginning of class or, for the sake of efficiency, submitted electronically and printed before class. If completed in class, small slips of paper or note cards may be used to record the submissions and distribute them to students.

Whether using desks and chairs or just chairs, teachers arrange their rooms so there are two concentric circles of chairs facing directly across from each other in pairs with possibly a desk in between. Each student is given a card/slip of paper with one question or passage. Then, each pair has three minutes to present their prompts and accompanying insights to each other before time is called. The teacher then directs all students to hold on to their prompts as only students seated in the outer circle move one position clockwise to a new partner. Only at this point do the new partners exchange prompts and begin new three-minute discussions. This same cycle continues for as long as the conversations seem fruitful and time allows before regathering as a whole class to discuss and exchange insights.

As teachers circulate, monitoring the paired mini-discussions, they may note comments that merit further exploration in whole discussions. With only one or two minutes for each student's expression of ideas, there will remain a lot to be said. The goal is to have all students actively and continuously participating within a class period and learning from each other. Students who may hold back from expressing ideas and insights in a larger class discussion respond more readily to speaking to one other student. The format also asks them to participate in a less formal and shorter way. Ideas may be repeated and extended or challenged as mini-conversations continue.

A limited snapshot of speed discussions regarding selected passages from chapter 6 of *In the Time of the Butterflies* might look like this, where the prompts are highlighted in bold:

> Tara (*in the outer circle facing Shira and reading her slip's quote*): **#1 "He is as close to a toad as a man can look. A heavy-set mulatto with mirrored dark glasses that flash my own scared look back into my face" (109).** This is a description of El Jeffe's enforcer Magic Eye. Toads are really ugly and have big eyes. It is interesting that he seems to hide his "magic eye" from others with the mirrored glasses. This makes him seem even more intimidating and powerful.

> Shira (*reading her quote and checking the context in her text*): **#2 "I look down at the lopsided scales as he puts his dice back. For a moment, I imagine them evenly balanced, his will on one side, mine on the other" (115).** This quote is after Minerva and El Jeffe roll the dice for what each one wants. They both use the loaded dice so they both win. El Jeffe says it can be a draw or they can both have what they want. Minerva calls for a draw. The most interesting thing to me is the "lopsided scales." The scales of justice are supposed to be even, but in Trujilloland, Trujillo tries to tip the balance of everything in his favor.

> Tara (*picking up her text and quote slip and moving clockwise to the left before exchanging quote slips with her new partner Monee. She then reads Monee's quote slip.*): **#3 "We've traveled almost the full length of the island and can report that every corner of it is wet, every river overflows its banks, every rain barrel is filled to the brim, every wall washed clean of writing no one knows how to read anyway" (117).** This is the last sentence of the chapter. Minerva, Mama, and Papa are traveling home after finally freeing Papa from prison. The whole island is bogged down in the rain. Maybe it's even a metaphor for how bogged down the whole country is because of Trujillo. "Every" is repeated four times. That means no place and no one escapes, just like the Dominicans under Trujillo.

> Monee (*reading and responding to the quote slip Tara gave her*): **#1 "He is as close to a toad as a man can look. A heavy-set mulatto with mirrored dark glasses that flash my own scared look back into my**

**face" (109).** This is when Minerva is hoping to free her father and meets a general and Magic Eye in an office. This describes Magic Eye. He is called this because he sees what others miss, but here, Minerva sees only her own scared face being mirrored back to her from Magic Eye's mirrored glasses. It says, "flashed my own scared look back into my face." If she sees her own fright, it must double it and make it stronger.

Tara (*picking up her text and quote slip and moving clockwise to the left before exchanging quote slips with her new partner Ray*): **#4 "I stepped on the gas. From the corner of my eye I saw him, a figure growing smaller and smaller until I left him behind me" (88).** This is after Minerva finds out about Papa's secret life and second family and rams the jeep into Papa's Ford. She is literally driving away, so Papa is getting smaller and smaller in the rear-view mirror, but Minerva's discoveries and anger at her father, who before was the "big man" in the family, make him seem smaller in her impression of him.

Ray: Nice idea. What I noticed about this quote was that Minerva seems to see everything from "the corner of her eye." This phrase is repeated several times in the chapter. If you see something from the corner of your eye, you are just getting a glimpse of it. Maybe for the first time. Maybe you don't see the whole thing, but you definitely see a part. This could relate to Minerva seeing her father in a different way for the first time.

Ray (*Ray will continue by reading and then giving his comments on the passage Tara gave him.*): **#3 "We've traveled almost the full length of the island and can report that every corner of it is wet, every river overflows its banks, every rain barrel is filled to the brim, every wall washed clean of writing no one knows how to read anyway" (117).**

Imagine twelve or more conversations similar to these continuing through the classroom. A little noisy, yes, but everyone is simultaneously involved in speaking, listening, reflecting, expanding, and connecting. In this format, each student reflects on a passage twice, once as a speaker and once as a listener. Some observations will be repeated, expanded, and added to as Ray did above for quotation number 4. He was able to add his own observation from a previous discussion and connect to what Tara was observing in the quotation. When differing ideas are tried out and potentially linked to earlier conversations, further exploration of diction, tone, character, mood, setting, and concepts is done.

This process will run more smoothly if teachers facilitate a few procedures. First, whether questions or passages, teachers should monitor the prompts to ensure there is no repetition. Second, teachers should ask students to have their texts with them for reference so they can begin discussion by orienting their quotes with context. Since the quotes appear in no particular order, it is especially important to ground them in context. Finally, teachers with a set of finger cymbals, a bell, or a buzzer will find them useful in signaling discussion end times.

After speed discussions, teachers may reserve some time to reconvene the class as a whole to ask questions such as, "What passage particularly interested you?" "Did you find repeated ideas or insights?" "What's a new idea you encountered?" Teachers may also find that reluctant speakers, having had the opportunity to rehearse their thoughts, will be more open to sharing in the larger group.

## THE WHOLE PICTURE

For illustrative purposes different literary texts have been referenced throughout this chapter. However, the importance of making a classroom discussion-based requires continuous planning and commitment on the part of the teacher. The strategies presented here are not meant to be a one-off or a quick change of pace. Students need to feel the value of their contributions and ideas as they are explored and developed over time.

There is a certain comfort level in the activities in which everyone shares a chapter title or an important word or phrase without further initial comment. Teacher questions can then help students to explore these initial observations further. With experiences such as these, students can easily transition to activities such as descriptive reading. Discussing differing responses to real questions that arise from the text also offers students opportunities for extended exchange.

In these cases, the teacher becomes the prober, the clarifier, and the facilitator as discussions unfold. For maximal time-on-task discussion, formats such as Socratic seminars, fishbowls, and speed discussions can be repeated and utilized to enhance a classroom environment of comfort and inquiry.

Just as students develop skills in discussion through extended and sustained practice, they also gain insights through extended inquiry into a topic. Complex concepts such as "justice," "independence," or "courage" require and deserve extended exploration over time and texts so that ideas might be formed and developed. Alice Walker's "Everyday Use" stands on its own, but how much more might it yield within an extended exploration of "motherhood" and "heritage" coupled with such texts as Amy Tan's *Joy Luck Club*, Nathaniel Hawthorne's *Scarlet Letter*, Tennessee Williams's *Glass Menagerie*, Jamaica Kincaid's *Annie John*, Alice Munro's "My Mother's Dream," or Teresa Palomo Acosta's "My Mother Pieced Quilts," among many others.

**Textbox 3.1. In Dialogue with Oneself**

Within a unit focusing on the Vietnam War and concepts of courage, my students began by completing an opinion survey in which they ranked different descriptions of Vietnam War participants for their courage. The descriptions included everything from infantrymen on patrol to nurses in M.A.S.H. units, generals making tough calls, and draft resisters. Students then went on to read first-person accounts of the war from *Patriots: The Vietnam War Remembered from All Sides* followed by selected poems and short stories before tackling Tim O'Brien's *Things They Carried*. It was during a discussion of this text that one student commented, "I'd like to change my rankings on the opinion survey we filled out at the beginning of the quarter." Of course, we discussed her change of heart and her reasons: Why? Why now? But just as important for me was the internal dialogue/discussion that the student had been carrying on with herself. The concepts within the texts were "alive" for her and remained open for further consideration.

## A WORD ON VARIATION AND THE VALUE OF PURPOSEFUL GROUP WORK

Teachers need options to accommodate various class personalities and times of day and skill sets. Thus, none of the ideas presented here are set in stone; try the descriptive reading activity by using it to "read" a painting or one frame of a movie. Does the novel already have chapter titles? Have students create subtitles for sections within the chapter or suggest alternatives to the given title.

Or turn the activity in which each student offers a chapter title into a small-group activity in which individual students decide which of several offered titles they prefer for a chapter. Like-minded students can then form small groups to create reasons their choice should prevail. A group's presentation of these reasons might almost take the form of a sales pitch for their chosen title, giving each group a stake in the outcome.

Small groups give students a greater opportunity for expression since there are fewer voices to be heard. However, it is important to remember that small groups work best, just as whole-class discussions do, when there is a genuine problem to solve or a controversy to explore. Students in groups work well with defined options beyond "Discuss and then write down your answers to the following questions." The activity sheet presented in textbox 3.2, used with *Romeo and Juliet*, is an example of a question for discussion.

**Textbox 3.2. Example of a Question for Group Discussion**

Text: *Romeo and Juliet*, act 3, scene 5
　　1. Think about the actions and contents of *Romeo and Juliet*, act 3, scene 5. Which of these titles would you select?
　　　a. Betrayal
　　　b. Farewell
　　　c. Extreme Passions
　　　d. More Light and Light It Grows, More Dark and Dark Our Woes

Teachers might create possible titles or use titles generated by another class or from a previous year. However, it is preferable to begin with a fresh list in which students do not have a predetermined bias. The template in textbox 3.3 offers a framework for use with any text and offers students the opportunity to practice argumentation skills of identifying and explaining reasons in support of an opinion.

**Textbox 3.3. Template for Group Discussion of Text**

Text _____
　　1.　Think　about　the　actions　and　content　of
_____. Which of these titles would you select?
　　　a.
　　　b.
　　　c.
　　　d.
　　As your teacher directs, form small groups to make a case for your selection. Complete the following in order to most effectively present the case for your group's choice.
　　Group Members:
　　Title Choice _____
　　What makes your choice the best one to encompass and represent this scene? List as many specific reasons as you can, referring to specific characters, actions, wording within the scene, and multiple possible meanings. Be ready to make the most persuasive case for your title choice.

1.
2.
3.
4.
5.

As you listen to the reasons given for other choices, what makes your choice the strongest selection?

## CONCLUDING THOUGHTS

Although not explicitly stated, classroom seating for any of the activities in this chapter is optimal if students can face one another in a circle or horse-shoe formation. For a variety of reasons, this may not be possible, but comments made to the back of another's head are not as conducive to discussion as those made face-to-face, so teachers must think carefully about how they might arrange their rooms to best foster discussion among students.

In a student-centered, discussion-based classroom, teachers take on the important role of facilitators who create an environment and climate of trust and inclusion, and who know their students and their developing skills in reading, writing, and thinking well. Rather than the dispensers of knowledge, teachers become fosterers, creators, and monitors, the ones who make things happen, enabling students to make their own discoveries.

## REFERENCES

Alvarez, J. (1994). *In the time of the butterflies*. Chapel Hill, NC: Algonquin.
Friedman, C., & Jaffe-Notier, T. (2011). James Baldwin: A futuristic voice from the past. Presentation at the National Council of Teachers of English Convention. Chicago, November 17–22.
Hurston, Z. N. (1990). *Their eyes were watching god*. New York: Harper Perennial.
Santa, C. M., Havens, L. T., & Valdes, B. J. (2004). *Project CRISS: Creating independence through student-owned strategies* (3rd ed.). Dubuque, IA: Kendall/Hunt.

*Chapter Four*

# Daily Classroom Discourse That Supports Speaking and Listening Goals

## Kimberly R. Gwizdala

In a traditional public speaking course at the secondary or college level, students typically learn classical concepts of rhetoric, practice ways to successfully communicate with different audiences, and develop and present speeches to the class. The ultimate goal of these courses is to provide students with the tools and experiences necessary to become effective communicators.

However, in recent years, many secondary schools and districts have moved away from requiring students to take a separate public speaking course. For example, in 2009, York Community High School in Illinois removed the one-semester speech class requirement after determining that the skills taught, practiced, and assessed in a speech class could be, and in most cases were already, addressed in the other disciplines. This removal was done with a conscious effort to continue to "map the curriculum in a manner that advocated the direct instruction of listening and speaking in all classes, not just English," according to Joe Flanagan, former York English Department chair. The move reflected a desire to view public speaking as not an isolated experience but rather a skill that should be incorporated in all subject areas.

The rationale behind the removal of a specialized speech class is understandable, but without a specific course for public speaking, the ultimate responsibility for teaching and assessing speaking and listening standards invariably falls to the English teacher. Within the Common Core State Standards, for example, Speaking and Listening is listed as a category under the larger English Language Arts umbrella. While some may see this as a burden, an additional item on an English teacher's plate, teaching speaking and listening is a natural and essential part of literacy learning.

## IMPORTANCE OF DEVELOPING
## SPEAKING AND LISTENING SKILLS

Teachers recognize that students will be asked to communicate in a variety of ways throughout their lives, yet students are not always prepared for these interactions. This lack of preparation can lead to miscommunication and missed opportunities. In this increasingly connected world, students need to be prepared for all interactions—be it in the classroom, in their relationships, at home, or in their future workplaces. By incorporating strategies to explicitly teach, practice, and assess speaking and listening skills, English teachers can help students effectively communicate regardless of context, purpose, or audience.

Beyond improving a student's communication skills, purposefully designing discussion opportunities can positively affect a student's social emotional development. Self-awareness, self-management, social awareness, relationship skills, and responsible decision-making are all aspects of social emotional learning (SEL) that can be improved when teachers take the time to help students engage in classroom discourse with intentionality.

Illinois SEL Standards (2004) such as "Use communication and social skills to interact effectively with others" and "Demonstrate an ability to prevent, manage, and resolve interpersonal conflicts in constructive ways" call upon teachers to address the following goals: (a) improve the quality and complexity of class discussions; (b) support students in their speaking and listening skill development; and (c) provide students with strategies to create and foster healthy interpersonal relationships now and throughout their lives. Through purposeful design of discussion experiences, teachers can accomplish these goals.

Furthermore, many speech-related standards are a part of a teacher's professional responsibilities, as indicated by the popular Danielson model. Taking time for intentional speaking and listening development can help both students and the teacher reach their goals.

## MISCONCEPTIONS OF DISCUSSION

Understandably, many English teachers see themselves as first and foremost teachers of reading and writing and may feel unprepared to teach and assess public speaking skills. Therefore, the use of discussion within the classroom is often used primarily as a means to an end goal, whether by helping students better understand a passage or preparing them to write.

What's more, speaking and listening opportunities are often separated from the rest of the curriculum, taking the form of "discussion day" or "presentation day." By separating these experiences from everyday learning experiences, teachers prevent discussion from holding a natural place in the classroom. In 2015, the satirical newspaper the *Onion* published an online article that perfectly represents this issue with the following title: "Oh God, Teacher Arranged Desks in Giant Circle." The article continues: "'I have no idea what's going to happen here, but it can't be good,' said a visibly shaken Katie Wahl, 11, who according to reports began steeling herself for whatever awful group project, class discussion, or sharing of personal experiences the sixth-grade teacher might have in store for them" (2015). The dread experienced by the imaginary Katie is understandable and common. The notion that conversations must be an isolated experience is detrimental to listening and speaking skill development. Rather, discussion should be the foundation of every class. It is when we normalize discourse and make it a natural place that students are able to have the time and space to practice, reflect upon, and improve their communication skills.

## STRATEGIES FOR IMPROVING SPEAKING AND LISTENING SKILLS

Recognizing the demands placed on English teachers and the needs of their students, this chapter seeks to provide specific ways a teacher may use discussion as a means to improve students' speaking and listening skills. Below are the four primary strategies examined in this chapter:

1. Support student preparation for discussion
2. Provide students with strategies to clarify, verify, and challenge in discussions, offering a variety of ways to enter the conversation through discussion moves
3. Encourage diverse perspectives and create a culture of critical reflection
4. Provide feedback to students to support growth

## SUPPORTING STUDENT PREPARATION

The phrases "share with your group" or "discuss with a neighbor" serve as invitations to discuss and collaborate, but often teachers find this directive is interpreted—and misinterpreted—in far too many ways. Some groups may remain hesitant to share, perhaps mumbling out a sentence as they wait for the next activity. Other groups experience an imbalance in the discussion with some members taking control of the conversation while the others sit back.

While there are the rare few groups who can easily find a rhythm to the conversation, naturally making connections, offering challenges, and digging deep into the text or concept with all members equally involved, this is not a natural state for students. By providing students structure and guidance for their interactions, teachers can help students make the most of these conversations.

## DISCUSSION FRAMEWORK

At times, students can see discussion as an activity that one "gets through" rather than an opportunity for deeper learning. Teachers can work to address this misconception by helping students see the power of conversation through a reflective discussion template. Originally proposed by Lemov (2017), a discussion template can easily help students see the necessity of discussion in helping strengthen their original ideas.

A template similar to the one in table 4.1 allows for students to see exactly how discussion can transform and strengthen their ideas. For example, when asked to explore Tim O'Brien's message regarding the power of storytelling in *The Things They Carried*, a student reading the final chapter may recognize that storytelling can "bring the dead back to life," but only through a comment provided by his peer does he realize storytelling can bring the long-gone versions of ourselves "back to life" as well. On a single sheet of paper, a student can see how his ideas were enhanced through conversations with peers.

While this simple yet powerful approach does not alone help an educator teach and reinforce specific speaking and listening skills, it does help students see the significance and necessity of discussion for reaching deeper levels of understanding. Further, this structure demands active listening from

**Table 4.1.   Sample discussion template**

Prompt:

Initial response:

Peer                              Comment

Revised response:

*Source:* Modified from Lemov (2017)

the students in order for them to be successful in the process. This design helps students place a mindful ear on the specific comments and moves made by their peers, thereby preparing them for the deeper tracking activities offered later in this chapter.

## SETTING THE AGENDA

After examining a prompt, students may have ideas as to what they want to discuss. Depending on the level of preparation expected, they may have those ideas written out in a formal organized response. Yet rarely does a student's individual planning and preparation contribute to a larger group goal created *before* the conversation begins.

Before a conversation regarding a text or issue, students can work to develop an agenda or list of topics they agree to cover in the conversation. By placing the list on the table or board, the group or class has committed themselves to covering those particular topics. This gives shape to the discussion while still allowing flexibility to explore the topics in any order for as long as needed.

Further, this approach supports students who need prompting as it offers a list of topics they may want to bring up in discussion. Care must be given to make clear that these are not the only topics allowed to be examined in the discussion. For example, in a discussion over chapter 7 of *The Great Gatsby*, students may agree to discuss (1) how Fitzgerald builds tension, (2) Tom's confrontation style, and (3) Gatsby's inability to accept Daisy's love for Tom in the past; but they may find themselves naturally moving into a larger examination of the limitations and advantages of reading the story solely through the narrator Nick's perspective.

Negotiating and prioritizing the topics of a discussion are essential skills that teachers can help develop within their students by allowing them time to establish a discussion agenda prior to the start of the conversation. Asking students to evaluate the quality and completeness of the agenda after the discussion can also help students make better judgments on appropriate and important topics to address during discussions.

## PROVIDING OPPORTUNITIES TO
## CLARIFY, VERIFY, AND CHALLENGE

When it comes to skill development, in many ways, a teacher is similar to an athletic coach. In a sport, a coach's job is to teach particular techniques or moves, give the players opportunities to practice those techniques in low-risk environments, and then guide the players in implementing the technique during a game. No baseball player can throw a curveball upon first attempt;

the body and brain must first understand and practice the processes involved in that particular pitch. So, too, must a teacher coach students in the art and science of discussion.

## DISCUSSION MOVES

The first step in this process is to help students identify the qualities of an effective discussion. While asking this without any guidance may result in generic and vague suggestions from students (e.g., "good flow"), teachers can elicit more specific responses from students through modeling. Teachers may choose to show students a recording of a roundtable discussion, a long-form interview, or even a class discussion from a previous year. Students should be asked to track one individual over the course of the discussion, identifying the specific ways the individual entered and continued on in the conversation. Teachers may need to stress that the focus is not necessarily on content but rather on the approach.

Working together, teachers and students might develop a list similar to the one below, taken with permission from the Glenbard West High School English Department in Illinois:

- Asked a question
- Asked an open-ended question that invited different ideas
- Asked a closed-ended question to check positions
- Asked for the speaker to reword their response
- Made eye contact with the speaker
- Moved the conversation to a new topic
- Invited a quieter participant to share through a question
- Checked to ensure they understood the idea
- Provided direct evidence
- Connected the ideas of two other speakers

With the established list, a teacher can begin coaching the students in these moves. Practicing with just one or two moves at a time, a teacher can isolate that particular characteristic, allowing students the opportunity to both try it themselves and see it used by their peers.

As a way to further the practice, teachers could provide students with one to three slips of paper with discussion moves on them to try during a conversation. When a student completes the challenge, he or she can flip over the slip. While directing students in such a way may seem inauthentic, allowing students opportunities to practice the different ways to enter and remain in a discussion is crucial. Students need to know what the moves feel like to be comfortable in using them without direction. With practice, students will internalize the strategies and, over time, may find themselves extending beyond the original list. These characteristics may also be used to give feedback, as will be explored later in this chapter.

## SENTENCE STARTERS

Just as students might be inexperienced in using a variety of oral discourse moves, they may find themselves wanting to enter a conversation but struggling to find the right words to do so. In the same vein of Graff and Birkenstein (2010) in *They Say/I Say* with academic writing, teachers can offer students sentence starters as a way to help them enter the conversation. Organizing the ways to enter into three primary categories—clarify, verify, and challenge—teachers can use the sentence starters below as ways for students to enter and stay in a conversation. Below are suggested sentence starters created by the English Department at Glenbard West High School.

CLARIFY: To make an idea or interpretation easier to understand

- What did you mean when you said . . . ?
- So you're saying that . . . ?
- I'm not sure I understand what you mean when you say _____? Can you elaborate?

VERIFY: To confirm the accuracy of an idea or interpretation

- What evidence suggests that this is true?
- In what other ways might we be able to interpret this line/idea?
- Did anyone else in the group see this line/idea differently?

CHALLENGE: To say or show that an idea or interpretation is not yet fully developed

- I agree with . . . , but we also have to consider . . .
- I have a slightly different way of looking at this line/idea. [Then offer your idea or interpretation.]
- The evidence I see suggests something a little different. [And then offer evidence that doesn't fit the idea or interpretation.]

Ultimately, teachers want students to feel comfortable and competent enough in discussions to use their own words, but providing students with the language to enter the conversation is a necessary first step in skill development. Furthermore, using the sentence starters can support student listening skill development, as they will be able to more easily identify when a peer clarifies, verifies, or challenges and thereby respond accordingly.

## SUPPORTING STUDENT QUESTION DEVELOPMENT

Originating from the work of the Right Question Institute, teachers can support student speaking and listening skill development by teaching them how to design meaningful questions. The Question Formulation Technique (QFT) begins with providing students an artifact such as a quotation or a picture. Students are then encouraged to write as many questions as possible in a short amount of time without censoring themselves or editing the questions. The questions created would then go through a vetting process where students would ultimately refine and select the strongest questions to use in a discussion. For example, students examining Thoreau's "Civil Disobedience" could be given the following quotation and may ultimately develop the questions below:

> There will never be a really free and enlightened State until the State comes to recognize the individual as a higher and independent power, from which all its own power and authority are derived, and treats him accordingly.

- Who is the "State"? Is it always the government?
- Who is more important today: the individual or the society?
- Is it ever possible to entirely separate yourself from the constraints of society or the government?
- What is the "power" that the individual possesses?
- Does each individual possess the same level of authority and power?
- What would Thoreau's suggested world even look like?
- What does it mean to be enlightened? Is it necessary?

While not every question in the list would be examined over the course of a class discussion, any of them could lead to a rich conversation designed entirely by the students. This process helps students see the important role they can and should play in a discussion while supporting creativity, close reading, and problem-solving skills.

## ENCOURAGING DIVERSE PERSPECTIVES

Perhaps the most difficult task in clarifying, verifying, and challenging is challenging. To be clear, the term *challenge* is not meant to advocate for an adversarial or hostile classroom environment. Rather, this chapter encourages teachers to promote critical reflection and responses from students not only to the text but also to each other. Unfortunately, classrooms—and perhaps society as a whole—have become echo chambers; students no longer know how to, or feel that they should ever, disagree with a peer, so instead we get "piggybacking." Consider the common scenario below in which students responded to the following question: "To what extent are Holden Caulfield's problems self-created?"

Sheila: Holden Caulfield is to blame for his struggles. He's rude to Ackley, who is probably the closest thing he has to a friend.

Mike: I agree. Holden Caulfield is his own enemy. He gets into a huge fight with Stradlater just because Stradlater wouldn't tell him about his date, which really wasn't Holden's business anyway.

Ali: To piggyback off of Mike, Holden makes problems for himself that weren't issues in the first place. He didn't need to lie to the mom on the train.

Madison: Right, and now if that mom talks to her son about her conversation, it might just make more issues for Holden later on.

This is a very friendly conversation *that doesn't go anywhere.* The students have decided, in their planning or in the moment, to follow a fairly straightforward narrative; instead of examining the *extent*, they have identified the different ways Holden may have made his life more difficult. The students demonstrated uptake (though a rudimentary form of it) by first responding to the previous speaker before adding another comment, but few other speaking skills are present in the scenario.

It may very well be that, in an attempt to create a culture of respect and rapport, teachers have diminished the value of healthy debate. Promoting civil disagreement within the classroom can be difficult, but below are some strategies that may push students toward using "radical candor" where students can challenge directly while also showing they care personally for their peers (Scott, 2017). Teachers need to encourage students to not settle for the low-hanging fruit of agree + build, but to stretch to the sweeter fruits found through authentic discourse and debate.

## MAKING ROOM FOR NON-CONTENT-SPECIFIC CONVERSATIONS

Often, students can feel ill equipped to challenge ideas presented in texts as they do not feel like experts and therefore that they should not question the content. As a way to combat this notion, teachers should allow for opportunities to step away from the text and provide questions that encourage debate. As students are always passionate about food, I humbly submit the following prompt: Is a hot dog a sandwich?

> Elizabeth: What? No. Absolutely not. A hot dog just can't be a sandwich.

> Amy: Okay, but why?

> Elizabeth: Well, a hot dog is in a bun.

> Carson: I think it is a sandwich. Elizabeth, you said that it can't be because it's in a bun, but isn't a sandwich just meat encased in bread?

> Owen: Yes, but the bun is just one piece of bread—not two slices as in the case of a traditional sandwich.

> Amy: But then what are we to make of sub sandwiches? Those aren't always fully cut into two slices; it's all still one piece.

Yes, the conversation veers into the absurd, but students are authentically engaging in the question and directly responding to what their peers are saying. They have all seen if not eaten a hot dog in their lives. They feel comfortable in making claims, challenging the other side, and qualifying earlier responses.

Without fail, this single prompt has engaged even the most reluctant of speakers. In part, it is the insignificance of the topic that allows students to feel comfortable expressing their positions and challenging the positions of others without falling into a hostile territory sometimes associated with more significant topics. While this conversation is still a far cry from the work ultimately desired of students, by engaging students in non-content-specific debates, teachers give students the chance to practice discussion moves— especially the difficult process of critically responding to peers—in a low-pressure environment.

The key is to start with a two-sided debate in which the positions are clear (e.g., yes/no) but the reasons need to be identified. When students are ready, teachers can elevate their prompts, making them perhaps more consequential, by identifying the interests of their students and the issues of the day. Below are other prompt questions that may engage students in debate before the addition of content:

- Should our school put tracking devices in student IDs?
- Should students be able to grade their teachers?
- If it is so dangerous, should football be banned at the high school level?

- Should completing one hundred service hours be a requirement for graduation?
- Should parents have access to a student's school email account?

As noted in earlier chapters in this volume, authentic discussion requires students to explore questions without pre-specified answers (Nystrand, 1997). As a way to support a student's ability to challenge another's ideas in discussion, teachers should use prompts that allow for debate, beginning with non-content-related questions before adding the complexity of a class text.

## PHYSICAL DISCUSSIONS

Students may be hesitant in disagreeing with their peers because they do not know where their other classmates stand. It can be intimidating to speak up, and if students think they would be the only voice of opposition, many may elect to remain silent or go with the majority opinion. Therefore, discussions paired with physical movement can allow for a student (and teacher) to visually see the positions of all students before the conversation begins.

Having students move to a corner of the room (to reflect a position from strongly agree to strongly disagree), line up according to the extent to which they agree or disagree with an idea, or even use a staircase to show their position are all ways to engage students physically and cognitively in the conversation. It is important to allow students the flexibility to move to another corner or position at any point when moved by the conversation, thereby encouraging healthy debate for the purpose of persuasion and discovery.

## IDENTIFYING THE CONTINUUM

To further help students feel comfortable in a debate environment, teachers can help students more easily identify the larger conversation and the different positions taken in the debate. For example, students in an advanced placement (AP) language and composition class might be asked to determine whether or not their school should enforce an honor code (a question that appeared on an AP exam). Before beginning the discussion, a teacher may ask each student to identify a position between the two poles and predict and plot three to four other potential arguments along the continuum.

This process encourages students to consider perspectives across the spectrum, recognizing the nuances between positions while keeping them away from resting too much on one extreme or the other. By visually plotting out the potential positions of others, students can better see where they stand in relation to others, thereby helping them prepare for an effective discussion.

**Figure 4.1.   Sample continuum design for honor code prompt**

Another continuum activity would be for teachers to use resources such as the *New York Times*' Room for Debate articles or showing students a debate from Intelligence Squared US, a nonpartisan, nonprofit organization dedicated to restoring reason and civility to public discourse through debate events. Having students plot out the continuum as they read or watch is an alternative to class discussion that still supports students' close listening skill development while preparing them to be effective communicators who can discern the various perspectives in a debate.

## PROVIDING FEEDBACK TO SUPPORT GROWTH

When a teacher views discussion as merely a mode of transportation (idea → writing; idea → reading), the teacher places little emphasis on helping students develop and strengthen their communication skills. When a teacher considers discussion assessment, it typically comes in the form of a rubric at the end of the discussion. While this type of feedback can be helpful at times, it is certainly not the only possible form of formative assessment, nor is it the most effective way to provide feedback to students. When the strategies above are paired with specific and timely feedback that focuses on growth, students can make significant improvements in their speaking and listening skills over time.

## SELF AND PEER TRACKING

As referenced earlier in the chapter, students can develop their speaking and listening skills through active awareness of the discussion moves they and their peers use during a class conversation. Teachers can structure discussions in a way that allows students to identify when they have used a discussion move through providing move slips of paper they can flip through or a checklist with all the moves. These trackers should be minimal in terms of the work required to complete them as the focus should still be on the discussion itself.

Another option would be to have students track their peers during a discussion through a similar checklist or through backchannel digital means using websites such as TodaysMeet.com. This approach works best when there is a small group verbally communicating in the center with an outside group tracking them silently or digitally.

## HALFTIME

Incorporating a discussion "halftime" allows teachers to essentially reset the discussion and give short, specific feedback to students before the discussion continues. This is an opportunity for teachers to use the language of the discussion moves to identify where students have found success thus far and what they may need to try in the second half. Furthermore, establishing a guaranteed halftime prior to the discussion enables the teacher to more easily break into the discussion, support students who are struggling to enter the conversation, and allow all students the opportunity to reflect and adjust.

## METACOGNITIVE REFLECTIONS

Students need to be given opportunities to reflect upon their speaking and listening skills throughout the skill development process. While reflections can be a valuable tool to help students bring closure to a discussion, they can also be used to support metacognitive reflection in which students consider how particular aspects of the discussion affected their understanding, what they did in the discussion to push the conversation forward, and when and how they made adjustments to their own discussion approaches. These discussion reflections could be holistic, as in the following example prompts: To what extent did the discussion enhance, challenge, or modify your original ideas? How did your peers affect your understanding through particular discussion moves?

An alternative to the holistic prompt would be to ask students to look specifically at one particular moment in the discussion, using a template similar to the following: "When we were talking about _____, I _____. My peers responded by _____, which resulted in _____." Short enough to be completed on a Post-it note, this cause/effect mini-reflection may help students see how the choices they make in a discussion have a direct effect on the conversation and on their peers.

These reflection structures can be used as a way to prepare students for the next discussion opportunity as well as preparing them to read or write. Teachers can then use the reflections to determine the extent to which students have internalized the discussion moves, help students set goals for future discussions, and provide feedback on the areas of need. It is important to note that feedback does not necessarily need to be tied to a grade, as explored in later chapters.

## CONCLUDING THOUGHTS: PROMOTING SPEAKING AND LISTENING SKILL DEVELOPMENT

Discussion is an invaluable part of any classroom experience. In discussions, students are able to work through complicated ideas and expand their understanding of class concepts and texts. These discussions can prepare students for more challenging readings and for advanced writing activities, but the benefits can extend beyond preparation for other tasks. Teachers can use daily discourse to support the development of communication skills while doing so in ways that enhance the other aspects of the class. Small adjustments to activities already present in the classroom can ensure student growth in the areas of speaking and listening, thereby helping students more effectively engage in discourse regardless of context, purpose, or audience.

## REFERENCES

Graff, G., & Birkenstein, C. (2010). *They say/I say: The moves that matter in academic writing* (2nd ed.). New York: Norton.

Illinois State Board of Education. (2004). Social/Emotional Learning Standards: Goal 2—Use social-awareness and interpersonal skills to establish and maintain positive relationships, standards 2C and 2D. Retrieved July 19, 2018, from https://www.isbe.net.

Lemov, Doug. (2017, October 27). A front the writing discussion template. Retrieved July 19, 2018, from http://teachlikeachampion.com.

Nystrand, M. (1997). *Opening dialogue: Understanding the dynamics of language and learning in the English classroom.* New York: Teachers College Press.

*Onion.* (2015, April 13). Oh God, teacher arranged desks in giant circle. Retrieved July 19, 2018, from https://local.theonion.com.

Scott, K. (2017). *Radical candor: How to be a kickass boss without losing your humanity.* New York: St. Martin's.

*Part II*

# Reflecting on Practice to Foster Engagement and Learning

When a conversation matters, when context demands a give-and-take exchange of ideas, and when there is a pressing need to communicate clearly, directly, and accurately, what mode of communication is most effective?

Imagine for a moment awaiting medical diagnoses or test results, or perhaps the need to coordinate or resolve a pressing issue with a partner or significant other, or addressing a significant academic or social-emotional concern with a student, which would you do?

a. Write a letter to be sent by mail
b. Draft an email or text message
c. Have a conversation and engage in dialogue

Most of us would immediately (and laughably) eliminate the first choice, writing letters, because the excessive time required to write and respond through the mail is highly impractical. Many of us like to send emails or text messages, but those formats are also susceptible to long waits or concise exchanges that may impede important context, tone, and inflection.

The fact is that when conversations really matter, we speak. When the answers matter, and people need clarity, understanding, and resolution, they talk. So, why do teachers often avoid that native literacy, speech, shared among all students? Research about language development and acquisition tells us that we learn to speak, in almost every case, before we read and write. Perhaps this fact often relegates speaking and listening to a realm on the outskirts of the language arts classroom. Maybe we assume that speaking gets enough practice simply by its constant use in the real world and that calling explicit attention to speaking in the classroom detracts from the ways teachers support and instruct reading and writing.

Shifting a classroom and curriculum to authorize student voices will change how many traditional classrooms work, but that shift won't change the fundamental values we share as language arts teachers. Making room for speaking and listening can have significant positive effects on reading and writing, yet some teachers remain hesitant to include opportunities for their students to talk in class. What we have traditionally valued as knowledge in the language arts classroom, reading and writing, has been slow to invite speaking and listening as equal and integral partners in literacy development.

A move toward a dialogic classroom may alter the hierarchy in a classroom as the teacher entrusts students to make meaning, which initially can be inefficient, clunky, and imprecise. Turning the inquiry over to students can be unnerving and challenge teachers' perceptions of their *roles as teachers*. Discussions can be difficult to assess without a framework and rubric that moves beyond the frequency with which students speak. Traditions in which student achievement and aptitude is a function of the individual possession of "knowledge" and content can cause some to be reluctant to embrace a co-constructed model for learning. Furthermore, many teachers have simply not had the opportunity to witness the interconnectedness of speaking with writing and reading. Teachers, after all, are charged with *causing* learning, and that is no trivial responsibility, which is why knowledge of how and why to implement, foster, and sustain discussion is so critical.

The chapters that follow outline what teachers can do to transform their classrooms into dialogic communities. These steps include crafting curricula that authorize student voices and embracing an instructional role that doesn't diminish or silence these voices. The teacher must learn to facilitate and not dominate discussion by reflecting on how often and how long the teacher interrupts student conversation. These interruptions will decrease if the teacher creates discussion sequences that teach students what academic conversation is, including a framework of argument that mirrors writing expectations. Discussions won't work if students don't know how to use uptake to respond to others, support claims with evidence and explanations, and reflect on their contributions to improve a conversation's quality. The teacher's approach must be principled even when discussion wanes, ceases, or spins out of control—the teacher must problem solve, oftentimes with students, to always honor discussion and the students' voices.

We admit that a discussion-based classroom changes the way teachers and students spend their time together by shifting the control of classroom activity from the teacher to the students, but this shift isn't one that damages learning. In fact, discussion actually increases academic performance, if a teacher can design inquiry units that compel students to talk with each other to create meaning. But adopting a dialogic approach goes beyond improving academic performance—it has an impact on students' engagement and their experience of classroom community. Because classroom conversation relies on student voices, students take more ownership of the class's discoveries and find joy in learning. When students talk to each other face-to-face every day, a community forms. This community is one that offers support, embraces difference, and enjoys the journey together.

The following chapters explore the teacher's role in creating classrooms that foster discussion and in preparing students to embrace and thrive in dialogic classrooms. Chapter 5 illustrates how teachers can improve as facilitators of discussion by reflecting on their practices and collecting data during discussions to enhance the students' experience of the inquiry and improve the discussion. Chapter 6 offers a procedure for teaching students to participate and reflect on productive and civil academic conversations by using argument as a framework to navigate essential questions that complement the skills expected in writing. Chapter 7 acknowledges the challenges that using discussion holds and recommends specific troubleshooting strategies that allow the facilitators and conversants alike to recover from these difficult moments and recapture the discussion's flow. These chapters provide teachers with practical strategies to make discussion a guaranteed and viable instructional approach to improve students' literacy skills.

We must stop talking about speaking and listening and start teaching it.

*Chapter Five*

# Seeing and Hearing What Actually Happens

## Dawn Forde

*Empower* means to give authority over to another. Teachers often use this word to describe what the end goal of their instruction is—to empower students, to make them authorities in their own right. Teachers want students to have the command of writing or the capacity to make complex inferences or the ability to read insightfully. This *command*, this *capacity*, and this *ability* is the evidence of learning—that under our watch students have developed into critical thinkers and concerned citizens when they read, when the write, and when they speak.

Teachers would like to think that they have authorized students to be active participants in their learning, and through this authorization, they have grown academically, socially, and emotionally. This growth can only be realized if students can actively negotiate ideas with their peers, determine the course of classroom discourse, and pursue answers to their emerging questions.

Teachers who foster these skills understand that they can relinquish control of classroom discourse to their students by embracing the roles of teacher as curriculum maker and researcher. As the curriculum maker, the teacher creates the learning experiences that students will have and so the challenge for teachers is to ensure that the design of classroom conversations simultaneously authorizes student voices and ensures that students develop as critical thinkers. As researchers, teachers can observe students' responses to discussion activities and use these observations to improve their roles as facilitators, teaching students to exist within a dialogic community. A teacher can embrace a principled approach to discussion by adopting instructional practices that foster discussion, nurturing an environment that encourages conversation, privileging the students' voices over their own, and utilizing transcripts to enhance the overall quality of the conversation.

## REFLECTION ONE: WHICH APPROACHES PROMOTE AUTHENTIC DISCOURSE? USING INQUIRY AND THEMATIC UNITS TO ENHANCE DISCUSSION

In his article "Is It Time to Abandon the Idea of 'Best Practices' in the Teaching of English?" Peter Smagorinsky (2009) proposed that teachers might abandon the notion of "best practice" in English education, given the demands of national and state testing, teacher preference, and district mandates. George Hillocks Jr. (2009) responded to Smagorinsky's proposal, in "Some Practices and Approaches Are Clearly Better than Others and We Had Better Not Ignore the Differences." Hillocks concluded his rebuttal by noting that "if the teacher is the only one who counts in these matters, then perhaps one practice, method, or paradigm is no better than any other. But if the learning of students counts, then there can be no question that some methods, practices, and paradigms are better than others" (p. 29).

Hillocks's claim notably urges educators to put students and their learning first when it involves curricular and instructional choices. It means that a teacher's preference, comfort level, and interest should not take precedence over a student's opportunity to learn. And if discussion is a method that enhances a student's opportunity to learn, then a teacher must attempt to foster conversation.

Using inquiry, an approach guided by essential questions and a sequence that capitalizes on students' prior knowledge, can enhance the success of a classroom that adopts dialogue at its core. Unlike traditional methods that put the teacher and the content first, inquiry and a structured process approach honors student interest while refining skills, increasing the probability that students can engage in effective dialogue in order to read accurately and write skillfully. Since teachers are still responsible for creating the conditions where students can and do learn, then we must not *ignore* Hillocks's assertion that there are better practices and approaches when we design discussion opportunities in class.

In *Curriculum as Conversation*, Arthur Applebee (1996) contends that "students are more likely to take interest in and derive satisfaction from their work" when questions are authentic. If we want students to engage in meaningful conversation, then we must consider what essential questions will compel students to speak. Some questions resonate with middle and high school students more than others, and teachers must purposely design units around these questions.

Questions about fairness and privilege, conformity and rebellion, and freedom and imprisonment will probably pique students' interest more than questions about texts as reflections of history or specific literary movements—it is not that the answers to such questions are unworthy pursuits but that this information is only relevant to middle and high school students when they contribute to their understanding of fairness, conformity, or freedom.

While questions about the historical significance or the literary significance of a text often possess only a few responses or even one answer, the importance of the essential question is that a single answer will not suffice—that multiple answers result through the negotiation of multiple perspectives and contexts. The essential question requires conversation.

Consider an exchange between students who are evaluating the success of Alex Fulton, a college student who parties in his fraternity and rarely goes to class, landing a job at his father's Fortune 500 company. This activity served as gateway activity to an extended inquiry into success where students would eventually read texts such as *Death of a Salesman* by Arthur Miller, *Outliers: The Story of Success* by Malcolm Gladwell, and a series of thematically related short stories, including Stephen Crane's *Self-Made Man* and F. Scott Fitzgerald's *Winter Dreams*. Using Alex's story as a hypothetical situation, students might negotiate what *success* means in the following ways:

Drew: In no way is Alex successful. He is supposed to go to college to learn, not waste his parents' money. Just because his parents own a Fortune 500 company doesn't mean he can do whatever he wants. This guy is not successful. He's pathetic.

Alejandra: I agree with Drew's assessment of Alex. Who goes to college and just plans fraternity parties? He isn't successful because he is only relying on his parents' money. He isn't working for anything.

Trent: While we might not like what Alex is doing, we can't say he isn't successful. He's the director of sales at a Fortune 500 company. He is successful. He has a good job that makes a lot of money. The director of sales has to know a lot about what consumers will buy, and Alex was able to throw "legendary college bashes." I think that his time at college was well spent, just not the way college students should spend their time.

Drew: So, Trent, if I understand you correctly, you think that Alex is successful? You have to work hard to be successful, not party all the time. We don't even know if Alex earned a degree. The scenario points out that "he spent four years at college," but we don't know if he graduated. Just

because Alex's father is successful doesn't mean he is automatically successful.

Albert: Although I agree mostly with Drew and Alejandra that Alex
didn't work hard for his success, I think that Alex's story illustrates that
sometimes people have perks or advantages, like economics, which allow
them to become successful. We can't discount that Alex ended up successful—at least up until this point.

This discussion illustrates the lively debate that can result when teachers use
questions with multiple answers. In addition to discussing Alex Fulton's
case, the students explored six more successful individuals in order to determine what criteria must be considered to define success. Not only does this
conversation invite multiple perspectives, but it also applies to the students
themselves, who often measure their own success based on academic performances or cocurricular accomplishments.

Teachers must remember that discussions will have the most value if
students can transfer these conversations to other contexts both inside and
outside the school's walls. Prioritizing issues pertaining to students' social-
emotional development and local, national, and global issues will undoubtedly hone the teacher's ability to craft questions that initiate classroom conversation.

But developing an engaging question is not enough. The teacher must
consider how the discussions will help students navigate the essential question. The teacher's practice and approach here is critical as they value or
devalue conversation since the teacher is decidedly in control of whether
discussion and student voices will be honored.

Ralph Tyler notes that "the environment in which people will continue to
develop is one where goals require effort and problems must be solved"
(Nowakowski, 1983, p. 29) and that a teacher must always consider "the
learners: what they have already learned, what their needs are, and what their
interests are and build on them" (p. 27). Tyler's recommendations suggest
that the teacher's primary responsibility is to build a classroom that authorizes students to collaboratively create solutions to problems while improving the students' capacity to do so—essentially tailoring the environment to the learners' concerns and needs day to day. Teachers, therefore, can
empower student voices without abdicating their responsibility by creating
experiences that promote learning.

Teachers might first design a series of gateway activities that introduce
the students to the issues, the vocabulary, and the skills necessary to navigate
the question's possible answers. Gateway activities that foster classroom
conversation include opinionnaires (an inquiry into students' opinions) and
surveys, scenarios and role-playing activities, and case studies and simula-

tions. Because gateway activities typically precede major texts, students have the advantage of designing a conceptual framework before applying and testing their understanding against other authorities such as their teachers or Toni Morrison or F. Scott Fitzgerald. When teachers employ these activities as part of their practice, they position students as authorities since their observations, interpretations, and questions make the concept, the skills, and the texts worthy of study.

To begin a unit on the extent to which technology hindered or fostered relationships with others, for example, students explored a series of scenarios in which technology created a problem for a central character. In one such case, students discussed the effects of online gradebooks and learning managements systems on teenagers' relationships with their parents. Jack Castro, the scenario's central character, finds the online technology helpful since he knows his grades, what assignments are due, and how to contact his teachers, but since his parents also have access to these sites, Jack feels his parents are overly concerned about his progress. An excerpt from this conversation reveals that students sympathize with Jack's situation, knowing all too well the costs and benefits of technology:

> Shivani: Jack's situation is just like ours. I am sure that we are constantly waiting for our teachers to update our grades. Whenever I hear my notifications ring, I am scared to look at my grade. If my grade is good, an A, I am pleased, but if I don't do so well, I worry about getting my test back.

> Benjamin: Shivani, I know how you feel; whenever my math teacher posts quiz scores, my entire lunch table stops whatever we are doing to check out our scores. If the scores are good, then we carry on with whatever we are doing. If the scores are bad, then we talk about how worried we are about our grades, especially since my parents will ask me what went wrong.

> Mary: Yeah—not only will they ask me what went wrong; they will want me to meet with my teacher—even if the whole class does poorly. I try to tell them that one five-point quiz doesn't matter, but it doesn't help. Jack's parents need to give him some space. It's not like he can meet with his teacher on Saturday when the grades are posted.

> Kamen: Well, Mary, your parents are only trying to help you. They are worried about whether your grades are good enough to get into a good college. It's what parents do. They think they are responsible for how well you do in school.

> Shivani: Kamen, that may be true, that parents want what's best for us, but Jack's parents need to lay off. The problem is Jack's parents are

pressuring him so much that I think he's going to rebel. I think that the online gradebooks just cause more arguments between parents and students. They don't really improve relationships. Parents only swoop in when tests and quizzes are low; parents never address when grades are good.

In this short exchange, students expose that Jack Castro's situation is a problem that they face daily. Comments by Shivani, Benjamin, and Mary demonstrate the pressures and stresses that students experience when using online gradebooks while Kamen's contribution reminds the class that parents feel obligated to support their teenagers' learning. All comments demonstrate that these students know the issues that arise as parents and children use online technology in school.

Imagine how students' authority will empower them as they analyze E. M. Forster's *The Machine Stops* or Ray Bradbury's *The Veldt*, two stories that reveal how technology can pose problems between parents and their children. If teachers want to position students as authorities, then it is critical that conversations rely on the expertise of students.

When entering a text, such as *Romeo and Juliet*, *A Tale of Two Cities*, or *The Sound and the Fury*, teachers may feel the need to assume control since Shakespeare's language and syntax, the tumultuous history of England and France, or deciphering stream-of-conscience writing seem essential to navigating these texts—and while work on these challenges might be necessary, teachers who desire to empower student voices should design ways to achieve these goals while still honoring discussion.

Teachers can ensure that curricular conversations continue after prereading sequences by using the knowledge and the questions developed in the gateway activities as the inspiration for "during reading" sequences. For example, if prereading conversations about leadership suggest that students believe followers respond better to democratic rather than autocratic rulers, it appears the teacher must design discussions around the littluns' response to Jack and Ralph as leaders in *Lord of the Flies*.

Similarly, if students judge rebellion as a moral response to an unjust government after reading Martin Luther King Jr.'s *Letter from Birmingham Jail*, the teacher must have students explore the morality of Montag's rebellious actions in *Fahrenheit 451*. An effective strategy is to use the class's conversation in the prereading to create the next conversation. It is a simple strategy, but a strategy that requires the teacher to listen to the current conversation and prepare for the next one. It is a strategy that requires patience, discipline, and restraint.

## REFLECTION TWO: DOES THE ENVIRONMENT ENCOURAGE OR STIFLE STUDENTS' VOICES? CREATING AN ENVIRONMENT THAT HONORS DISCUSSION

Once teachers embrace conversation as an essential mode of instruction, they must dedicate themselves to creating an environment where discussion can thrive. Students entering a dialogic classroom may need to be convinced that student voices matter. In *Opening Dialogue: Understanding the Dynamics of Language and Learning in the English Classroom*, Martin Nystrand (1997) reports that his research revealed that "on average discussion took 50 seconds per class in eighth grade and less than 15 seconds in grade 9" (42). These statistics suggest that students are often passive spectators rather than active participants in classroom discourse.

Teachers must remember that much of a student's experience at school is working independently and listening to authority. Whether it's lectures and vocabulary study or silent reading and in-class essays, students have been conditioned to see their teachers' voices and the work they assign as more important than their own voices and their interests. When teachers ask students to participate in authentic discussion, to see their contributions and the contributions of their peers as legitimate sources of knowledge, then these requests go against what their experience of school has been.

Teachers, therefore, must implement strategies and adopt dispositions that don't dishonor students' agency by treating students as vessels to fill. Just as the teacher's theory of instruction can increase the success of using discussion in the classroom, the teacher can arrange the environment to have an impact on students' perception of discussion as useful and essential in creating a community of learners.

First and foremost, teachers must consider how often their students are given opportunities to discuss. If we say discussion matters, then it must matter, and so we must frequently engage in it. Students should be conversing with each other early in the school year, perhaps the second or third day of school. Introducing discussion early will immediately display that the teacher values student voices. Students then should anticipate conversing publically with their peers every week, not just once a unit or, even worse, once a quarter or a semester.

A final discussion activity on whether George's mercy killing of Lenny in *Of Mice and Men* was moral, or a research unit on a current topic like gun control culminating in a debate, isn't going to convince students that their voices matter. These are onetime, however enjoyable, epochal moments that do not invite students to see their voices as the most important tools and resources in the classroom. So, if the teacher is new to discussion as the primary mode of classroom interaction, then he or she must complete an inventory of the discussions students have or will have over the course of a unit, a semester, and a school year. Intentionally creating frequent discussion opportunities encourages students to see themselves as intellectuals in their own right.

Once a teacher designs these opportunities for dialogue, the teacher must also understand that large-class discussions, particularly those that rely on essential questions, may take more than forty or fifty minutes, especially if the teacher expects students to carefully negotiate ideas. In fact, if teachers want all students to participate in a discussion at least twice, and a typical classroom has twenty-five to twenty-eight students, then it will probably take at least two class periods. Dedicating this time not only allows students to practice listening and speaking skills but also communicates to students that *all* voices matter—not just those who are extroverted, more confident, or quicker thinkers.

Early in the school year, the conversation may even take longer, but this time is necessary so students can learn to function within a dialogic community. Some teachers might hesitate to invest in this time—after all, the teacher can simply transfer this knowledge more efficiently and more accurately than a student-led discussion can; however, if we believe that classroom instruction should enhance students' skills and understanding, and not the teacher's ability to deliver content, then we must provide time for discussion to work.

Every aspect of the classroom environment should contain evidence of the teacher's values. If the teacher values discussion and student voices, the physical space needs to mirror this value. Desks in rows, in table groups, or in a circle display whose voice matters. Desks arranged with the teacher as the focus put the teacher's voice at the center of the universe rather than the students' voices. If we want authentic discourse to occur, then students must sit facing each other.

It seems simple, but when students engage in full class discussion while sitting in rows or small groups, they fail to honor each and every voice. In the case of rows, students rarely turn to face their peers, and they direct their comments to the teacher who endorses or alters their contributions. The teacher then must determine the order of speakers since students are not aware of whose hands are raised and whose are not. Having students converse with one another and noting who has and hasn't contributed are potential challenges when students sit in rows.

Although many teachers have redesigned classroom spaces by arranging desks in groups to foster collaboration, this arrangement, too, can present an obstacle for large-group discussion. In this configuration, the happenings of the small group can distract tablemates from the large-group discussion as students seem to be more aware of what their tablemates do or say rather than the conversation's focus.

When teachers desire to have a large-group conversation, they should place students at the center. Having students move the desks and tables so they can see all the participants engaging in discussion cues students into the primacy of the activity—that we are now arranging the class so our voices can be heard and our ideas can take shape together. Before any conversation, whether small group or large group, take a moment to note how students are arranged—if the teacher wants students to value their peers' voices, then take a few minutes to create a space that respects all participants.

## REFLECTION THREE: AM I SPEAKING TOO MUCH? ENSURING STUDENT CONTRIBUTIONS (NOT THE TEACHER'S MONOLOGUES) DICTATE DISCUSSION

Even if teachers adopt a theory of instruction that promotes conversation and arranges a space that puts students at its center, it doesn't guarantee that students will feel empowered to speak, so teachers must constantly reflect on whether their voices dominate discussion. For years, parents, teachers, and administrators have conditioned students to listen to their teachers, to silence their voices, and to listen to the authority, for the authority has both the knowledge and the discipline to help learners succeed in school—and students want to be successful. Students, therefore, might easily surrender to the teacher's voice if the teacher decides to use it.

If teachers want classrooms that empower student voices, they must acknowledge that every time the teacher speaks, students will defer to the teacher's contributions and questions as "the right answers." These "right answers" will carry more weight than their peers' contributions, and the class will regress into recitation, a question-and-answer session with the teacher, rather than engaging in authentic discourse, where students exchange contributions and challenge interpretations with each other.

Students may even want to assure themselves that the class's discussion is accurate by directly asking the teacher questions such as, What do you think, Ms. Forde? Ms. Forde, are we right? and, Do you agree with Carter's interpretation, Ms. Forde? These questions in conversations are critical because teachers can either empower student voices or their own voices—and teachers need to act literally in seconds to value the former and avoid the latter.

It would be remiss if we did not acknowledge that teachers may feel frustrated by facilitating discussion initially, particularly if this practice is new for them. Teachers may find themselves wanting to correct interpretations, respond to questions, and alleviate awkward silences, but the guitar teacher does not strum the strings for her aspiring musician, nor does the soccer coach dribble the ball for his athletes. Instead they invite and encourage their novices to play the instrument or the game in order to improve their skills and understanding of the endeavor. Teachers, too, must allow students time to practice and to participate in discussion not only because it is the nature of learning but also because acclimating students from quietly listening to actively engaging takes time. The teacher, therefore, must expect misinterpretation, refrain from answering questions, and find comfort in silence.

A teacher must limit teacher-talk time. As much as teachers want to ensure that students emerge from discussion with a nuanced interpretation of Emily Dickinson's poem "Much Madness Is Divinest Sense" or a thorough characterization of Kurtz as Byronic hero in Joseph Conrad's *Heart of Darkness*, teachers must allow students to negotiate meaning. This negotiation includes providing possible explanations of Dickinson's definition of madness or Kurtz's tragic actions, asking peers to clarify their interpretation of the word *sense* or Kurtz's actions as Byronic in nature, and challenging students' readings of the poem's attitude toward society or Marlow's empathy for Kurtz. While the teacher may know the many and varied ways to explain, to interpret, and to challenge these analyses, the students in all likelihood do not, and so in service of discussion, the teacher should refrain whenever possible from entering the conversation.

What if students want teachers to enter the conversation? How should teachers respond? Although teachers may feel compelled to answer questions, especially those directed toward them, or to provide accurate interpretations, particularly when students misread, teachers should refrain from providing answers. Teachers can use a number of strategies to prevent usurping the conversation from students and interrupting the flow of ideas. The goal is to redirect the conversation back to students so they remain in control.

If the teacher feels compelled to speak because of misinterpretations or unexamined perspectives, the teacher can enter the conversation with a question. By responding to students through questions, the teacher will imply that student responses are just as important—and even more important—than teacher responses. Eventually students will direct their questions to each other, knowing full well that the teacher won't be providing answers.

If the teacher enters the conversation, it is to the teacher's advantage to ask questions that elicit multiple responses. This questioning technique reinforces that most questions, problems, and texts have multiple answers, a series of solutions, and competing interpretations and that each answer, each solution, and each interpretation has advantages and disadvantages, costs and benefits, and potentials and limits.

To reinforce the complexity of thinking, the teacher may even count the number of explanations or interpretations by saying, "We are not moving forward until we have at least three different interpretations of Dickinson's use of *sense*," or "How many possible explanations of Kurtz's behavior can we derive?" Have students assess these interpretations, evaluating which interpretations are feasible and which interpretations are limited. Allow them to reflect on what possibilities exist so that students understand that the discussion helps articulate what *is* as much as what is *not*.

In addition, couch any question using the students' previous comments to refocus the discussion on *their* understanding, *their* epiphanies, and *their* struggles. By using the students' names, their words, and their phrasings, the teacher reaffirms the students as authorities and meaning-makers in the classroom. Students will eventually adopt the same strategies as the teacher and direct their questions to their peers.

Last, the teacher needs to authorize the conversations as communal understandings—not what the authority wanted the students to remember—so students feel their ideas and questions are determining the course of learning. At the end of each conversation, students should reflect and respond to the following questions: Have we accomplished the discussion's goal? What truths has this discussion revealed? And what questions has this discussion raised? This series of questions reinforce that students' contributions are central to the class's understanding and ensures that the conversation has value. This discussion sequence also requires students to identify where conversations need to go, aiding curricular design for future conversations.

## REFLECTION FOUR: WHAT'S THE TEACHER'S ROLE IN THE CONVERSATION? TEACHER AS SCRIVENER—THE POWER OF THE TRANSCRIPT AND DATA COLLECTION

Teachers can improve the quality of public discussion and their abilities to facilitate it by listening to their students and transcribing these conversations. Creating transcripts allows teachers to evaluate themselves, their students, and the overall quality of the conversations. Studying these artifacts can reveal the extent to which the teacher's essential question is engaging, whether the talking in class is actually recitation or authentic conversation, and if the teacher dominates or facilitates a discussion. If transcribing seems too much of a chore, the teacher can use audio or video recordings to capture these conversations. Observing these discussions in real time (through transcribing) or upon reflection (through audio and video) will ultimately highlight the successes and growth opportunities for teachers and students alike.

As a recorder of her students' interpretations and insights, the teacher will be less likely to speak and more concerned with accurately depicting the students' exchanges and ideas. These transcripts will serve as texts that teachers can use to analyze their role as facilitators as well as to design future activities. If the teacher does not have access to audio and visual recording, the teacher might collaborate with a colleague who is willing to observe the teacher's class. By working together, the teachers can refine the strategies and behaviors necessary to privilege authentic discourse over teacher talk.

Julie Nelson Christoph and Martin Nystrand (2001) compare starting a discussion to starting a fire—"with enough kindling of the right sort, accompanied by patience, ignition is possible" (250). The teacher can "kindle a flame" by using the transcript to design conversations that incite interest and cultivate an understanding of the essential questions and texts that the course explores. As the teacher examines the transcript, the teacher might reflect on the following questions:

- What issues, comments, and questions incited passionate responses from the participants?
- What characters or plot points intrigue students? Which characters or story lines seemed to resonate with students?
- What examples did students use from their own lives to navigate this conversation?
- Are these examples autobiographical or reflections of current/historical issues?

As the transcript reveals these questions, the teacher will gain insight into the students' cares and concerns, their talents and expertise, and their political and moral perspectives. This information is essential in designing curriculum that both empowers students as authorities and speaks to their passions. Students will feel compelled to speak if they feel their expertise will enhance the conversation.

The transcripts can also reveal how the teacher's students behave in discussion and what skill must be practiced if the students' contributions will reflect the academic discourse that transfers to the reading and writing experiences students will have. The transcript will allow the teacher to make the following considerations:

- Who speaks? For how long? Who doesn't speak?
- Who poses questions? Who likes to answer?
- Which students jump right into the discussion? Who waits to synthesize ideas? Who likes to have the last word?
- Are students negotiating ideas, or are they reporting or even lecturing?
- Are students listening or more concerned with their own voices?

Knowing which students thrive in discussion and which students struggle will allow the teacher to provide feedback that will improve each student's speaking and listening skills while enhancing the quality of the conversation at large. The more conversations students have, the more they will improve as individual contributors and as a community of learners.

Not only will transcripts invite the teacher to consider their students' interests and expertise, but also the transcripts will reveal the students' competence in curricular content. Conversation requires that the participants are familiar enough with the themes, characters, and literary techniques to develop positions, ask questions, and challenge interpretations. Reviewing the transcripts will reveal what conversations need to be had:

- What do students know about the essential question or the text? What have they yet to expose?
- What conversation comes next given the teacher's knowledge of the inquiry, texts, and literacy techniques that students will encounter?
- What questions did students raise? Were they all answered? If not, how will the design of future discussions answer the questions raised in this discussion?

The student exchanges will expose the extent to which they understand the theory of white privilege or the plot in William Shakespeare's *Macbeth* or Sydney Carton's transformation in *A Tale of Two Cities*. The teacher will use these insights to design conversations that will develop more thorough and complex understandings of the essential questions and the materials.

Most importantly, written and recorded transcripts will expose the extent to which the teacher enacts the principles necessary to authorize student voices. If the teacher is new to this practice, then audio/video recordings will probably reveal more about whether the teacher's contributions extinguish or spark discussion than a written transcript.

- How many times does the teacher talk compared to the students?
- Does the teacher interrupt students or the flow of conversation with commentary?
- How long are the teacher's contributions compared to the students' contributions?
- Are the teacher's contributions directing students to specific interpretations?
- Does the teacher's contribution resemble mini-lectures?
- Has the teacher allowed students to pursue their own questions—even if the pursuit takes longer than expected?
- Does the teacher praise or dismiss contributions, privileging some contributions over others?

If the transcript or recording contains mostly student voices, then the teacher can continue to plan with the students' interests, content knowledge, and skills in mind; however, if the transcript reveals that the teacher's voice dominates the discussion, then the teacher should use the responses to these questions to change the practices that diminish the students as authorities and silence their voices.

## CONCLUDING THOUGHTS: HEARING THE VOICES THAT MATTER MOST

In the preface to *Reflective Teaching, Reflective Learning*, George Hillocks Jr. (2005) observes that what the teacher values emerges from the teacher's practice—what is actually seen and heard—and not what the teacher says she values from what she thought she saw and heard. He declares that "saying we care is easy and trivial," but "making such care manifest itself in every class is neither easy nor trivial" (xx).

This manifestation of care requires teachers who design curriculum that fosters discussion to accurately characterize the classroom conversations that they witness and then reflect on ways to improve these experiences to enhance students' abilities to speak logically, listen attentively, respond appropriately, and question critically. In order to guard against the lip service Hillocks notes, we should adopt a principled approach to discussion to prove to our students that we do indeed believe their voices matter most.

## REFERENCES

Applebee, A. N. (1996). *Curriculum as conversation: Transforming traditions of teaching and learning.* Chicago: University of Chicago Press.

Christoph, J. N., & Nystrand, M. (2001). Taking risks, negotiating relationships: One teacher's transition towards a dialogic classroom. *Research in the Teaching of English, 36*(2), 249–286.

Hillocks, G., Jr. (2005). Preface: What have I tried to teach my students. In T. McCann, L. Johannessen, E. Kahn, P. Smagorinsky, & M. Smith (Eds.), *Reflective teaching, reflective learning* (pp. vii–xxii). Portsmouth, NH: Heinemann.

Hillocks, G., Jr. (2009). Some practices and approaches are clearly better than others and we had better not ignore the differences. *English Journal, 98*(6), 23–29.

Nowakowski, J. R. (1983). On education evaluation: A conversation with Ralph Tyler. *Educational Leadership, 40*(8), 24–29.

Nystrand, M. (1997). *Opening dialogue: Understanding the dynamics of language and learning in the English classroom.* New York: Teachers College Press.

Smagorinsky, P. (2009). Is it time to abandon the idea of "best practices" in the teaching of English? *English Journal, 98*(6), 15–22.

*Chapter Six*

# Inviting Student Reflection on Participation

## Andrew Bouque

When faced with struggling readers, do colleagues ever suggest that they should no longer instruct their students to read? Where are the teachers who, when faced with struggling writers, would conclude that they should no longer instruct their students to write? Teaching students to read and write well has always comprised the fabric of the language arts profession, and few would disagree that teaching students to read, write, and communicate with fluency is critical to their development as educated, literate, and engaged citizens.

But when faced with a class of students who struggle to engage in sustained and meaningful academic discourse, teachers might reconsider the expectation that students engage in frequent academic dialogues. They may even urge their colleagues to abandon classroom discourse altogether.

It's no wonder teachers sometimes retreat from the expectation that students should talk in class. Few language arts experiences are as awkward and uncomfortable for students and teachers alike than a discussion gone badly. Nevertheless, who among us would dispute that our collective charge as literacy instructors means that our students become competent readers, writers, *and* speakers? While many of the rich student discussions on literature, life, and meaning take place in the language arts classroom, it took the introduction of the Common Core English Language Arts Standards to elevate and articulate explicit standards for speaking and listening and place them as equal partners with reading and writing in the education of a well-rounded and literate student.

Some of the most exciting and rewarding moments in a language arts classroom occur when students engage deeply in meaningful dialogue about works of literature or relevant issues. In those flow experience moments, time seems to pass swiftly; students eagerly participate, finding their voices with passion and conviction; and the classroom becomes a place of authentic engagement as all are compelled to contribute, explore, create, solve, refute, and defend positions. The ending bell comes as a surprise; students plead to discuss again tomorrow, and others continue their dialogues into the hallways as they gather their materials and head to their next classes.

How do teachers capture those "lightning in a bottle" moments and make them more a part of the day-to-day literacy experience in the classroom? How can teachers lay the groundwork for rich, dialogic exchanges among their students? If the goal is to foster deep, sustained dialogues in our classrooms, teachers must commit to allowing their students to use their voices with frequency. Teachers will have to commit to valuing classroom discussion as an equal partner to both writing and reading, as they teach their students how to talk to one another by supporting their own reflection on classroom discourse as well as feedback on how their conversations can improve.

## WHY A FRAMEWORK OF ARGUMENT MATTERS IN TEACHING STUDENTS TO DISCUSS

It's hard to dispute that young adults like to talk to one another, and teachers would well serve their students' literacy development by capitalizing on this truth. When a teacher commits to fostering dialogue in the classroom, the teacher needs to also commit to *instructing students how to talk to one another*. Authentic conversations undoubtedly serve many purposes in our lives, but in the classroom, the purpose of dialogue should be predominantly academic; therefore, choosing a framework that is also academic, like *argument*, provides a variety of useful instructional benefits:

- a common vocabulary to describe the contents and types of contributions students make during and after discussion as students participate and reflect upon theirs and others' contributions
- a consistent underlying framework for preparation, contribution, and response in a discussion
- a consistent and transferrable model for student writing
- a reliable feedback mechanism for assessment and growth over time

Just as instructors would teach students how to write or to read, preparing students to participate in academic discourse can benefit from some thoughtful sequencing of instruction. Introducing students to an argument framework prior to discussion will help foster a classroom in which sustained and meaningful academic dialogues occur.

One of the clear benefits of argument is that it establishes a common vocabulary for both spoken and written contributions. Students need not only a way to address the content of their peers' contributions but also a framework that identifies the component parts of the contributions. Students who prepare to discuss by crafting arguments with claims, evidence, and warrants around important inquiries or issues will have the raw materials they need to engage in meaningful inquiry. Booth, Columb, Williams, Bizup, and Fitzgerald's *Craft of Research* (2016) and Hillocks's *Teaching Argument Writing, Grades 6–12* (2011) provide useful definitions for essential terminology:

- *Claim, or point.* The student's assertion; what the student is trying to prove, argue, or demonstrate. At minimum, a claim should be a point that is debatable or contestable and requires an argument to support.
- *Evidence or data.* The necessary explanation or analysis of it which will likely include the supporting texts, verbal and nonverbal, and surveys and samples. In language arts classrooms, these are most often the works of fiction or nonfiction, and visual or audio texts that comprise the data relevant to a given discussion or inquiry.
- *Warrant.* The commonsense rule that people accept as generally true laws, scientific principles or studies, and thoughtfully argued definitions that "justify" how or why evidence actually supports a claim.

A framework of argument is useful from a teacher's perspective as well in that it provides clarity and specificity of feedback for instructional and assessment purposes. Argument can help demystify a teacher's discomfort about how to assess student contributions in a discussion. For those who are required to assess student growth with respect to literacy targets, a framework of argument provides the underlying "rubric" to assess this growth.

Teachers who support student discussion know that some student voices resonate while other students are more reserved, preferring to listen than to offer verbal contributions. Evaluating student performances in a discussion can be challenging, and while we likely want all of our students to engage freely in every discussion, *frequent and quality contributions are not always the same.*

Students who speak often may earn high marks for participation, but those students have not necessarily displayed proficiency in argument without demonstrating facility with making claims and supporting those claims with logical reasons, textual evidence, and appropriate warrants and backing. Likewise, more reserved students who only contribute to discussion once or twice may demonstrate proficiency or even mastery of argument through the quality of their contributions with respect to claims, evidence, warrants, and backing. Without a framework for what makes a quality contribution in a discussion (which a framework of argument provides), teacher feedback may be limited to urging students toward greater (or less frequent) contribution or possibly some constructive social-emotional considerations, neither of which are academic in nature.

Furthermore, adopting a framework of argument for discussion has powerful transfer benefits for student writing. A framework of argument in speaking supports and reinforces the ways of thinking, analyzing, and responding to others that many teachers expect in their students' written arguments. As argumentative discourse mimics arguments in writing, discussions become the testing grounds upon which students practice their interpretations and positions by making claims, introducing and explaining evidence, and engaging in close analysis.

The classroom is an authentic, live audience (in contrast to the imagined audience of most writing assignments) as student contributions receive feedback in real time, often from a multitude of classmates, whereby they must refine and revise their thinking in order to articulate their arguments and interpretations with greater precision, clarity, and awareness of audience and the ubiquitous opposing viewpoints. Adopting a framework of argument from day one through one hundred and eighty can be a powerful approach in supporting students across all literacies, especially speaking and listening.

## PREPARING STUDENTS FOR A DIALOGIC EXPERIENCE

Every language arts classroom makeup is different, and all teachers must implement instruction that responds to the various needs of their students. Often there is no guarantee that incoming students will have had much instruction in how to engage in discussion or why they even should engage in discussion. It is rare, indeed, that teachers begin a new school year or semester with students who have been taught how to speak to one another, and rarer yet that students experience vertically aligned or programmatic instruction and assessment in speaking and listening. Laying the groundwork early and providing frequent opportunities for students to speak to one another across the entire semester or, even better, the entire year will provide significant growth opportunities for nearly all students.

Imagine incoming freshman students entering a dialogic high school classroom where the teacher has planned to engage the class in a short inquiry into the nature of being a successful student. Students begin the year with a short and focused unit on argument, a critical unit in the initial instructional sequences that will establish the framework for how students engage in discussion, writing, and thinking. Preparing students to learn how to discuss in an inquiry environment should happen immediately, as the necessary negotiations that must occur throughout the school year will be frequent and essential to preparing students to write.

Following the short argument unit, the teacher asks students to review a collection of documents (statistics, nonfiction articles, testimonies, and a short video) to support an inquiry into the question *What makes a successful student?* This particular inquiry is appropriate at the beginning of a school year for several reasons: students explore a variety of perspectives on the definition of academic and scholarly success as well as competing definitions of a student versus a learner. Students select and organize the data within the documents and craft a claim as an answer to the question *What makes a successful student?* As they test and refine their claims through the initial discussion, they will apply their new insights days later to Paulo Coelho's *The Alchemist*, their common summer reading assignment, as they analyze Santiago, the main character, as a successful student.

The early stage objectives for teaching students to engage in all-class discussions are fairly straightforward. The teacher must convey a consistent and frequent expectation that classroom discussion is about including all student voices in an effort to refine and strengthen everyone's arguments as well as develop deeper literal and inferential comprehension of texts and problems within the inquiry that is the discussion. On the first day of discussion, we want our students to engage freely with one another, testing and revising their claims, supporting and challenging one another, and asking the questions that complicate the discussion or even take it in new directions.

There are some key considerations that the teacher might emphasize in the early stages of preparing students to talk. First, students must be prepared with content to contribute to a discussion. Without prepared content, there won't be a sustained discussion. In every planned class discussion, the use of graphic organizers is absolutely necessary. Students must be prepared to talk by offering claims, as well as a variety of supporting evidence and reasoning.

Next, we want our students to have a civil and respectful way of addressing one another, demonstrated through uptake of ideas and the acknowledgment of their classmates by name. Every effort to build a respectful and collegial tone contributes to a positive classroom community that will support authentic discussion throughout the year.

Third, we want our students to understand that a discussion is the collective processes through which they are working through problems by making arguments. The teacher should reinforce the message that discussions support everyone by developing deeper, collective understanding of the issues/topics/problems and questions of the classroom.

These new understandings can be made permanent through strategic reflection during a discussion—reflection after or through essays/writings that relate to the discussion topics.

- Students must be prepared to enter the conversation. Effective preparation requires time and a structure like a graphic organizer or planner.
- Students must be civil and collegial to one another by acknowledging each other by name and using uptake in their contributions.
- Students must engage as a community working toward a deeper collective inquiry into the discussion topics.

Several days prior, students prepare their arguments for the discussion question by reading the text they will use in the conversation. Graphic organizers should include at minimum the critical questions or inquiry as well as sufficient room to write a claim, a series of reasons or subclaims, and evidence and explanations (which would include warrants). A completed organizer should be initially considered a student's preparation, and on the day of the discussion teachers should take the time to visually check every student's organizer and record its relative "completeness." As students enter the classroom for the first discussion, this particular seating arrangement will consist of two concentric circles (or squares/rectangles, whichever structure can distinguish between those discussing and those listening).

There are a few factors to consider: (1) The students who will begin the discussion, the conversants, should be seated in the center of the classroom in an arrangement that allows all of the students to address one another face-to-face. (2) The students seated on the outside, the listeners, should be arranged so they are close enough to the conversants to clearly hear everything that is said. And (3) the arrangement of desks or tables should be such that allows free movement into the center and back out to the perimeter. For expediency's sake, the teacher should make every effort to arrange the room and publicly display the names of students who will begin the discussion on the inside and who will be on the perimeter.

Once everyone is seated and ready with their prepared materials for the *What is a successful student?* discussion, the teacher should quickly check each student's preparation for relative completeness. Such checks can be completed in various ways depending on the technological supports available to students and classrooms. Some students have access to iPads or tablets while many still prepare on paper organizers. Regardless, it is important to have a clear sense of how prepared students are upon entering a given discussion because there are often clear correlations between quality of preparation and effective contribution.

Providing class time to prepare for discussions is time well spent in these formative stages of learning how to discuss. Naturally, as students become more familiar and proficient with the procedures of discussion, teachers may limit class time for preparation. Observed preparation for each student is a critical data point that a teacher will find useful as part of the individual student assessment picture throughout a school year.

## THE DAY OF DISCUSSION: WHEN THE ONLY QUESTION THAT MATTERS IS, *WHAT MAKES A SUCCESSFUL DISCUSSION?*

The initial conversation for any group of young students serves a multitude of purposes, but none is more critical than inviting students to reflect on how they and their peers are doing in their first discussion and what they think they can do to improve the overall experience. Getting to the heart of the question or the inquiry is less important than inviting students to reflect on the demonstrations of the process themselves.

In these formative discussions, teachers should get involved, but not in the actual student conversation. The teacher should take an active role in pausing the discussion for the sake of metacognition so that students invest in the process of reflecting on how they are doing. These reflections should be documented on the board and used to generate a class rubric, or at minimum the criteria by which students aspire to be proficient speakers and listeners.

For students, the initial class discussion will be a nervous moment in which they are "formally" presenting their voices in a performance-like setting. The discussion might be choppy and disjointed, lacking a natural rhythm or flow that will develop over time. Students will be nervous and unfamiliar with how to proceed. The teacher should be patient, supportive, and reassuring throughout this process. Emphasize that these discussions are practice and that the class will work together to generate the characteristics of strong and effective discussion.

The teacher should inform students that he will support them by building in pauses when they can reflect on how the discussion is going. These teacher cues are a critical scaffolding practice that should be used early on, but not overused once students have internalized the habits of mind and procedural knowledge for how to discuss. With enough practice and frequency, students will be able to sustain full class periods and more without any interruption from the teacher, with the exception of occasional cues to keep the discussion focused, efficient, and all-inclusive.

For the first discussions, establish some basic parameters that can be easily seen by everyone in the classroom. A few simple directives will go a long way to clarify the "rules." Since students are divided into two groups, speakers and listeners, it will help to clarify the expectations of each role. Students who begin the conversation will probably want to know what to do:

- *How should I start?* Introduce yourself by name each time you speak. Try to refer to one another by name if you address a point that person made.
- *What can I say?* Offer a claim, reason, or evidence from your organizer. Make a comment or pose a question about something heard or something from the data set.

Students who begin as listeners are going to provide feedback not by listening to what is being said about successful studenthood but by observing key details about how their classmates are doing and what they see as strengths and areas of improvement in the discussion:

- *What should I look for?* Are the students who are talking introducing themselves and offering claims?
- *What should I write down?* Ask yourself what is going well and how you think this group could do better.

Once the responsibilities are clear, the discussion can begin.

## WHAT DO THE EARLY STAGES OF DISCUSSION SOUND LIKE?

The transcript below reflects typical contributions from freshman students in the *What is a Successful Student?* conversation:

Amanda: I'm Amanda. My claim is that hard work and dedication are two of the qualities that one should possess in order to be successful. My main evidence that led me to believe in this was in document B. It says, "Successful students do all of their homework and never turn in work late. The key to doing well in school is responsibility. The successful student is the responsible student." I believe that's also dedication because if you're dedicated to your work and dedicated to what you're doing, you will do well and get all your work done and your grades will improve, so in order to be as successful as possible, your grades need to be good.

Bernard: Uh, Bernard. To a certain extent I agree with you, Amanda. I feel like working hard is really important, and I feel like to go beyond that, a successful student should be passionate about their studies and doing what they want. That's like, hardworking is just doing it just for the grade. Being passionate is going one step further and doing it because you want to do it, and you want to do well.

Sonya: Um, Sonya. I agree with Bernard and sort of disagree with Amanda because I said a successful student is someone who doesn't always focus on the grade but the aspect of growth and development like a learner, and I used evidence from document C. I said that the students were dropping out of college to become like inventors and they were becoming successful without the college education.

Jonathan: Um, Jonathan, um, okay. So, I agree with Sonya and Bernard. I said, my claim was a successful student is one who strives for a higher level of knowledge, a growth inside and outside of the classroom, and one of my reasons was a student who always strives, or one of the reasons I believe the claim is true is a student always strives for growth and will always improve. And I used those from the sources Sonya did, source C, talking about how they dropped out of college to pursue what they wanted to do and grow outside of the classroom.

Margie: Um, Margie. I agree with Bernard because I think that a successful student reflects a hardworking, diverse, and determined and passionate individual, and I found evidence for this, that a determined individual perseveres through challenging situations, in source B when it says, "Many students do well in school with these assets but the truly successful student is the one who doesn't give up when faced with academic challenges." I thought that working through a challenging situation can be just as important as solving an equation at times, and intelligence would be the road to nothing without the determination and passion to do well in school.

Teacher: Okay, so that was the first five comments. I would like you all to take a minute, and in your notes on the inside I would like you to think for a bit and write something down about what you have heard that was new, different, or supports what you were thinking initially. On the outside, I would like all of you to write down a couple of things that you observed this group doing well and maybe one thing that you think they could improve upon. Now, I know you have only heard five contributions, but how are they doing and what could they improve? Inside, what have you heard that was new to you or that you didn't think about? It could be vocabulary, it could have been a certain criterion, it could have been a perspective, and so forth.

(*Students reflect and write for approximately one minute.*)

Teacher: Okay. Stop writing. Outside listeners . . . for the plus column. What do you think they are doing that is really good?

Jamie: Um, I think they are doing a good job at addressing previous comments that were said before.

Teacher: Okay, nice job of addressing previous comments. Keep going, let's hear some more positives.

(*Teacher writes criteria on the board as students reflect.*)

Emmet: Somebody was always speaking.

Teacher: Okay. Someone is always ready to go.

Taylor: Um, their voices were projected loud enough so everyone could hear them.

Teacher: Is that true? Could you all hear what your peers were saying? You have to be honest about that because if you need them to speak louder you have to ask.

Sara: Everyone always has evidence to support their claim.

Teacher: Okay, you heard everyone use evidence for claims. That's a good start. Is there anything they could work on or improve?

Crystal: I did hear a bit of repetition of other people's ideas. I was actually hoping for something new to come up.

Teacher: Okay, some repetition. I am actually going to put a star by that because that's not necessarily a criticism. I think it could be as the discussion goes on, we hear a bit more of the same thing, but you are also working off the same body of evidence and source work, so that's something to be aware of.

Bree: I saw that some people were kind of just staring down at their iPads and not making eye contact.

Teacher: Okay, eye contact. Anything else? Inside group, please consider the feedback you have received from your class that I have recorded on the board. Continue to address previous comments, be ready to contribute, keep projecting your voices and using evidence. Be mindful that you are not simply repeating other ideas, and make sure to make eye contact when you speak. Okay, then, we are going to continue. Now, when I open it back up to you, I am going to let it go for more than five contributions. We were just taking some time to reflect. I would highly encourage you if your thinking has changed and you want to address that or if you want to ask somebody a question now that you have taken a moment to reflect on what others have said to do precisely that.

Trey (inner circle): Can we use like outside sources other than the homework that we did?

Teacher: Let's ask your class what they think. Are all of you okay with using evidence or sources that were not in the texts provided? (*Class response is positive.*) I get the sense that your class feels fine about using additional sources.

Grace (inner circle): Do you want us to note if a student has a different opinion than we have?

Teacher: Because you are in the inner circle, yes. I want you to be focused on *what* you are discussing. I don't want you to be focusing as much on *how* you are discussing. That's the job of the listeners. Your job now is to address the question *What is a successful student?* Anything you hear about that question that helps or challenges the answer you prepared is your territory for notes.

The first, brief round of discussion and shared reflection lasted approximately eight minutes, and in that time thirteen students raised their voices either to offer a claim and supporting evidence about what it means to be a successful student or to provide qualitative, reflective feedback on the process of engaging in discussion.

Among the several features that stand out in the initial five contributions is that students identify themselves and address one another by name; they all state a claim and each contribution that follows Amanda's, the first, offers a claim that agrees or disagrees to some extent with a prior position; most contributions refer to a specific source as support; and most contributions use the vocabulary of argument (claim and evidence) to describe the content of their contributions. During the reflection phase, the class generated six criteria for effective discussion (four positive and two critiques), which were written on the board and included as expectations for improvement as the discussion continued.

As the discussion progressed, the built-in pauses continued to generate reflective feedback. Approximately halfway through class, the inner and outer circles of speakers and listeners were switched. By the end of the period, all students had an opportunity to participate to make arguments and reflect on *What makes a successful student?* and *What makes a successful discussion?* respectively. Even toward the end of the discussion, students continued:

Teacher: Pause. On the inside right now, what I would like you to do is go down to the bottom of your notes where it says "My evolving thinking" and reconsider your definition of a successful student based on what you have heard. What would you add, subtract, or change? You are synthesizing everything you have heard, which is kind of a challenging task right now, but that's what we need to do in discussions. If you are on the outside, I would like you to reflect on the list of criteria that you have noted on how the discussion is going, and I would like you to put a plus next to things that are positive and a minus next to things that could be improved.

(*Students reflect and write for approximately one minute.*)

Teacher: Okay, everyone can stop writing. I would like to hear from the outside. So, as much feedback as you have right now. What are you observing? There's no judgment here. Just what are you hearing?

Anders: I heard that a lot of people were just saying the same thing over and over and over again. I heard branching off of what this person said or based off [of what] this person said, they were saying the same exact thing with different evidence, but it doesn't change the fact that they haven't introduced anything new in the discussion.

Teacher: Okay, so you feel like something that needs to be improved is there was an idea offered and then each contribution that followed was repetitive?

Anders: Yeah.

(*Teacher writes criteria on white board.*)

Teacher: Okay, what else did you see or hear?

Rachel: I was seeing that everyone was saying, "Okay, my claim is . . ." and they would say theirs but no one actually came in and responded to someone else's idea and caused a discussion about that idea. It was just everybody stating their idea.

Christine: I said that they sounded confident and persuasive.

Teacher: Alright. Feel free to talk while I am writing, I can add more . . .

Samuel: They were supporting ideas well, but they weren't tying them back to their claim.

Teacher: Interesting. Over here?

Max: There was good flow in the discussion. It wasn't all cluttered. Everyone waited nicely.

Teacher: That's a nice compliment. Max said you aren't all piling on one another. You are being respectful and letting one another speak. I actually think there was a moment when two students wanted to talk at the same time and they were like, "No, you go," at the same time, which was great. When that happens, and that will happen, somebody just go, but it's a courteous thing that when you are done, you invite that student to make the next comment. If you are in a discussion group and you hear that, please be sensitive to the fact that two people want to go and don't jump in afterward to make a comment until both students have had an opportunity to contribute. What else?

Anders: I remember in middle school that a lot of people would stay on the sides and just not talk, and just five or six people would just rant the entire time. But almost everyone here has said something.

Teacher: And I paused the conversation, so I bet we would hear from even more. This is a good start, and I thought you were doing well. There are several good points of feedback here. When we open this back up, let's look closely at this one (*points to "Responding to someone else's idea"*). I really want you to think about the comment that comes before yours. Whatever you hear when you enter the conversation, I want you to *acknowledge* the comment that came before.

For example, one way you might do this is to say something like, "Sam, you bring up a really interesting point about perseverance as a quality of success, and I would like to develop that more with the following example." So work on trying to transition that idea to the next idea. That doesn't mean you can't change the topic—you can—but always try to let the speaker before you know that you heard them and recognize the importance of their comment. That reinforces the value of every voice, and that is really powerful in academic discourse.

A close look at what the students offer one another as feedback in this excerpt reveals that they have prior knowledge of what effective discourse should sound like. They offer a rich mixture of qualitative, constructive feedback from the originality of the contributions to the need to build upon one another's ideas. There is praise as well, as students compliment their peers' confidence and tone as well as the fluency, rhythm, and high level of participation of the discourse.

During this reflective moment, the teacher's facilitation of student feedback ensures that the tone of the classroom remains positive and encouraging. The initial request to redefine and synthesize acknowledges the challenge of the task as it identifies it as necessary to academic discussion. Next, the teacher frames the feedback as judgment free and frequently restates and records student voices on the board to affirm their validity.

During Max's comment about the rhythm of the discussion, the teacher celebrates the compliment and uses it as an instructional moment to address how the flow of a discussion can be an issue, suggesting a polite method to navigate awkward moments. Prior to reopening the conversation, the teacher challenges the group to incorporate specific feedback by highlighting Rachel's comment about everyone starting with their own idea (Rachel was reacting to the lack of uptake) rather than building upon one another.

At this later point in the discussion, students have continued to observe and critique their own participation as they set goals for improvement for the entire class. As many more participants engage in making arguments about what it means to be a successful student, the pause and reflective moments should address the academic content of the discussion as well as the quality of the discussion itself.

By the end of this first discussion, students have experienced what academic discourse sounds like and feels like; they have entered into the discussion through direct participation in the question or by providing constructive feedback on the process; they have articulated criteria for effective discussion that can be used on a rubric to evaluate their learning; they have tested and revised their original claims on what it means to be a successful student through the consideration of divergent opinions and counterclaims; and they have actively built the foundation of a strong classroom community in which all voices are heard, respected, and acknowledged by name. At the end of class, students should reflect on their preparation for the discussion as well as how the discussion changed their thinking, their participation with respect to the evolving criteria for successful discussion, and a few explicit goals for the next discussion.

## Textbox 6.1. Qualities of Effective Discussion

(*Student-generated criteria*)

- Use appropriate volume and clarity.
- Dedicate yourself to your opinions.
- Engage in contribution (let ideas flow).
- Encourage participation from all.
- Use evidence/sources.
- Agree to disagree politely; be nice and respectful.
- Focus on a central topic.
- Support your thinking with reasoning + evidence.
- Respond to someone else's ideas.
- Make eye contact.

- Have a positive flow/rhythm.
- Project a confident and persuasive tone.
- Let each other talk and finish.
- Elaborate details in explanation.
- Incorporate new ideas.

Within two days after this initial discussion, students prepared to apply their revised perspectives on *What makes a successful student?* to Paulo Coelho's *The Alchemist*, their common summer reading assignment, as they analyze the main character, Santiago, through this inquiry. The transcript that follows reveals the immediate transfer of many of the qualities of effective discussion that students recently generated:

Callie: My claim is that while Santiago may have become an excellent student at the end of the novel, I felt that at the beginning he was simply a learner—not simply—he was constantly learning from what was around him, and he didn't necessarily have someone there teaching him and telling him what to do. Some evidence that I used was "but ever since he had been a child he had wanted to know the world and this was much more important to him than knowing God" (8). The fact that he left the seminary to follow his dreams shows me he is more driven by his own desire to learn than necessarily to learn specific things, like God or sermons.

Erin: If I understand you correctly, you are saying he is very motivated by himself to learn because he didn't really have anyone else guiding him?

Callie: Precisely.

Erin: I would agree with that because it says, "The boy felt jealous of the freedom of the wind, and saw that he could have the same freedom. There was nothing to hold him back except himself" (28). He's basically making the decision on his own. He doesn't have anyone pushing him to do it. He doesn't have anyone telling him he can't. He realizes that it's all up to himself at that point.

Martina: I agree with the fact that in the beginning he wasn't much of a student. I also saw that a student is someone who is willing to take challenges and be willing to do something new that they hadn't done before.

Callie: I have something I think we should clarify before we keep diving into whether Santiago is a student or a learner. How are we going to define student and learner in this discussion?

Ana: I think that a learner is someone who is independent and follows his own path, while a student is more directed and taught by someone.

Martina: I do agree with Ana's difference between a student and a learner, but I still believe that a student is one who has a leader, or a teacher. I also believe that a student is one who is willing to take the challenges that are given to them and doesn't just give up. I found evidence to prove that Santiago was not like a student in the beginning. He asks, "Well how am I going to get to Egypt? I only interpret dreams. I don't know how to turn them into reality. That's why I have to live off of what my daughters provide me with. And what if I never get to Egypt?" (15). I said that he was never willing to take the challenge, like all he kept on doing was thinking, oh, I'll never get there. He didn't really want to do it. He was just trying to make excuses up, not willing to do the challenge, and that's something that is not a student. A student is willing to take the extra step and do the challenge and learn from it, but Santiago doesn't want to.

Ruchi: I agree that students have to be willing to face challenges. And I agree when you say he wasn't willing to take challenges, but later in the section he kind of was willing. It ends with him working at the crystal merchant shop, and so he was willing to put the time and effort into making money for his journey.

Alice: I have a specific quote which is proof he is willing to face challenges because in this moment when he is robbed by the thief, rather than turn away and go back and sell what he has and become a shepherd again, he decides to figure it out and keep moving forward. The quote is, "As he mused about these things he realized that he had to choose between thinking of himself as the poor victim of a thief and as an adventurer in quest of his treasure. 'I am an adventurer, looking for treasure,' he said to himself" (42). This is the point where he decides to keep continuing forward because he's an adventurer. Bumps in the road are going to happen, but to keep moving forward and not give up shows he is willing to persevere through difficulties.

Erin: From what I am hearing from you is that Santiago has gone through a lot of character development to get to that point. Later on in the book when he says, "And after another long silence, he added, 'I need money to buy some sheep'" (47). I think this also shows not only his character development but also that he focuses on personal growth because he understands that in order to get to Egypt he is going to have a lot of different steps along the way, and he accepts that it's going to take more time than he originally thought; because he is willing to take on those challenges, he has come to the realization that he needs to go slowly and understand everything that he needs to in order to arrive at his destination. I think he is more a learner at this point because he reflects on his personal growth, but has qualities of a student too.

Undoubtedly, students use the discussion to test definitions of *student* and *learner* in order to improve the precision and accuracy of their claims about Santiago. During this exchange, the process of defining is evident in every contribution, as Callie offers a claim that *Santiago is a learner*, and Erin employs an uptake phrase ("If I understand you correctly") to clarify and then support the idea that a *learner* operates independently while a *student* has someone else pushing or guiding him or her. The last contribution in the excerpt, also by Erin, opens the possibility that Santiago is both *learner* and *student*. Complexity grows as students contribute.

Unlike the previous discussion transcript where Rachel pointed out that contributions did not build upon one another, this excerpt reveals a constant building, refining, and challenging of the extent to which Santiago is a *learner* or a *student*. Most of the participants use direct textual evidence to support their claims, and each adds new vocabulary in the form of criteria to build a definition of learner/student: independent versus directed/taught, willing to accept challenges, perseverance, and reflection on personal growth.

Although clearly in a formative stage, students are practicing the moves they will make when they write an argument on the same question, *To what extent is Santiago a successful student?* Even a casual examination of the transcript of Callie, Martina, Erin, and Alice reveal the features of strong argumentative writing, minus the obvious first-person perspectives. Such exchanges illuminate the intimate connections between the arguments students speak and the arguments they write. The excerpt that follows is a passage from the culminating activity, a written argument by Callie, which reflects similar negotiations made in the discussion.

## EXCERPT FROM CALLIE'S COMPOSITION

While Santiago may have been a student for brief periods throughout his journey, he can be more appropriately classified as a successful learner rather than a successful student due to his self-guidance, the way he learns from his environment, and his motivation to better himself in the world—all of which stem from his natural desire to learn. . . .

[Santiago's] relationship with the church supports the notion that he is a learner rather than a student because it highlights a key difference between students and learners: students are taught what they need to know by someone else, while learners increase their knowledge out of their own desire. . . . Santiago has not only yearned to better understand the world—he did understand the world. His natural desire to learn is a quintessential trait of all learners, and it is one that most prominently distinguishes them from students.

Santiago's curiosity in conjunction with his personal growth, from clueless boy to understanding the language of the world, supports the claim that he is a successful learner. Many will argue that Santiago is actually a student because he is constantly being taught by the desert, the Alchemist, the camel driver, the crystal merchant, and so forth. However, they would be mistaken because Santiago was drawing his own conclusions from all of these people, not being told what to think.

In fact, the Alchemist himself stated to Santiago, "I only invoked what you already knew" (154). When under the guidance of the Alchemist, Santiago was the closest to a student he could be along the duration of his journey due to the intentional tutelage the Alchemist provided; however, Santiago's motivation was never to become rich from his treasure . . . his decision to follow his heart, his own beliefs, over those of the Alchemist further confirm his position as a successful learner, not a student.

Callie's claim, the support that follows, and even the acknowledgment of her opposition ("Many will argue") depends almost entirely on the negotiations that occurred during three full days of class discussion. Her ability to navigate the prompt, move between competing definitions of *student* and *learner*, and apply those definitions to a work of literature was made possible by the feedback of her peers through a series of opening discussions that generated not only the criteria and content of her essay but also the standards by which she and her classmates would engage with one another in discussion as civil, academic argument.

Rich and productive class discussions don't just happen spontaneously; rather, with a deliberate eye toward planning and a supportive, patient optimism, teachers can foster classrooms in which student voices emerge in powerful ways. Students arrive on the first day of class as thoughtful and reflective persons, eager for a framework that will free them to make and negotiate meaning of complex texts, issues, and inquiries.

The opening sequence of discussions serves critical roles in teaching students how academic discussion works and why they engage in discussion at all. Providing even a little argumentative framework will go a long way in reinforcing the similarities between speaking and writing—a powerful combination in literacy instruction. In embracing a framework for reflection, in which students work together to identify, define, and apply the qualities of successful and effective discussion, teachers authorize their students to inspire themselves and their peers to live the literacies the language arts profession values.

## REFERENCES

Booth, W. C., Columb, G. G., Williams, J. M., Bizup, J., & Fitzgerald, W. T. (2016). *The craft of research*. 4th ed. Chicago: University of Chicago Press.

Coelho, P., & Clarke, A. (1998). *The alchemist*. New York: HarperOne.

Hillocks, G., Jr. (2011). *Teaching argument writing, grades 6–12: Supporting claims with relevant evidence and clear reasoning*. Portsmouth, NH: Heinemann.

*Chapter Seven*

# Planning, Managing, and Troubleshooting for Rich Discussions

## Andrew Bouque and Dawn Forde

Engaging students consistently in authentic discussion presents a number of challenges. Teachers report that typical problems they encounter when trying to engage in authentic discussion include the following:

- Lack of student participation
- Aggressive or disrespectful behavior
- A few speakers dominating the conversation
- Participants all talking at once or talking over each other
- Conversations that are primarily unsupported claims or off-the-cuff opinions
- Frequent off-topic or off-point comments
- Participants speaking without regard for any connection to what others have said
- Round-robin, turn-taking participation rather than dialogic exchanges among participants
- Teachers frequently feeling they have to fill a void and end up doing most of the talking

Experiencing one or more of these challenges sometimes results in teachers abandoning the goal of authentic discussion or attempting it infrequently. However, we wouldn't consider abandoning reading or writing because students are experiencing difficulty. Instead, teachers would design instructional strategies that would ultimately improve the students' skills in these areas.

So since "dialogically organized instruction . . . had a strong, positive effect on achievement," as Nystrand (1997) concluded (57), it makes sense to find ways to "troubleshoot" these difficulties. This chapter presents numerous strategies that teachers can use to address the variety of challenges involved in discussion-based approaches.

To a great extent, these challenges can be avoided if students are equipped to engage in civil discourse; therefore, do not underestimate the role preparation plays, particularly when students are new to the experience. As students internalize the criteria for strong contributions and learn to work with their peers, they will not need as much time to prepare themselves for discussion as novices do; however, in order to increase the likelihood that the discussions will be as productive as possible, the teacher should build in planning time for students before every discussion just as the teacher would encourage prewriting and planning strategies before students compose each essay.

## HELPING STUDENTS PREPARE FOR DISCUSSION

Teachers ought to share with students the question or problem before the conversation occurs so students can reflect on how they will want to respond. In addition, materials should accompany the prompts. Students shouldn't be blindsided by topics or themes. They must understand the nature of happiness, obligation, or redemption, if the discussion prompt requires them to do so.

The discussion prompt might also necessitate that students know literary terms such as *narrator reliability, extended metaphor,* or *symbol.* In these cases, students should have procedures for determining whether a narrator is reliable and a method for explaining how extended metaphors and symbols work. Don't just "see what students know" about topics, themes, or literary terms—it typically won't go as well as a deliberate plan that considers how discussions need to be sequenced in relation to topics, themes, and terminology.

If the discussions revolve around concepts like strong leadership or disillusionment, for example, then the teacher should provide resources for students. If the theme is leadership, then teachers might use philosophic commentaries on the nature of power and news stories about current world leaders to help students define the qualities of an effective leader. In a discussion about teenage disillusionment, teachers might provide psychological texts about the teenage brain and poems about growing up, such as "On Turning Ten" by Billy Collins or "Crossings" by Judith Ortiz Cofer, so students can come to understand that there are physical as well as emotional changes during this period of adolescence.

A new topic or theme requires a new understanding so, as a result, students need to prepare for these moments as a result. For example, a discussion that invites students to consider punishment in schools in preparation for discussing Hester's punishment in *The Scarlet Letter* might require students to explore the differences between shame and embarrassment, the consequences of intrinsic versus extrinsic motivation, and the evolution of the American justice system from stocks to prisons to rehabilitation.

Applying social, psychological, and historical contexts to the way schools and governments apply punishments requires planning time in order to make a rich discussion. Preparation for discussion may look like preparation for an essay with students composing claims, finding supporting evidence, and explaining and warranting evidence, all skills necessary for strong written responses. In *Transforming Talk into Text*, McCann (2014) describes these exchanges as "exploratory dialogue," conversations necessary to "discover positions, identify examples, and respond to counterarguments" (82). This preparation will reinforce writing skills while giving students a framework for reading—and the teacher should require this type of preparation and provide feedback for it.

Although some might contend that this type of preparation seems scripted, these plans are critical for students new to academic discussion as there may be too many concerns to navigate in real time, including displaying an understanding of the topic and texts, constructing quality contributions that reflect one's thinking, and ensuring that the class's conversation is generative and democratic. Just as a coach would have students practice individual skills before scrimmaging and game time, so too should the teacher who uses discussion in class.

The preparation might also require that students take into account the various formats and structures used in discussion. If the teacher uses a fishbowl configuration, a format where the outer circle responds to the inner circle, then students need to know what their responsibilities are in either circle. The inner circle must come prepared to share their arguments while the outer circle must craft questions to challenge these arguments in order to create a deeper understanding of the texts and question involved.

Another format may require students to take on a particular perspective or interpretation. For example, simulations may require students to take on the role of parent, an administrator, or a counselor. Before negotiating the issue with their peers, it is advantageous for students to consider how these lenses shape the topic and what texts or parts of texts this stakeholder might use to develop her argument and challenge others' arguments.

When the conversation follows a debate format, students should consider the limitations of their own arguments by predicting what objections might be raised. These considerations will prevent the conversation from descending into awkward silences, since students have reflected on how to respond to these challenges. Changing the formats of discussion and then using each format at least two to three times in the school year not only allows students to internalize the structure of each but also prevents any format from becoming overused and then losing authenticity.

## WHAT TO DO WHEN STUDENTS DON'T PARTICIPATE

Inevitably, every classroom will have a population of students who are reluctant to engage in discussion. There are a variety of challenges for students in adapting to a classroom that emphasizes discussion, especially large-group or all-class discussion. Many students find the shift from small-group discussion groups of four students or fewer to a group of twelve, fifteen, or more with an audience just as large to be intimidating and uncomfortable.

Students who are hesitant or uncomfortable in discussion typically have good reasons for being so, and each student may need some personal attention in order for the teacher to understand the particular context and individual challenges students face. The following strategies can help students raise their voices for the first time and can function as supports for students to develop increasing confidence and comfort as they work toward improved participation.

### Brief Meetings with Students

Teachers can provide students with an initial boost of confidence by finding time to meet with them to review their preparation prior to the day of discussion. These meetings can be brief, but they should engage the student in informal discussion about the prepared claim, reasons and evidence, and ask questions about what aspects of the preparation the student feels most confident. Then, ask the students how they plan on contributing to the class discussion. These short meetings can do a great deal in getting students to commit to participating in discussion.

### Goal Setting

Another effective strategy for reluctant students, which is also useful for all students, is to have them set realistic goals for themselves. Some of the suggestions listed below may help, and the point here is that students commit to making a verbal contribution to discussion. Initially, a realistic goal may be as simple as offering one contribution. As students become comfortable with making a single comment, they should be challenged to increase the frequency and variety of their contributions. Students should reflect on the kinds of contributions that exist in most argumentative discussions and find out what they are most comfortable trying.

## The First Voice

Navigating the ebb and flow or rhythm of a discussion can be like merging onto a highway for the first time. Soon after a discussion begins, it develops a momentum of its own, and students who have a difficult time finding their entry point in a discussion will benefit from the opportunity to start the discussion as the first voice. Instead of asking the class who would like to begin, teachers can offer these students the opportunity to open the dialogue by sharing a claim and supporting evidence. Sometimes this is all that is needed to get a student involved at the onset.

## Lower Stakes Contributions

Another way to invite students into the conversation is to have them consider "lower stakes" contributions as alternatives to the claims, evidence, and explanations that they have prepared. For example, sometimes students are more comfortable with posing a question or asking for clarification of another student's point. These contributions are lower stakes in that they don't require a student to offer an original interpretation or explain evidence. Instead, clarifying questions tend to help all participants follow the conversation and comprehend/interpret with clarity and help some students raise their voices in a conversation.

## "She Said What I Was Going to Say"

A common obstacle for students in discussion is the perception that the evidence they identified and analyzed has been "taken" by another student and therefore is no longer valid. Encourage students who feel that others have addressed all of "their" preparation to listen carefully and offer alternative interpretations or nuanced ways of using the same evidence. There are always multiple ways evidence can be used and interpreted. In the case of identical evidence, students can acknowledge that they also had the same evidence but then share how they used it for a different reason or interpreted it in a different manner.

## Fear of Disagreeing

Sometimes students feel that their unique interpretations isolate them from engaging with a larger group. Students might say they prefer not to participate because they don't agree with what the rest of the class says. In cases like these, encourage students to embrace their disagreement and offer a challenge or an objection to a claim, interpretation of evidence, or a warrant. Such disagreements often elevate the complexity of the discussion.

Sometimes, students find it liberating or "easier" to disagree with another student's contribution by offering a different perspective or alternate view of a claim, evidence, explanation, or warrant. Typically, reluctant students are reserved or shy but not lacking strong opinions or viewpoints on the discussion topic. Disagreement is essential to any effective discussion, but playing the role of contrarian should include an explanation of how or why one disagrees.

## Hearing All Voices

Teachers should be mindful to build in opportunities to hear all voices. Even with a variety of strategies and setting individual discussion goals, some students will not engage. A teacher can build in pauses during and at the end of discussions to invite voices that haven't been heard. Asking, "Is there anyone who would like to offer a comment, claim, or interpretation who hasn't had the chance to contribute?" can provide the inroad that some students need to participate.

Another strategy during conversation is a simple reminder that not all voices have been heard and that the students themselves should be mindful of the patterns and frequency of voices. With some consistent messaging via verbal cues and reflection on the democratic nature of discussion, students will develop a keener awareness of the communal nature of the dialogue and begin inviting their peers into the conversation directly.

## Fighting to Be Heard

As student competence and comfort in discussion grows, so will their confidence. Several factors can shift an otherwise congenial and polite conversation into a more aggressive interaction as students clamber for "airtime" and voices become competitive rather than generative. In a sense, this is a "good" problem to have because it is evidence that students want their voices to be heard, but it can also be a sign that students have forgotten the purpose of the discussion and are focused only on their own participation rather than the collective inquiry.

If a teacher focuses too much on frequency of discussion contribution rather than quality, students may be more likely to compete for opportunities to talk, leaving other willing, but less aggressive participants on the sidelines. Unfortunately, simple reminders do not always correct discussions that become aggressive and competitive, but it's a good idea to take the time before each discussion to remind students of the shared responsibility to provide opportunity for all student voices to be heard. If the discussion becomes too aggressive, the teacher should stop the conversation and ask students to reflect on the tenor of the conversation and suggest some strategies for addressing the competitiveness.

## Students Directing the Discussion

Another strategy is to have students call on one another after a contribution, rather than a more free-form open dialogue. After a student makes a contribution in discussion, others will want to respond, but they must raise their hands to be called on by the last speaker. This can be a really effective method provided no student is repeatedly denied an opportunity to speak. If the dynamic limits students who are actively trying to contribute, consider placing contribution limits on participation until all students have had the opportunity to speak.

Some teachers monitor the discussion from the white board or through a projector, writing names down in order as students raise their hands. This approach guarantees each student secures an opportunity to speak, but it will impact the free-flow exchange of ideas and may demand creative uses of uptake to transition from one contribution to the next. It is sometimes necessary when students struggle to show restraint or self-awareness. Obviously, interventions that restrict flow experiences and authentic engagement are not optimum, but when students struggle to show restraint or self-awareness, ground rules are sometimes necessary to guarantee opportunities for all students to speak.

## WHEN CONVERSATION STALLS

Even if students are prepared and understand the importance of each and every peer's contribution, there will be moments when conversation stalls. These moments will happen more frequently when students are first learning how to participate in discussion, particularly when the students' have either failed to prepare enough or don't feel comfortable enough to move away from their prepared arguments to the arguments that the discussion necessitates.

Even when students are experienced speakers, every now and then the conversation may stall given the difficulty of the topic, the text, or even time of year (near winter and spring final exams, before extended breaks, or even in October and April, months that present challenges for teachers and students alike). Instead of abandoning the conversation, the teacher should use these opportunities to improve the students' abilities to navigate discussion by recognizing the nature of the difficulty and then encouraging students to refocus on the conversation.

Teachers have all been there—expecting a conversation to take thirty minutes or the entire period but the class decides it's finished after twenty minutes. Although the quality of the conversation isn't the problem and the exchanges between students have replicated academic discourse, the students believe they have explored all possibilities when, in fact, as the curriculum maker, the teacher knows there is a lot more to explore. The teacher, therefore, should not remedy the situation by entering the conversation but have strategies that will revive conversation when it ceases.

A useful strategy that will keep the discussion's focus while honoring student voices is to use the last contribution given to propel the conversation forward. The teacher may invite students to create a contribution that supports or opposes the last speaker's interpretation by requiring students to find additional examples and counterexamples or to create different interpretations for the evidence given.

In a discussion where most students blame Lady Macbeth for Macbeth's immoral actions and the conversation halts, the teacher may invite students to consider other factors that influence Macbeth, including Macbeth's ambition, the promises of the witches, or the political upheaval of Scotland. Rather than expecting students to make these moves immediately, the teacher should give students time to prepare these responses before initiating the conversation again. And if students appear to struggle independently, have students work with a partner so this conversation will enhance the larger conversation. When conversation begins again, students will have created another set of ideas to explore as well as strategies for moving with the conversation after they have conveyed their prepared arguments.

## WHEN A DISCUSSION IS FLAT

Another learning opportunity for students arises when the conversation isn't reflecting the speaking and listening criteria generated in class. A teacher's transcript might reveal limited evidence of uptake with students listing rather than synthesizing ideas, no direct support as students summarize events rather than read direct quotations, and long periods of silence rather than a steady flow of contributions. When discussion devolves into this situation early in the discussion, rather than stopping the conversation, let the conversation go for around five to seven minutes, and then stop to allow students to reflect on the conversation.

Acknowledge the discussion is not working, and then have students reflect on their conversation. Draw the students' attention to the class's discussion rubric, and use the following questions to guide the reflection:

1. Given our conversation thus far, what is going well or what should we continue to do?
2. Using our conversation, what needs to be improved?

3. Given what needs to be improved, what steps can we take to ensure we do improve the conversation's quality?

As students discuss each question, encourage them to give examples from the conversation to reinforce the argumentative framework used in class. When they offer ways to improve the conversation, write these fixes on the board so students can use them as guides. For example, if a student identifies a problem with uptake, then write the student's suggested transition move on the board, or if a student identifies that contributions are limited to one chapter or one character in a novel, then the student might recommend where more evidence can be found or which characters should also be explored. This reflection puts students in control of the conversation as they actively remedy the conversation's quality, so even when discussion doesn't go as expected, the teacher can still use discussion to enhance the students' literacy skills.

## NAVIGATING CONTROVERSIAL CONVERSATIONS

Nussbaum (1997) maintains that a democracy requires its citizens to possess the "Socratic capacity to reason about their beliefs in genuine dialogue" in order to "unmask prejudice and secure justice" but that this requirement "take[s] time and practice" (19, 81). Nussbaum's observation suggests that the teacher's responsibility is to build an environment that revolves around developing, supporting, and authorizing students to engage in classroom conversation so they may develop into socially responsible critical thinkers.

Most teachers want dialogue to be authentic, but this desire means that students might share personal stories, expose moral principles, and critique political perspectives as they navigate discussion together. A student may reminisce about a family friend suffering from addiction or contextualize a contribution through a religious lens or even critique current school or public policy. The students' willingness to share these stories, principles, and perspectives demonstrates that the teacher has built a classroom community where the participants view the academic world as mirroring their social and emotional world. At the same time, the teacher will want to create strategies that will ensure that students respond to these discussions in civil and just ways.

It is often advantageous for students to understand issues from multiple viewpoints before students enter politically charged conversations. Although students may have immediate responses and even positions regarding these topics, the teacher may want to introduce students to a continuum of positions so students don't devolve into binary arguments or either-or propositions. The teacher can use simulated experiences that invite students to role-play parts so that students encounter these diverse views and rehearse the arguments before abandoning these roles and entering the conversation from their own points of view.

Role-playing activities may even require students to support a position with which they disagree. For example, in a case where students explore the effects of online gradebooks on student-parent relationships, a student who believes that technology has hurt his relationship with his father may have to adopt the role of a father himself. Through this lens, the student will encounter the challenges of parenting that he hadn't considered up until this point and may even develop more empathy for parents trying to motivate their children. Rather than dismissing a parental point of view, this strategy allows a student to reflect on how he will respectfully disagree with voices that oppose him.

Uptake during contentious issues is critically important because the speaker and the listeners need to agree on what a contribution means so the participants know how to frame positions that agree or disagree with it. An effective strategy using uptake is one where students give consent to the rephrasing of their ideas before a new speaker contributes. This consent gives speakers the opportunity to clarify any misconceptions or misspeaks before the conversation proceeds. As each speaker contributes, the speaker must ask the previous speaker if her interpretation of the contribution is accurate—the speaker might ask, "Is that what you were saying?" or "Have I misquoted you?" These questions allow the previous speaker to amend or clarify the comment before discussion continues as characterizing another's contribution is often the cause of conflict.

In fact, if students don't ask clarification questions, set up a protocol where any student (or teacher) can say "speaker out of order" if one's contribution doesn't contain a clarification question. This protocol reminds the entire class that their contributions need to accurately address the issues before them. If students use this procedure with a topic that isn't as contentious, they will have practiced the moves before, internalizing some of the moves necessary to create a common understanding.

## CONCLUDING THOUGHTS

The troubleshooting strategies in this chapter provide a series of solutions to challenges that teachers face as they attempt to facilitate classroom conversation. Once teachers have diagnosed these challenges as concerns about individual students or classroom dynamics, they can use this information to work with students to improve the quality of the conversation. Just as teachers wouldn't give up on their students if they faced setbacks as readers and writers, teachers shouldn't abandon conversation when it fails to meet their expectations. Instead, teachers should embrace these moments as important academic, social, and emotional opportunities that will invite students to take ownership of their learning.

## REFERENCES

McCann, T. M. (2014). *Transforming talk into text: Argument writing, inquiry, and discussion, grades 6–12*. New York: Teachers College Press.

Nussbaum, M. C. (1997). *Cultivating humanity: A classical defense of reform in liberal education*. Cambridge, MA: Harvard University Press.

Nystrand, M. (1997). *Opening dialogue: Understanding the dynamics of language and learning in the English classroom*. New York: Teachers College Press.

*Part III*

# Expanding Conversations

Even though students may enjoy classroom discussions, often they—and sometimes teachers—do not view them as significant learning experiences like writing essays, reading texts, listening to lectures, taking notes, or reviewing quizzes and tests. Students sometimes do not see how an open-ended discussion of a poem or a scene in a play leads to understanding or learning. As different views, questions, or confusions are expressed, students sometimes beg the teacher, "Just tell us the answer so we can move on. You're supposed to teach us, not confuse us." A class discussion about a recent event in the news or in school may be interesting to students and may be seen as a positive bonding experience among students and the teacher. But at the same time, students may see it not as an important learning activity but as a nice break from classwork or, more negatively, as a waste of class time.

Given the research findings presented in chapters 1 and 2 revealing the strong relationship between discussion and student achievement, an argument can be made that any instance of authentic classroom discussion focused on academic concepts and positive, productive interaction has value for student learning. But it is also important that students themselves experience participation in classroom discussion as valuable for their learning and not just as a nice break from what they consider "real" classwork.

The chapters in part 3 focus on how teachers can move beyond approaching discussion as one of several different options in their repertoire of classroom strategies that can be used to provide a variety of approaches to "keep things moving and changing." The chapters address ways discussion can be frequent and extended, expanded, and built upon over time to enhance and enrich student learning.

The contributors to part 3 demonstrate not only how discussion can be integrated throughout a unit for literary works such as *Romeo and Juliet, The Brief Wondrous Life of Oscar Wao, The Catcher in the Rye*, or *The Tempest* but also how a series of discussions can be designed so that each builds a foundation for the next. For example, for a unit on *Romeo and Juliet* exploring the concept of decision-making (How do others influence our decisions? How do our decisions influence others? How often do we think of the consequences of our decisions?), early discussions engage students in debating their own views about such questions as whether teens can make important decisions on their own and whether teens jump into things without thinking them through. In the next set of discussions, students are "expert panelists" reporting on research on teen decision-making, including brain research. In later seminar discussions, students focus on Romeo and Juliet as good or poor decision-makers. Hence, each discussion supports, as well as enriches and expands, the next one.

Chapter 8 addresses how teachers can enhance learning through units that incorporate "layers of discussion," starting with discussions based on students' personal views that serve as warmups, followed by expert panel report-outs based on research, and concluding with student-led seminars interpreting a major literary work.

Chapter 9 illustrates how teachers can design discussions within an eight- or nine-week inquiry unit to create a conversation that grows richer with each text as students develop deeper interpretations and apply the concepts to their own experiences.

Chapter 10 explores how teachers can use digital discussions to enhance face-to-face interaction, to increase student participation, to spotlight the relationship between writing and discussion, and to allow students to practice writing through public conversation. The chapter highlights the value of bringing the technology that is a standard way of life for today's students into the classroom.

Chapter 11 examines ways teachers can effectively navigate the different challenges of facilitating naturally occurring discussions and planned class discussions, particularly when they involve dialogue about controversial issues. The goal is to create discussion-friendly classrooms that model democratic pluralism in which individuals value and protect an array of competing or conflicting views.

Together these chapters model the processes of designing instruction to incorporate authentic discussion that engages students in extended inquiry.

*Chapter Eight*

# Layers of Discussion

## Lisa Whitmer

> According to social constructivist theory, learning is a process of actively constructing knowledge through social interaction with others.
>
> —Vygotsky (1978)

Let them talk. Let them examine. Let them share. Carefully designed curriculum allows student discussion to ebb and flow within a unit and honors the learning that comes from talking, examining, and sharing. A few simple built-in practices use initial conversations and discussion to build upon further conversations and discussion, and as each experience evolves, so do the thinking and the skills, in a meaningful and natural way.

Teachers should consider discussion design in three simple stages for students: initial, midpoint, and end; however, each stage allows students to examine and share ideas at levels appropriate to what they are reading and writing and how they are asked to explore their reading and writing.

Mindful unit design aids in scaffolding levels of discussion where each conversation builds upon the next conversation for progressive and enhanced literacy experiences. The initial stage of discussion lays the groundwork for deeper concepts found in upcoming texts, and it also helps students ease into collaborative work and speaking experiences. Midpoint experiences use the previous established work to help students dig deeper, explore more challenging relationships, and examine more hidden complexities.

In the end, students have landed in a place that is more meaningful, more complex, and even more personal. It's a place of ownership for students as their voices have helped to shape, examine, and dig deeper into what they study. Their own ideas have helped to drive the learning, for their choices were decided upon after careful consideration and analysis of many ideas, and in the end, the claims they create are their own. Their discussions are rich and provocative; they matter to the student, and they are important considerations for society. Carefully constructed curriculum design helps students to find and raise their voices.

## STRUCTURING DISCUSSION WITHIN A NINE- TO TWELVE-WEEK UNIT

In a unit designed for college-bound freshmen on *The Tragedy of Romeo and Juliet*, students explore the following essential questions:

- How do the others influence our decisions?
- How do our decisions influence others?
- How often do we think of the consequences of our decisions?

## LAYING CONCEPTUAL GROUNDWORK: FRONT-LOADING TO INITIATE DISCUSSION

Often, teachers design a unit to begin with some type of anticipation guide, opening students up to concepts, experiences, and actions that will eventually appear in the text studied; however, most statements on the guide are designed so students relate more personally with upcoming topics. A few examples are as follows.

> I believe love at first sight is possible.
> I believe my parents or guardians have my best interests at heart.
> I believe there are a lot of support systems available for struggling teens.
> I believe it is important for teens to push against adults at times.
> I think we should test kids early on for signs of depression or possible signs of suicide.
> I think my parents or guardians should have a say in who I date.
> I think my parents or guardians would support me if I ran away with someone I loved.
> I think it's okay to disagree with my parents or my teachers at times.
> I tend to jump into things and make quick decisions without thinking them through.
> Teens can make important decisions on their own.
> There are only a few adults I'd listen to for advice.
> My parents provide me with good advice.
> I believe my parents/guardians could choose a good person for me to date.
> I believe teen suicide can be prevented.

The intentional design of the anticipation guide is to get students "warmed up" for eventual topics and concepts that will later appear in the text, and work with the anticipation guide creates fodder for writing and discussion that will lay the groundwork for future discussions involving the play.

Leading a quick discussion about the above topics and asking students to write about one or two that resonate with them begins the path for layered discussions. Through this prereading activity, students already have a beginning base of reasoning, claims, and evidence that they can use to later explain, defend, and support as they begin to read the anchor text.

Using the anticipation guide as a start, students learn that the above questions actually correlate with specific research topics, along with the anchor text of study. Students are asked to choose a research topic of interest to begin the inquiry, and then they move to the library databases to retrieve articles about their chosen research topics:

Teen rebellion/brain research (TR)
Teen decision-making (support systems/brain research) (TD)
Teen suicide and prevention (anxiety/depression/support systems) (TS)
Family conflict against and within families (support systems) (FC)

At this time, students acquire research information for a more enriching experience with the anchor text. While the research information is rich and powerful in itself, it also serves the purpose of laying meaningful groundwork for deeper understanding that will come later in the unit.

## EXPERT PANEL REPORT-OUT

Once students obtain research on a chosen topic, they are asked to participate in an "Expert Panel Report-Out." This experience for students is a less intimidating form of speaking, although it's not necessarily discussion. The structure or setup for this activity is merely reporting out information in a nonthreatening yet purposeful manner. This experience begins to teach students basic ways to segue off of a peer's statement or idea, the sophisticated skill of uptake.

From the research students have gathered, they read and annotate articles and create a Cornell note (CN) for each piece. Using their CNs, students sit as a panel up in front of the room, based on their research topics (TR panel, TD panel, TS panel, and FC panel). Students are now seen as the "experts" on this topic as they will be providing information from the research they have acquired. It is their job, individually, and as a panel, to teach and inform their audience (the remaining students). They are asked to share two of the strongest ideas found in their research. Meanwhile, the audience is provided with a Cornell note and must summarize the information presented by the expert panelists, also recording the student name, the "expert" who is speaking.

As students proceed to share their findings, audience members listen and record information. When the first "expert" finishes, other panel members are asked to consider an angle or idea from what was stated to form a "segue" into their own research. The segue or "uptake" skill actually asks the listeners to consider points or ideas stated by the presenter that they can use to enter into the panel report-out; it also requires some careful listening in order to find the opening and be able to acknowledge or even gain a "gist" of the speaker's idea before bringing in his or her own.

For this activity, the following, more basic segue or uptake frames help to support students practicing this skill. However, these frames become increasingly sophisticated as the unit continues. These uptake frames are versions of the ones suggested by Gerald Graff and Cathy Birkenstein in *They Say/I Say: The Moves that Matter in Academic Writing* (2012). Examples of such uptake frames include "Joseph, your point about ———— is similar to the idea in my research that ————," or "Matthew, my research article said something a little different about ————. It stated that ————."

Providing segue frames for students is crucial as it allows students to more skillfully enter the conversation, since many students struggle in seminars or collaborative activities because they do not know where, when, or how to enter. The following transcripts reflect student application of the segue/uptake frames.

## Family Conflict

Amanda: My research discussed how in a dysfunctional family, children are left to take care of themselves and they have to make decisions about school, jobs, money, and relationships on their own.

Sandra: Amanda, my research on family conflict also discussed the dysfunctional family and how a dysfunctional family household often lacks love, compassion, and communication.

Liz: Like Sandra's research, my research also discussed how important communication was, saying that "to have a strong family relationship, one needs strong communication and a strong support system."

## Teen Rebellion

Julio: Research on teen rebellion discussed how "the reason that the teen brain stands out is because the teen is at an age where he or she starts making decisions poorly, and they interpret things differently. They are not mature yet."

Gisselle: My research is similar to Julio's in that it discusses how the frontal lobe in teens is not as developed as an adult's, and this controls reasoning, impulse control, and planning, Therefore, the actions of teens often appear as rebellious.

## Teen Suicide and Prevention

Leo: My research stated that suicide is the eighth leading cause of death.

Octavio: My research seems a bit different than Leo's data because it states that more teenagers die from suicide than other means, and that for fifteen- to twenty-four-year-olds it is the third leading cause of death.

Adriana: And the research also discusses the signs and states that depression is a main cause, and the signs can be loss of appetite and a sense of hopelessness.

Gabby: I'd like to add to Adriana about the signs of suicide because my research suggests that ways to help or prevent these feelings is to turn to key supports and not isolate oneself and get more involved.

By the end of the Expert Panel Report-Out, students have shared deep reading of research articles, created their own notes, and obtained information about all research topics by listening to panel presentations. All of this information is in their portfolio. At this point, students are well equipped with conceptual knowledge, personal connections and reasoning, and actual research in order to more deeply attack the anchor text. Of course, this is when the anchor text is revealed—*The Tragedy of Romeo and Juliet* by William Shakespeare (although most have figured it out by now).

## INITIAL SOCRATIC SEMINAR

Following the Expert Panel Report-Out, students begin reading the anchor text, *The Tragedy of Romeo and Juliet*, beginning with an introduction of all characters and a close reading of the prologue. Armed with their newly acquired research, students begin to annotate the prologue. Where they see a connection in the text with research topics, they mark TR (teen rebellion) or TS (teen suicide) or FC (family conflict)—their connections are evident almost immediately: "From ancient grudge break to new mutiny" (FC), or the line "A pair of star-crossed lovers take their life" (TS or TR). As we begin act 1, scene 1, the connections grow even stronger: "Do you bite your thumb at us, sir?"; "I hate the word as I hate hell, all Montagues, and thee!" (FC); or

Romeo "pens himself up and locks fair daylight out making himself an artificial night" (TS).

As students read acts 1 and 2, the above annotations and deeper thinking continues because of the work students completed during the Expert Panel Report-Outs. At this time students are asked to share their deep reading and analysis with others in their first of three Socratic seminars. Using individual information from acts 1 and 2, the prologue, and research, students prepare for and participate in their first discussion, making predictions based on what they've read so far. In preparation for the seminar, students are asked to consider the following questions:

- At this point in the play, whose actions or decisions could contribute to Romeo's and Juliet's decisions to take their lives by the end of the play?
- Where or how do we see aspects of our research topics of teen depression, teen rebellion, family conflict, support systems, and teen suicide playing a role in the teens' decisions?
- How do the aspects of tragedy, character flaw, or fate contribute to the decisions the teens make?

The overall inquiry for this seminar asks students to choose a research topic, a character, or a tragic element at this point in the story that could contribute to the tragic deaths of Romeo and Juliet. In this seminar, students use what information they have acquired so far to predict events and decisions at the end of the play. Students prepare by addressing the question and finding *evidence* in the text to support their *claim*. They are also asked to interpret and justify their evidence in order to convincingly argue their claim. As students move forward, the work they do in correlation with the anchor text is, for the most part, framed in the skills of argument. The following transcript demonstrates how the students use the knowledge from expert panels to make sense of the play:

> Yannet: Well, I thought that Benvolio is to blame at this point. He is the one who vowed to get Romeo to forget Rosaline. He tells Lord Capulet that he'll "pay that doctrine or die in debt." He's expressing that he's making a promise to Romeo to ensure that Romeo will find another woman even though he is heartbroken and depressed at the moment. He encourages Romeo by saying, "Examine other beauties," which basically means look at others girls, implying there are other fish in the sea. Because Benvolio strongly insists that Romeo go to the party to check out other women, and he makes a promise to Lord Capulet that he will cure Romeo's heartbreak, his actions definitely play a role in Romeo and Juliet finding each other and then dying in the end.

Octavio: I hear what you're saying about Benvolio, Yannet, but I felt that the Friar might be to blame because he is the one who helped bring Romeo and Juliet together.

Paula: I don't agree with either of you, even though Benvolio did get Romeo to the party, but I see fate and timing contributing to the tragedy. First, it is seen when the servant delivering the invite to the Capulet party can't read and just happens to run into Romeo in the street to ask him to read the invite. And later, fate and timing come up when both Romeo and Juliet only find out after they fell in love that each is the other's enemy: Even Juliet says, "My only love sprung from my only hate. Too early seen unknown and known too late." Juliet is suggesting that she fell in love before she found out the truth and, because of this, she can't turn back. Her love has happened first and overpowers the news that he is her enemy. She also reveals that if she would have known he was an enemy before falling for him, she may not have loved him.

José: I agree with both Paula and Octavio, but I think Yannet's idea about Benvolio makes a lot of sense because, if Benvolio had not promised to help Romeo and push him to go to the party, they would have never met.

Monica: I think all of your ideas are good, but I was leaning toward the research topic of teen rebellion because, first of all, Romeo rebels by going to the party, and he rebels again by falling in love with the enemy. And he also sneaks into Juliet's garden, which is like dangerous rebellion, and then they eventually get married, secretly, and they know they are enemies and shouldn't be doing this.

Octavio: Monica, I like your idea because there are so many strong examples, and I like the idea of rebellion. I hadn't thought of Romeo's actions as being rebellious, and that's pretty interesting, and it also ties into our research about how teens may make poor decisions, and it is seen as rebellion by adults, but really they are practicing how to push the limits in order to grow their frontal lobe.

This activity moves students into their first attempt to address the anchor text at a deeper level. They are beginning to synthesize research and their peers' interpretations of the play. All the while, students are gathering notes and building a greater understanding of the text as the activities unfold. Moreover, students are practicing initial skills of uptake and using peer ideas not only as entry points but also as ideas to judge which interpretations are more valid.

In José's response, he already considered which of the two peer ideas merits the stronger argument. Then he continues to justify his decision with further reasoning. In his excerpt, we see how considering more than one idea gets him thinking, and it also requires him to explain himself using the skills of argument. In Paula's statement, she rejects both peer ideas; however, she recognizes some positive elements of one of the arguments, a concession, and then moves into her point. Octavio seems to be forming his claim as he is listening and making connections to the research, the beginning steps of synthesis, and he even attempts to support his thinking by referencing more specific information from research. The skills of argument are evident in this conversation as well, for in Yannet's opening to the seminar, her claim includes evidence that she explains by interpreting the text and tying it back to her idea.

When students move to the Socratic seminar, this is also an important time to reinforce "uptake or segue" skills. Since all the students have created their own claims, selected evidence, and interpreted and justified their evidence, a variety of ideas are expected in the seminar. Because of this, students are reminded to "segue" off of the speaker's ideas into their own. This activity will require a variety of segues, and a half sheet of "uptake" frames is provided to all students before we begin.

### Textbox 8.1. Uptake/Segue Frames in Socratic Seminar

- If peer idea is similar to your own: "Joseph, our team, thought the same thing. We also felt that ———."
- Add additional information/evidence to a point of similarity: "Sanjana, our team also felt that ———, and we supported that by mentioning ———." Or, "You may also want to consider the evidence that ———."
- Point of disagreement or differing perspective: I understand what you are saying about Romeo here, Maria, but I felt it was more an act of ——— than ——— because ———.
- Point of clarification: "Jordan, you stated that ———, but I don't understand what you meant when you said, "———.""
- Faulty reasoning: questioning of evidence/interpretation/justification "José, I understand your idea that ———, but I don't see how your evidence supports your idea. But I don't understand your interpretation of your evidence when you say, ———. But I don't see how your explanation proves your point; how does it relate to your point?"

Obviously, students will create their own more organic segues; however, frames provide entry points for those who struggle. These also remind students of the different angles they can consider when listening and, eventually, when writing. Segues and uptake serve an important purpose in a carefully designed unit because students are able to continually practice this sophisticated transitioning skill in each discussion activity they experience. And as literacy is recursive in nature, uptake in a discussion activity also reinforces the skills of transitioning from idea to idea when writing.

For example, when students need to elaborate in their own writing, it's similar to adding additional information in a seminar. When they are asked to include an opposing idea or differing perspective, they have already practiced dissent in their discussions by disagreeing with a peer idea or listening to others disagree. And concessions, qualifiers, and rebuttals may all be found in peer notes if ever needed to refer to for additional ideas in their writing.

## MIDPOINT SOCRATIC SEMINAR

At this point in the unit, previous student speaking opportunities have prepared students for a much deeper and more meaningful relationship with the anchor text. These discussions have also prepared them for higher levels of comprehension, moving beyond literal comprehension levels of basic stated relationships to much more inferential understandings, and even considerations about an author's craft. They are additionally beginning to synthesize ideas from the anchor text with research ideas in their notes and from their own research articles.

Synthesis also occurs more organically for students at this time because the range of peer ideas has been constant throughout the unit, continually adding to and challenging their own thinking. Students have acquired knowledge by listening to, recording, and studying past peer discussion ideas that unconsciously and consciously help to shape their thinking. As students complete acts 3 and 4 of the text, they revisit the three inquiry questions from the discussion on acts 1 and 2.

Revisiting prior inquiry questions, along with new questions from additional reading, begins a new conversation regarding the actions and decisions of characters, the relationship of events and actions to research ideas, and the continual examination of the effects that others have on the main characters, Romeo and Juliet. It is here that earlier claims, reasons, and ideas are reexamined, revised, and challenged. And from this new seminar, which is based on newly acquired information from the text, new, student-owned ideas emerge.

Again, students move in and out of the seminar discussion and, at this point, understand their responsibilities: they know to create new claims and ideas and acquire evidence from the text to support their newly formed ideas. They also need to be ready to discuss, explain, justify, and even defend how the evidence and examples from the text support their thoughts. Agreement and disagreement ensues.

A simple thought grows more complex as students engage in the discussion. They agree, disagree, or simply examine or reexamine the actions, motivations, events, and the more inferential aspects of the play. For students, the discussion is a constant examining, questioning, and connecting with complex issues, relationships, and decisions and actions of the characters. From this discussion, students are making careful considerations, noting important actions, and even gaining some personal awareness. Consider the following exchanges between participants:

Jocelyn: I am sort of rethinking my original claim about Friar Lawrence because he was, like sort of, a weak support system; although he talked Romeo down when Romeo freaked out about his banishment, he still set him up with a dangerous plan to hide him out in Mantua, and he didn't even tell the parents! He says in act 3, scene 3, "But look thou stay not till the watch be set / For then thou canst not pass to Mantua." Romeo's got to be careful and could be killed if found with Juliet. Why would he set Romeo up like this in such a dangerous way?

Vanessa: Yeah, I hear what you're saying, Jocelyn, and I didn't really think about how dangerous Friar's plans were. I mean I only saw him as someone who was trying to help them. When I first thought about the Friar, he was a really strong support system, but now I think he took a lot of chances with Romeo and Juliet.

Yari: Okay, I see how you can call Friar a bad support system, but what about both Romeo and Juliet; they are the ones reacting so stupidly! The Friar is always trying to guide them and like slow them down and stop them from freaking out. I mean Romeo is constantly jumping into things and not thinking them through. I mean he is freaking out about banishment, saying, "Ha, banishment, Be merciful, say, death," which means Romeo thinks banishment might as well be death, but it's way better than getting killed, and he almost kills himself just because of being banished! I was thinking how this really connects to our teen rebellion research about an undeveloped frontal lobe—he's got poor judgment.

Chris: Yari, I was just thinking that, about the brain research and how rash Romeo is being again, and that he just bursts out and reacts again and again. I mean he did the same thing when he killed Tybalt. He just let his emotions go crazy and went after Tybalt and then killed him! He didn't think about what could happen to him. He just goes after Tybalt once he hears Mercutio is dead and attacks, saying, "Away to heaven respective lenity, and fire-eyed fury be my conduct now!" I mean he says, "Fire-eyed fury be my conduct"; he is letting his emotions take over and drive him. His frontal lobe is really undeveloped! He is not thinking through any of this. His judgment is whacked!

Mary: Oh, my gosh! I am so like that! If I get mad, I can't think about anything but being mad, and I just jump in and go like all crazy. I totally can see why Romeo acts how he does. He's completely blinded by his anger and sadness over Mercutio's death. He's "savage." He can't think normally here. I get it. I'd be the same if that happened to my best friend. I'd have to jump in and fight for her!

Jane: So, we always talk about Romeo and his character flaw of being rash or "savage," but what about Juliet? At first we said she was basically like a pushover because she pretty much tells her mom she'll do what she's told about checking out Paris at the party and marrying only with permission from her mom, and she just totally goes along with Romeo when he says we need to get married now, even though she says that line about their love is supposed to be like a flower, and they need to give it time to blossom. Is she just still getting controlled by everyone? It was interesting when she had no idea what to do when she found out about him killing Tybalt. She was like really torn, but I think, for the first time, she had to make her own decision. She had to choose, and she chose Romeo, even though the Nurse cursed him saying, "Shame come to Romeo!" And Juliet responds saying, "Blistered be thy tongue!" I mean she like yelled at the nurse for that, so she's kind of changing, like she's getting stronger.

Erika: Jane, I don't know if Juliet looks stronger, just maybe really confused, I guess. It was cool when she had such mixed feelings about Romeo, when she loved him but hated him because he killed Tybalt, and she uses all those oxymorons to express her confused feelings like, "honorable villain," and "fiend angelical." That would have been really hard to feel both those emotions almost equally.

Anna: Back to what Jane said, really? You think Juliet is getting stronger? I still see her as a "doormat" like Victoria said at the beginning of the play. She's now like stuck in this stupid place because of Romeo, and she just keeps following him even though Romeo just killed her cousin, her family. She doesn't even stand by her family who she's known forever, but only by a guy she's known for like what, two days?!

Cameron: Anna, what you and Jane say about Juliet also connects to the frontal lobe research stuff that she is making bad decisions and shows some poor judgment.

In this midpoint transcript excerpt, we see how because the students have discussed most of the above ideas in previous assignments, the conversation begins to tackle some deeper nuances, and the reasoning and rationalizations are becoming tighter and stronger. They are also having to address opposition and consider differing views. Moreover, they are becoming ever-more curious, invested, and interested in the thoughts and ideas established and, perhaps, beginning to determine the ideas they feel more strongly about and wish to pursue.

In Jocelyn's opening response, we immediately see her reconsidering and even reevaluating previous ideas based on new information from the text. She also provides a quick concession before shifting her argument to the complete opposite of her original claim and even providing textual support. And Jocelyn's statement even influences Vanessa's as Vanessa begins to reconsider her initial interpretations of Friar Lawrence.

In Chris's comment, his segue is really an affirmation of Yari's ending realization in regard to the teen rebellion/brain research. Students are making connections here to previous work, synthesizing, and deeply analyzing the moves of the characters. These student comments reveal their ability to capture the characters' complexities. And in Chris's comment, he's almost naturally weaving in textual evidence as a means to supporting his thinking. In Mary's comment, she makes an immediate personal connection, even providing some modern-day slang.

Jane's response opens with a counterargument, where she is pushing against previous statements and transitioning into her new perspective. Her discussion moves through much of the text as she refers back to earlier parts to continually support her stance regarding current evidence supporting her claim. Jane also notes the complexities of Juliet's circumstances and decisions. All the while her examples and text references seem to flow out almost effortlessly. And Jane's thinking propels Erika, who enters into the conversation with a different angle in regards to Juliet and her actions.

What Erika's comment brings to the seminar is focus on the text structure and the devices the author uses to convey his point. However, this high-level analysis appears natural as if it makes perfectly good sense to notice the use of oxymorons to express Juliet's mixed emotions. In the end, Cameron's simpler contribution still holds weight as he helps to synthesize Anna's and Jane's ideas and make connections back to research, connections that seem meaningful to him. Without this ongoing, natural conversation, those speaking and those listening would miss out on the constant critical thinking, a devouring of the text, along with the provocative thoughts that are being constructed in front of all participants.

After the seminar continues for approximately two to three class periods, students continually take notes. And at the close of the activity, students are then left with some powerful seminar ideas. Options for note-taking may involve the teacher keeping a typed transcript while students talk, or assigning a student this task each day, but oftentimes students are responsible for their own note-taking. Students are also encouraged to share notes, revise notes, and seek clarity of ideas after every seminar session.

## REFLECTION, ANALYSIS, AND EVALUATION OF PEER IDEAS: METACOGNITION

To increase a deeper understanding of the text, students take time after each seminar or collaborative activity to review notes. They know by now to highlight the ideas that resonate with them, ideas that were powerful and important to them, but they also need to be reminded about ideas they had never considered and points and reasoning with which they disagree. Annotating notes beyond highlighting allows students to react, further analyze, and add additional connections or ideas.

At this point, the seminar notes of their peers have become a third source that students can use to increase their understanding of the text. After students have analyzed and annotated their notes, the teacher allows for some metacognitive "shout-outs." This is when students are asked to give a shout-out to a peer's ideas in their notes that they found particularly strong or changed their thinking in some way, or even one they disagreed with when reconsidering the ideas in their notes.

### SAMPLE OF METACOGNITIVE SHOUT-OUTS

Jason: I'd like to give a shout-out to Adriana who talked about Juliet beginning to grow stronger in these scenes. I liked that. I never thought about that.

Randi: I'd like to give a shout-out to Bryan. His idea about Juliet's support system not being her parents but rather the Nurse, who is like another adult she went to, related to our research on teen depression and support systems. That connects to research about how a teen may reach out to an adult but just not their parents.

Cameron: I'd like to give a shout-out to Jordan who said Juliet's parents totally walk away from her; she has lost all her support systems, and the nurse tells her to marry Paris, totally betraying her. That was strong.

At this point, students make a second visit to the library as many want to change the research they have acquired from the beginning of the unit to a topic that interests them more, or they want to retrieve even better, more specific information than the articles they have. This research has become more meaningful and purposeful for students because they now see the tight relationship it has to the text they are reading, and they have a firm understanding of the text; therefore, they know what kind of research they want and how to better select it in relation to the text that they now understand deeply.

With these experiences and ideas in their heads and in their notes and portfolios, students then move into the final phase of the unit and complete reading act 5 of the play.

## ENDING DISCUSSION EXPERIENCES

The final discussion allows the previous heavy lifting to find its purpose when students execute their final Socratic seminar. In preparation, students determine the ideas and questions that they still need to discuss and bring them to the final seminar. This last seminar is also where they begin to discuss the angles they find most interesting and have been leaning toward from previous discussions. These are the ideas that they may reference in their final essay. They may examine a variety of claims and test out evidence and explanations to see if they hold ground. Students can also ask how others feel about a specific angle and receive feedback.

In the final seminar, students discuss significant events in act 5 in relation to previously established claims, reaffirming or reevaluating their previous thoughts. Students may also find that earlier ideas no longer hold value as the ending of the text does not support their initial argument, and they continue to reshape and revise their thinking. Students revisit the same questions previously addressed with the addition of one more based on the closing lines of the play, capturing yet another angle to the couple's tragic end.

When Romeo and Juliet are found dead in the vault, Prince Escalus states, "Some shall be pardoned and some punished." The last discussion revolves around Prince Escalus's statement, "Who deserves pardon, and who deserves punishment?" where students use their reading of the play, the research from the panel discussions, and the tragic elements of character flaw and fate to navigate the discussion.

The final seminar symbolizes all of the layering that has been established from the beginning to the end of the unit. Students now form their own richer and deeper ideas with textual support and explanation, naturally. They understand that differing perspectives exist and may need to be addressed in order to strengthen their own ideas. Students, by this point, acknowledge how peer ideas have developed their own thinking. There is continued ownership in this work as all contributions, notes, and research belong to the class. They also see a more significant purpose to the research. As students begin to craft their own essays, they have not only practiced these ideas but also assimilated these examples and understood the importance of getting these skills right.

James: By the end, it's clear that Friar Lawrence really was a poor support system for both Romeo and Juliet. His plan for Romeo was flawed because information and the letter were unable to get to Romeo. He should have made sure Romeo could get information, especially information about Juliet not really being dead. He also created another dangerous plan for Juliet, not just Romeo. He gives her a potion that made her appear dead. That is dangerous. But I think the worst thing he did was leave Juliet alone in the vault with Romeo, who was dead. With Romeo laying dead right next to Juliet, the Friar says, "I dare no longer stay." And the stage directions even say "He leaves." He leaves. He just walks away from Juliet who is totally in shock! He was only thinking of himself. He just leaves. Clearly, he should be punished because he was the guide they leaned on, but in the end, he failed them.

Anna: I agree, James, that the Friar created dangerous plans for Romeo and Juliet, and it was really irresponsible of him to leave Juliet in the vault alone, but for the most part, everything he did was to help them. His intentions were pure. He did what he thought was right. Remember, Juliet threatened to kill herself if the Friar couldn't get her out of this marriage, so in a way, the dangerous plan actually saved Juliet. Overall, I think he was a support system looking out for the best for Romeo and Juliet. And he does feel really bad and even responsible in the end; he even says to the prince that he is willing to take the blame and be punished. He says something in the end when explaining his role in this to the Prince, something like if you think I am to blame, then "let my old life be sacrificed some hour before his time / Unto the rigor of severest law." He is willing to take the blame for the tragedy of Romeo and Juliet; he feels really guilty and sad. He thought he was just helping.

Alondra: Anna, I agree that the Friar does seem sincere in his actions, even though he did create some crazy plans, but I have to go back to Romeo and his rash character flaw. We already talked about all the examples from act 1 and all the way to act 5 of how he keeps jumping in without thinking. He totally does this again in the end. It's like he never learns and never changes. After receiving the news from Balthasar, he immediately jumps on a horse, buys a poison, stating, "Juliet, I will lie with thee tonight," and rides off to the vault to die with Juliet. Again, no thinking, just reacting emotionally, and being really impulsive. He shows all the signs of an underdeveloped frontal lobe.

Jocelyn: I agree, Alondra, but I really keep going back to the research on the underdeveloped frontal lobe too. I mean both Romeo and Juliet all along made such rash decisions and didn't think about the danger and consequences of their decisions. And they are just teenagers who totally fit the description from research that the judgment and decision-making parts of the frontal lobe are not really developed. Because of this, every move they make it seems is a mess. I mean, at the end, Romeo buys a poison and jumps on a horse to go die, then kills Paris at the vault. And Juliet is willing to take this dangerous "potion," even though it might kill her. What? Do they ever make a decision that is not impulsive and dangerous? Ahh, they are totally doomed and, like it says at the beginning, they are "star-crossed lovers," totally unlucky.

James: When I think about their rash decisions you are talking about, Jocelyn, and that they don't have developed frontal lobes because they are teenagers, I keep thinking about our other research about teen depression and suicide where it talks about support systems and how important they are. So, if Romeo and Juliet both make bad decisions, and all of this leads to making the really bad decision of committing suicide, then wouldn't having a stronger support system have helped them the most? I mean they can't change being teenagers and making dumb decisions, but they can be helped by adults who can like better guide them. Because they didn't have very strong support systems in any of the adults around them, there was no one to help guide them through their problems and the dangerous situations they put themselves in. So, I think not having support systems is really what contributed to their deaths. And their parents, Friar Lawrence, and the Nurse are really most to blame.

This conversation between students reflects some powerful thinking and progressive growth. First of all, student responses reflect that all students are not only referencing specifics from the first acts but also examining actions from the end of the story in connection to events throughout the text. There is evidence here of strong comprehension of an entire text and the complex relationships of characters and their motivations and the effects of their decisions.

In the final seminar, it is clear how students are all settling into their final claims, their final stances and beliefs. It is also clear that the final essay is unfolding before them. In simply rereading the above seminar discussion, one can see the conversation has always been built around students grappling with difficult concepts and a powerful text with rich and nuanced complexities, yet they are doing so together, out loud.

In a carefully structured curriculum, one that moves students from one level to a more complex one, each conversation is manageable; each conversation has a purpose, and the purpose is to support their thinking and better understand a difficult text. Yet, along the way, the students have been continually rehearsing, practicing, and listening to the higher-level skills of argument.

Moreover, the discussions have created an ending point that allows the student to more readily transfer these spoken ideas into powerful, meaningful, and purposeful writing. They have truly been writing their essays all along, and the work housed in their portfolios can attest to that. If one is intentional about layering classroom discussion, in the end, the product deemed from this is a piece of writing students own, a piece of writing that incorporates the high-level skills of argument, one that more naturally synthesizes research and peer thinking.

The conversation in a carefully designed curriculum is the cog in the wheel that allows the skills of deep reading and strong writing to continually show students how to use those skills for a purpose and how to use their voices to express their thinking. The conversation is the vehicle that makes the skills of reading and writing purposeful. And the conversation includes everyone; there is always a listener when there is a speaker. The conversation in our classrooms can become one of our strongest intellectual tools. When we as instructors allow students to raise their voices, we allow them to find their voices. Intentional curriculum design honors this power.

## REFERENCES

Graff, G., & Birkenstein, C. (2012). *They say/I say: The moves that matter in academic writing* (2nd ed.). New York: Norton.

Shakespeare, W. (1992). *The tragedy of Romeo and Juliet*. New York: Simon & Schuster.

Vygotsky, L. S. (1978). *Mind in society: The development of higher psychological processes*. Cambridge, MA: Harvard University Press.

*Chapter Nine*

# Extending the Conversation

*Discussion-Based Inquiry Units*

## Julianna Cucci and Zanfina Rrahmani Muja

Oftentimes in English classes, discussion is a brief, isolated activity that serves to check or expand students' current understanding of a reading. However, when discussion is thought of as inquiry, or a larger set of related conversations that extend over the course of a multiweek unit of instruction, students can begin to make powerful connections among the texts that they read as well as between the texts they encounter and their own lives. How can teachers construct instruction to engage students in authentic discussion so that students can make these powerful connections?

This chapter explores how a teacher might use the concept of borderland identity to create a unit in which students engage in a series of discussions about the ways that culture and multiculturalism impact identity. The unit involves inquiry into the concept of borderlands (Anzaldúa, 2007) and how one defines identity when parts of that identity are difficult to reconcile.

### ESSENTIAL QUESTIONS: ANZALDÚA'S THEORY OF "BORDERLANDS"

Gloria Anzaldúa writes about her experience as a Mexican American woman in terms of "Borderlands," a space both physical and psychological, where two or more cultures collide. She describes the experience of living in this multicultural space, saying, "The ambivalence from the clash of voices results in mental and emotional states of perplexity. Internal strife results in insecurity and indecisiveness. The *mestiza*'s dual or multiple personality is plagued by psychic restlessness" (Anzaldúa, 2007, p. 100).

Some of the dualities that Anzaldúa explores in her essays and poetry are Mexican/American, Indian/conqueror, gay/straight, male/female, and English/Spanish. Spanish-speaking conquerors that define her language are at odds with her Indian ancestry; the English that she speaks is at odds with the Spanish of her childhood. Unable to identify completely with any group, the border between the groups becomes a new kind of identity. Anzaldúa writes, "Like all people, we perceive the version of reality that our culture communicates. Like others having or living in more than one culture, we get multiple, often opposing messages. The coming together of two self-consistent but habitually incomparable frames of reference causes *un choque*, a cultural collision" (Anzaldúa, 2007, p. 100).

While students don't necessarily identify with the specific dualities of her experience, the lens of seeing the blessings and the curses of belonging to multiple groups that are in conflict with each other can be helpful in making sense of their own experiences in a diverse world. The theory can be used to think about writing that examines issues such as culture, race, power, class, and gender. A teacher might construct essential questions around Anzaldúa's theory (see textbox 9.1).

**Textbox 9.1. Essential Questions for Exploring Borderlands**

1. What is life in the "borderlands" like?
2. Why is the concept of the "borderlands" important for understanding ourselves and the world?
3. What actual borders impact our identities?

What happens when two groups or cultures collide? What is the experience of the borderland?

The power of designing opportunities to engage in authentic discussions around this line of inquiry comes from the teacher not knowing the answers. The teacher becomes a guide in how to engage in a conversation. She can speak articulately about ideas and about strategies for how to read and write about text but is not the sole "expert." The students bring their experiences to the conversation as well and learn to read and think critically about both literature and their lives.

## GATEWAY ACTIVITY: FRIDA KAHLO'S *SELF PORTRAIT ALONG THE BORDERLINE BETWEEN MEXICO AND THE UNITED STATES*

Frida Kahlo's 1932 painting depicts her standing on a block between a symbolic representation of the United States to her right and Mexico to her left. It is a good gateway activity for gaining conceptual knowledge for talking about borderlands because it is a highly engaging visual representation of the experience of belonging in two different, conflicting worlds.

A teacher might begin by telling the students the title of the portrait and asking, "What do you notice in this painting?" Students chime in immediately with comments about the factories, the temples, and the other colorful images they see. It doesn't take long for them to begin to interpret the purpose of what they notice. A student will usually say something along the lines of, "She likes Mexico more" or, "She thinks that America lacks nature." At this point, it's a good idea to point out to students that they are beginning to interpret, or answer the question of what she is saying to the viewer.

The teacher can follow up these comments with, "How do you know?" or, "Does that interpretation account for all of the details in the picture? Are there others that point to something else?" This prompts students to use specific details to support interpretive work they have begun and to deepen their understanding. Once students have articulated that Kahlo is saying something about Mexico, the United States, and herself, students can work in small groups to explore the message further. What is she saying to the viewer about Mexico, the United States, and her feelings about both?

After students discuss in groups, they can present their findings to the class. Next, teachers can ask students to write individually to a prompt about the image. Students who have analyzed and discussed in class typically have a great deal to say about a prompt such as, What does Frida Kahlo communicate about her feelings about being a part of Mexico and the United States?

## CULTURES IN ME

The visual nature of Kahlo's argument lends itself to a way for students to explore the borders impacting their own identities as well. A teacher might ask the class about what other kinds of borders exist in the world that might cause an individual to have complicated feelings, as in the case of Frida Kahlo's painting. In a class that engaged in this activity, students noted many boundaries, such as male/female, young/old, gay/straight, black/white, immigrant/native, Mexican/American, athlete/student, friend/relative, safe/threatening, personal thoughts/outer appearance, personal goals/parents' expectations, ethnic identity/American identity, mind/body, home life/school life, dominant culture/minority culture, online identity/in-person identity, home life/work life, and existing/living.

Students might create visual representations of a border or borders that they exist in. In a class that recently engaged in the unit, students created posters that included symbolic representations of many different cultures or groups that they belong to. One Mexican American student added a quote from the movie *Selena* across the bottom of her page: "We have to be more Mexican than the Mexicanas and more American than the Americans."

In later conversations, students referenced the quote to describe feelings of alienation in multiple groups. The discussion of Kahlo's painting supported the students in interpreting a complex concept and applying it to their own lives as well as making connections with classmates. It paved the way for future conversations about complex texts dealing with culture and identity.

## "BORDERLAND" AS LENS FOR INTERPRETING COMPLEX TEXT

Essentially, the borderlands is a way to conceptualize the experience of living in a diverse society and existing with others who view the world and experience differently than you, indeed who even view and define you differently than you might define yourself. After exploring the idea of borders and identity, it's a good idea to extend the conversation by exploring how writers have answered the essential questions of the unit.

There are many poems, short stories, essays, and excerpts a teacher might use, among them Zora Neale Hurston's "How It Feels to Be Colored Me" (1928), Samira Ahmed's "Red Thread at Fatehpur Sikri" (2016), W. E. B. DuBois's "Of Our Spiritual Strivings" from *The Souls of Black Folk* (1903), Richard Rodriguez's "Complexion" and "Aria" from *Hunger of Memory* (1982), Bharati Mukherjee's "Two Ways to Belong in America" (1996), Luis Rodriguez's "'Race' Politics" (1989), and Gloria Anzaldúa's "To Live in the Borderlands Means You" (1987). This list is by no means exhaustive but merely representative of the kinds of works that explore borderland questions.

In a large group, small groups, and individually, students can explore how the essential questions are answered by each text. A teacher might create a "live document" on which students track the different perspectives they have learned about the concept of living in the "borderlands" and see how each text they have read could be engaging in a conversation with other texts.

## APPLICATION TO CONSTRUCTED INQUIRY

After students have considered multiple perspectives about the essential questions, they are ready to explore a case study about a borderland conflict, "Mia's Dilemma" (see textbox 9.2).

---

**Textbox 9.2. Mia's Dilemma**

Dear Mrs. Muja,

I'm really sorry that I was texting in class today and that I've seemed really distant. I appreciate that you asked me if there was anything you can do to help me. Actually, I feel so confused. I don't know what to do. Lately, I've been feeling like I don't really belong anywhere.

As you know, I'm seventeen and finishing up my senior year here. Now that I'm finishing high school, I've been starting to feel like there is a side of myself that I never knew before. My dad moved to the United States from the Dominican Republic when he was eighteen years old. Since then, he has only visited one time and he has vowed to never return. When I ask him about the Dominican Republic, he says that it's a poor country and that it is still suffering from the aftereffects of Trujillo's dictatorship. He also says that I have grandparents who live there, but that I have not met them because they have not come to terms with everything that they experienced during Trujillo's regime. I also know that my dad used to have a sister and that she was killed by Trujillo's regime, but he never really talks about her. Whenever I do try to talk to him about it, he says that the past should be left in the past and that it's not worth discussing. Even though I've always been super close to my dad, lately I've been feeling very distanced from him, especially because he never talks about his life before moving to the US. I also think it's kind of weird that I've never met my grandparents, and I know they are getting old, so I feel like I'm never really going to know them. Basically, I feel like there's a whole side of my identity that I don't really understand.

Admittedly, I didn't really give the Dominican side of my identity much thought until I met this girl named Lola. She's a few years older than me. Lola visited the DR many times, and she is still very close to her grandmother, who still lives there. When I talk to Lola, she tells me all about life in the DR. She especially talks about how people who live there are very poor and that they believe that they have been cursed! Can you believe that? They think they've been cursed by the white man because of the fact that they've been occupied by the United States

---

many times! My mom is white, so I don't even know what to make of this! Lola also says that people there are still haunted by the aftereffects of Trujillo's dictatorship. One time, when I was telling Lola that I didn't really know much about my Dominican Republic background, she told me that she didn't either but that she started to have a strange feeling when she was my age and that this feeling made her want to go back to live there for a year. I guess Lola and her mom never had a good relationship, but once she visited the DR, her grandmother told her stories about her mom that she never heard before. Lola says that if it weren't for visiting the DR, she never would have understood herself and the history that her family, especially her mom, experienced. She's a whole different person because of this one experience!

Lola really made me think about my life in a different way. Sadly, I feel like my life so far has been super boring. Don't get me wrong; I'm grateful for all of the things I do have, but I feel like a big part of me is missing. The Dominican side! All of my friends are white and rich, and this neighborhood is filled with white, rich people! Now, I love my friends, but sometimes I feel like they don't fully get me. Dylan, my boyfriend, is great, too, but he sometimes doesn't get me either. He's French and German, and he plays baseball and is super sporty. He's been living in my neighborhood all my life. We practically grew up together. When I try to talk to him about how confused I've been feeling lately, he doesn't really know what to say. My mom doesn't really get it either. Unlike my dad, she talks a lot about her family and her past. She had what she calls the all-American life! She grew up in a nice neighborhood, and her house had a white picket fence. In high school, she was a cheerleader, and she dated the captain of the football team. My parents met in college at the café where my dad worked to pay his tuition. My mom paid for college with the trust fund her parents had established for her. I'm also very close to my grandparents on my mom's side; we even have dinner with them each Sunday! I don't think my mom can really understand how I feel even if she wanted to.

Sometimes, for instance, my mom and dad get into fights on the way home from my grandparents' house. They're super close to my mom, but they're sometimes condescending towards my dad. My grandfather always makes this lame joke about how he's so sorry that they didn't serve tacos and refried beans, and he jokes that he's glad my dad didn't force us to have Hispanic names. My dad gets frustrated by this, and I've overheard him tell my mom that he thinks my grandparents are racist because they think all Latin American countries are the same. The truth is, I don't even know if there are any differences between Latin American countries! I wish he would talk more about the Dominican Republic so I can understand what those differences are, if they are there. I don't even know if saying this makes me racist?

Anyways, I tried to tell both of my parents about the feelings I've been having lately. I told them that growing up, I thought I felt that I belonged, but I guess I never really did, even with my closest friends. I guess I feel lost because my entire life, I've been surrounded by people who are only like half of me, the white half. I wonder if I am seeing everything around me only through this perspective. I told them that sometimes, when my friends use stereotypes about people from Latin American countries, I can't help but feel like maybe, in a way, they are making fun of me. And I never know how to react in those situations because I don't even know enough about it to react. I also told them about Lola, too, and how she understood herself more by visiting the Dominican Republic. My dad basically said, "Oh, you're a teenager, everyone goes through this." But then my mom got this super excited look on her face and asked if I wanted to go meet my grandma and spend time with her in the DR. When she said this, my dad got so angry. I'd never seen him like that! He yelled and yelled and was saying that he would never let me visit a poor country with a bunch of people who can't move on with life. He even said that if I want to visit the DR, he would stop talking to me.

I thought his reaction was kind of weird because he got *so* angry! Like, if this wasn't that important, he wouldn't have reacted that way. And if my dad actually did move on with his life, why would he be so against the idea of me going to visit his parents and learning more about his history? His reaction actually made me even more curious about visiting! And now, since my mom mentioned it, the more that I've been thinking about whether I should go or not.

The problem is, it's the summer before college, which makes it so hard to make the decision. There are so many things my friends and I planned to do this summer! There are going to be parties practically every weekend since everybody will be leaving for different schools soon. Dylan and I also have a whole trip planned out. We're going to go to Europe to visit France, Germany, Italy, and Spain. He and I are going to different schools next year, and we're going to be five hours away from each other, so this two-week trip was supposed to be our chance to really get closer before we have to do a long-distance relationship. I told Lola that maybe I could go to the DR for about ten days or so, but she told me that it wouldn't be enough time! She said that if I really wanted to experience the DR and understand myself better, I would need to immerse myself completely in the Dominican Republic culture, which would take all summer or longer. So, I know that if I go to the DR, I'll be missing out on all these amazing things I had planned for the summer.

I also know that if I do go, my relationship with my dad will be completely ruined. Ever since the topic of my visiting, he has completely distanced himself from me, and he only makes small talk with me when he needs to. That's why I know he's really serious about not talking to me if I decide to go. My mom says that I should go, though, and that she will try to help my dad see things from my perspective. She says that after she suggested it, she kind of regretted doing so because I would have to spend the summer with people I don't really know. However, she thought about it some more and now she feels they must be good people since they did a good job of raising my dad, which made her less worried about it. I also know that if I spend the summer in the DR, I will learn more about my background and my identity, which may make me more prepared for college and beyond. At this point, though, I am running out of time to make my decision, and I am feeling extremely conflicted. I really don't know what to do.

### *Your Task*

Mia is not the first person to think about the unique position that she finds herself in, between two cultures, two places, and two parts of her identity. You and your group members will respond to Mia's dilemma by answering the following questions. For each answer you provide, you must include at least two pieces of evidence (quotes from an author) that support your answer.

1. What should Mia do? Why? What are the pros and cons of any decision that she makes?
2. What role should Mia's family or friends play in her decision? Why?
3. Should Mia consider the tension that her decision may cause between her parents when deciding what to do? Why or why not?
4. You have read authors with different ideas about borderlands and identity. How might any of these writers' ideas inform Mia's thinking?

After you and your group members have finished formulating your responses to the questions above, the whole class will come together in the form of a panel discussion, during which you and your group members will give advice to Mia. Remember that your advice should come from both a careful analysis of the case itself and your understanding of other ideas about borderlands.

A typical conversation about the case study and living in the "borderlands" goes as follows:

Anna: I think that Mia should go because she could learn to see the world around her in two ways if she does. W. E. B. DuBois talks about how he is able to see the world through two different lenses and Mia would have that advantage too.

Nico: I think she should go too because Bharati Mukherjee talks about how she learned to live in two cultures because she knew enough about both of them. So Mia needs to know too, so she can decide for herself.

Chrissy: I disagree with both of you because if Mia goes, she is going to ruin her relationships with everyone in her life and she is probably not going to fit in there.

Justin: Yeah, if Mia ends up going, she ends up losing more, and I agree that she probably won't even have an authentic experience there because she'll go as an American.

Anela: I see what you mean, Justin, because Samira Ahmed talks about how she goes to India but looks at India like a tourist would, and not like someone who lives there all the time. But I don't think that's a reason for her to not go. If anything, going there will teach her humility and give her a new perspective. Like every time I go back to Bosnia, I feel lucky to have the things that I have in the United States. I get reminded of how much my parents have done for me to be able to be where I am today.

Luis: I think that too. I go to Mexico very often with my family, and I appreciate what I have now so much more. Going to the Dominican Republic can also make it better for Mia because she can actually connect things about her father. She can get a better understanding of how. Like DuBois talks about, she can maybe look at herself through the eyes of others. She could try to listen to what is good for herself, but she might also learn to see things from the eyes of another person, like maybe her own father.

Sam: Yeah, but this can go either way. Even after she has this entire experience, she will go home to the United States and back to her own comfort so . . . maybe it's better if she learned about all of these things by reading about them rather than sacrificing all those relationships.

Luis: That's not the same experience as actually going. And because she's actually going there, she would have to actually wholly throw herself into the culture and life there. When I go to visit the village where my parents grew up in Mexico, I don't think I would be able to see what I see or learn what I learn by reading a book about it. She needs to actually go and throw herself there—even if, like some of these authors talk about, she doesn't like what she finds.

Illya: I think it's important for her to go too. I used to go to Romania when I was little. I hadn't been for a while, and I felt like I didn't really understand myself, and then when I went a few years later, I felt better and I still feel better.

Chrissy: Okay, but maybe she doesn't learn from a book, but maybe she can talk to her dad about all these things. Maybe she just needs to find a way to do that.

Anna: I don't think that would work because her dad seems traumatized by something there, and he doesn't seem like he would open up about things. Maybe that's even why he doesn't want her to go, because she might learn something he doesn't want her to know about. I still think she should go though.

Illya: Anzaldúa talks about how finding the strength to leave the comfort of her home and her surroundings is one of the hardest things she has had to do. But then she suggests that it was all worth it because otherwise, she never would have known who she really is. The same might happen to Mia.

Anna: Yes, and then she can sort of merge the double self she has into a new self, kind of like how DuBois talks about.

Yvonne: I disagree. She shouldn't go. She is losing way too much if she does. She should respect her dad and learn about her culture from him. My family is Italian American, and we don't need to go back to Italy to learn about it because we have continued the traditions here, and this is where we live now. You don't need to leave the country to learn about your culture.

Semra: I agree. I've been to India so many times, and I don't actually ever learn anything when I go. I actually agree with Samira Ahmed when she says that she wants to "scour India off her skin" because I want to do the same when I go visit.

Illya: Just because she wants to "scour India off her skin" doesn't mean she didn't learn anything. She learned a lot about herself and her relationship to her roots. Mia would not be able to decide for herself if she wants to scour it off because she doesn't even know what it's actually like. That's why she needs to go, so she can know for herself.

Anna: I agree with you, Illya, because I think she should go even if she doesn't like it. And even if it does change her completely because at least then she could understand herself in a different way.

The discussion provided here illustrates the kinds of connections students are able to make between the essays and stories that they have read, the essential questions about borderlands, and their own experiences. Students demonstrate that they have interpreted not only what the authors they have read say but also why their arguments matter. Anna does not stop at stating DuBois's claim but applies it to her advice to Mia. Semra builds on Yvonne's ideas with a quote from Ahmed's essay and how it relates to both her own experience and what Mia should do.

If the students had been handed a packet of short works, the case study, and the instructions to synthesize what different writers might say to Mia, they would have likely struggled and looked to the teacher for the right answer. However, because they have had a series of discussions about the concept, students as a group are able to synthesize and apply multiple works to Mia's case.

After students engage in discussions about Mia's dilemma, the teacher can prompt them to reflect in individual writing on the experience. Students can compose essays to the following prompt:

> What is your final advice to Mia? Why? In your writing, demonstrate that you have thought about different perspectives and experiences, including those of your classmates, and why you think your advice is the most appropriate for Mia. Be sure to include what others have written about borderlands, identity, and culture that helps you in deciding about how to advise Mia. Conclude by exploring what the dilemma and our discussion of it implies about what life in the borderlands is like. Why does it matter?

In a class that recently engaged in discussing Mia's dilemma, the discussion was so involved that it took two full class periods. When it came time to write, students had no shortage of ideas and experiences to bring into their final analyses. Students included evidence about their interpretations of the essays they had read and what they implied for Mia, but they also included comments from their classmates and experiences from their lives. The discussion had become another text for them to learn from and use in developing their interpretations about what the concept of living in the borderlands is like and why it is worth discussing/learning about.

## EXTENDING THE DISCUSSION TO A NOVEL

Once students have thought about and applied the concept of borderlands through discussion and writing, they have the core knowledge to analyze a longer text. One possible text is Junot Díaz's *Brief Wondrous Life of Oscar Wao* (2008) because numerous characters navigate life in the borderlands. Other choices include, but are not limited to, *The Joy Luck Club* (Tan, 1989), *Beloved* (Morrison, 2000), *Caramelo* (Cisneros, 2003), *The Namesake* (Lahiri, 2004), *How the Garcia Girls Lost Their Accents* (Alvarez, 1991), *American Born Chinese* (Yang & Pien, 2009), *Aristotle and Dante Discover the Secrets of the Universe* (Sáenz, 2012), and *The Absolutely True Diary of a Part-Time Indian* (Alexie, 2007). Regardless of novel choice, students who have participated in the discussion activities up to this point are ready to relate the concept of borderland identities to the development of characters in the novel.

A teacher can prompt students to consider how the characters and the situations they experience are representative of living in the borderlands. Some possible discussion activities are the following:

1. Role-playing activities in which students take on the perspective of a character and answer the essential questions as the character would. Throughout these role-playing activities, students take on the point of view of multiple characters in the text and engage in conversation with one another from the points of view of each character.
2. Character charts that ask students to consider what characters are like before facing or engaging in the thematic concept and how they change as a result of doing so. These charts may ask students to identify adjectives to describe the characters and support these adjectives with textual evidence.
3. Journal prompts that ask students to consider how they may respond to the dilemmas or situations in which the characters find themselves, supporting their responses with personal experiences or textual connections to other writings from the unit.

In these activities, students can draw on their understanding of the complexity of identity and culture that they developed in prior discussions. When they discuss what a character might do, they do so with confidence because they have already practiced giving advice to Mia. When they interpret a character's point of view, they draw on the skill that they developed when they interpreted Kahlo's point of view and discussed the points of view of their classmates. When they respond to the novel in journals, they are able to make generalizations about what the author's choices mean about borderland identity, as well as make generalizations about their interpretations, because they have had multiple opportunities to engage in similar inquiry in the unit.

## SYNTHESIS PROJECT: PULLING IT ALL TOGETHER

By the end of their inquiry, students have interpreted and discussed multiple texts that inform their understandings of the essential questions about borderland identity. A final assessment can ask students to address the essential questions using evidence from the authors they studied at the beginning of the unit, from a longer work, and from their personal experiences. Students choose from possible assignments (see textbox 9.3).

---

**Textbox 9.3. Synthesis Project**

To live in the borderlands means you . . .
—Gloria Anzaldúa

Overview: Throughout this unit, we have examined the concept of living in the "borderlands." We have used this concept as a lens for reading and understanding nonfiction essays and *The Brief Wondrous Life of Oscar Wao*. Using these texts, we have considered the following essential questions:

- What is life in the "borderlands" like?
- Why is the concept of the "borderlands" important for understanding ourselves and the world?
- What actual borders impact our identities?
- What is the experience of the borderland?

---

Your Task: Create a project in which you answer the above questions. Your project should incorporate evidence from one or more of the essays we have discussed in class and from *The Brief Wondrous Life of Oscar Wao*. You may incorporate evidence from your personal experiences to illustrate your perspective.

Here are some possible formats for completing your project. Choose *one* of these formats.

- Write a multiparagraph analytical essay exploring how you answer the questions, and how at least two works that we have read answer the questions.
- Imitating a BuzzFeed "list," create a "buzzfeed" page that answers the essential questions. Your page should include quotes from core texts as well as images that represent the concept of living in the borderlands and that will attract the reader's attention.
- Using an audio recording device, create a podcast in which you answer the essential questions. Be sure to use evidence from unit texts in your podcast.

At this point in the unit, students have more perspective and have developed more sophisticated understandings of the concepts. In a class that recently completed this unit, students confidently took ownership of the task and felt they knew enough about the concept to be able to write extensively about it. They had resources they could return to and review when writing their ideas. Some needed a little help structuring their essays but were eager to talk with classmates for support about what they were writing, as much as to talk to the teacher. They truly became the "experts" in addressing the essential questions. In reflecting on their participation in the unit and the final project, students commented on how they appreciated learning more about their classmates in conjunction with the texts, thinking about how texts relate to their lives, and finding ways to verbalize their conflicting feelings about belonging and not belonging in multiple cultures.

## CONCLUDING THOUGHTS

The borderlands unit serves as an example of how a series of discussions about a central concept can help students to build complex understandings about issues that matter to them. The discussions in this unit were more than isolated rehashings of a text or issue but rather part of a developing conversation that grew richer with each text. Students were able to develop deeper interpretations of multiple texts and to apply the concepts to the richness of their own experiences. However, this concept might not be the right choice for every class.

Teachers can work with similar types of units around concepts that matter to young adults. A teacher might choose to explore justice, friendship, the American Dream, empathy, gender roles, or ambition, to name just a few. Rather than frame a unit around a specific work, or a specific skill, teachers can frame the unit around the rich conversations they want their students to have about literature and their own lives.

## REFERENCES

Ahmed, S. (2016, June 26). Red thread at Fatehpur Sikri. *The Fem*. Retrieved from https://thefemlitmagazine.wordpress.com.

Alexie, S. (2007). *The absolutely true diary of a part-time Indian*. New York: Little, Brown.

Alvarez, J. (1991). *How the Garcia girls lost their accents*. Chapel Hill, NC: Algonquin.

Anzaldúa, G. (2007). *Borderlands/la frontera: The new mestiza* (3rd ed.). San Francisco: Aunt Lute Books.

Cisneros, S. (2003). *Caramelo; or, Puro Cuento: A Novel*. New York: Vintage.

Díaz, J. (2008). *The brief wondrous life of Oscar Wao*. New York: Riverhead.

DuBois, W. (1903). Of our spiritual strivings. In *The souls of black folk*. Retrieved from http://www.bartleby.com.

Hurston, Z. N. (2011). How it feels to be colored me. In S. Cohen (Ed.), *50 essays: A portable anthology* (3rd ed., pp. 182–186). Boston: Bedford/St. Martin's. (Original work published 1928.)

Lahiri, J. (2004). *The namesake*. New York: Mariner.

Morrison, T. (2000). *Beloved*. New York: Penguin.

Mukherjee, B. (2011). Two ways to belong in America. In S. Cohen (Ed.), *50 essays: A portable anthology* (3rd ed., pp. 280–283). Boston: Bedford/St. Martin's. (Original work published 1996.)

Rodriguez, L. J. (1994). "Race" politics. In L. M. Carlson (Ed.), *Cool salsa: Bilingual poems on growing up Hispanic in the United States*. New York: Henry Holt. (Original work published 1989.)

Rodriguez, R. (1982). Aria. In *Hunger of memory: The education of Richard Rodriguez* (pp. 9–41). New York: Bantam.

Rodriguez, R. (1982). Complexion. In *Hunger of memory: The education of Richard Rodriguez* (pp. 133–149). New York: Bantam.

Sáenz, B. A. (2012). *Aristotle and Dante discover the secrets of the universe*. New York: Simon & Schuster Books for Young Readers.

Tan, A. (1989). *The joy luck club*. New York: Putnam's.

Yang, G. L., & Pien, L. (2009). *American born Chinese*. New York: Square Fish.

*Chapter Ten*

# Digital Discussions

## Nicole Boudreau Smith and Mark Patton

In their seminal *They Say/I Say*, Gerald Graff and Cathy Birkenstein note that for students to "actually participate in [academic] conversations remains a formidable challenge" (2014, p. xvi). More than a decade later, many students still struggle to engage in classroom conversations, despite their increased use of social media. But strategic teachers can use digital platforms to help students improve the skills they need to successfully enter into academic debate.

There's a second, and more pressing, reason to embrace digital discussion: technology is here to stay as an integral part of our students' lives. In a recent study of how today's youth use technology, *iGen*, Jean Twenge reports that "iGen High School seniors spent an average of 2¼ hours a day texting on their cell phones, about 2 hours a day on the internet, 1½ hours a day on electronic gaming, and about a half hour on video chat in the most recent survey" (2017, p. 51). The point isn't that this amount of digital time is a problem but rather that this is the reality our students live in: students are engrossed in technology in more ways and in a greater abundance than were prior generations.

Also, our students are "digital natives" (Prensky, 2001), individuals that were born accustomed to smartphones, the internet, and social media; to digital natives, technology usage is seen not as an advancement but as a standard way of life. As teachers, our goal should be to bring a curriculum to students that is connected to real life, not detached from the experiences students are likely to have.

Furthermore, we must provide skills that will be useful to students now and in the future. In his article "Inquiry versus Naïve Relativism: James, Dewey, and Teaching the Ethics of Pragmatism," Jeffrey Conant Markham addresses the need for relevant skills and discussions: "All our students are genuinely concerned with how they might get the most out of their lives, and they have a natural attraction to ideas that seem useful to them" (2005, p. 21). In regard to "useful" skills and applications, professional environments are increasingly becoming digitized, and professionals are expected to leverage their capacities to use technology. Therefore, teachers should find ways to integrate technology in a manner that models the everyday experiences of students and also equips them for future opportunities.

We share much of the trepidation and alarm that many adults feel when we observe the use of technology in the lives of young adults. Ideally, technology should be used to enhance communication and relationships, and individuals using it need to be cognizant of when and how technology detracts from human interactions. All too frequently, there is a sense that our younger generation *and adults* alike are not as present in the conversations in which they participate; we are distracted by our devices. This is no small problem. Jean Twenge further reports that there is a strong correlation to a decrease in happiness or an increase in loneliness when technology is used improperly (2017). Therefore, teachers need to promote digital interactions that enhance learning and classroom activities and aim to minimize any improper usage.

This is also a significant rationale for why a discussion-based inquiry approach to the English classroom is transformative and necessary. Digital platforms within this approach can provide students with many opportunities to improve their discussion skills and expand their learning. While there are significant risks of technology compromising human interaction and overall well-being, this is not cause to eliminate digital spaces for educational purposes. In fact, it should be a rationale for the opposite: teachers should feel responsible for using the classroom as a space to empower students to use technology to foster meaningful interactions, using the instructional landscape to promote learning and foster human communications.

While we are well aware that digital platforms can enhance the quality of students' learning experiences, we also contend that digital dialogues should enhance face-to-face discussion, not replace it. In the digital age, teachers need to harness technological advancement, while simultaneously putting high priority on discussion-based approaches. We have the responsibility to teach students critical skills that will aid them in whatever endeavors they pursue throughout their lives. To that end, we see many windows for technology to foster and practice core content skills, and in keeping with many of the priorities in the current educational landscape, these opportunities align with Common Core Standards.

Through digital discussions, students can practice many significant discussion moves, such as citing evidence, demonstrating uptake, posing questions, or articulating reasoning. By approaching digital discussions with the goal of enhancing face-to-face interaction, not replacing it, there are practical benefits that support students not only in the mastery of core content skills but also, more importantly, in helping them become equipped citizens.

## IMPROVING UPTAKE THROUGH DIGITAL DISCUSSIONS

Literary theorist Kenneth Burke observed that entering academic discourse is a lot like attending a party: "When you arrive," he writes, "others have long preceded you, and they are engaged in a heated discussion . . . you listen for a while, until you decide that you have caught the tenor of the argument; then, you put in your oar" (1941, p. 110–111). Although an apt metaphor for those accustomed to asserting themselves in conversation, it can be a tall order for adolescents to decide what to say and when. In their haste to "put in their oars," students can forget to account for what their classmates are saying. But building upon others' ideas in order to offer one's own—what Martin Nystrand calls "uptake" (1997)—is an essential component of meaningful discussion, and students need many opportunities to practice it.

Even in the most carefully structured classroom conversations, an individual student might be able to demonstrate "uptake" with another student no more than two or three times. Technology offers a valuable and needed space for students to gain more practice. By combining digital discussion with live classroom discussions, a teacher can double or even triple uptake opportunities for learners.

For example, teachers might use online forums to help students practice uptake prior to a challenging whole-class discussion. At the conclusion of a memoir unit, students were to use their independent reading books to discuss how people overcome obstacles. Anticipating that students might find it difficult to connect their ideas when they had each read different books, the teacher initiated online chats the week preceding discussion.

Students joined mixed-book chat groups; within the chats, they could not reply to one another without first acknowledging a peer's comment and relating it to their own observations. When the day for whole-class discussion finally arrived, the students had each practiced uptake at least three times, and therefore were more skilled at navigating multiple titles in class. By using the digital space, the teacher ensured students had an even more successful learning experience.

Teachers can use online chats not only to prepare students for class but also to support students *during* class. For instance, while a circle of speakers initiates discussion, the remaining student listeners can participate in a simultaneous online chat.

**Textbox 10.1. Hosting an Online Chat Group**

The tools to host an online chat group are simple and inexpensive: sites like Google Classroom, Go Soapbox, and ReCap offer free, easy-to-use, safe spaces to host educational discussions; as long as students have access to the internet and a connected device (their own or school issued; students can even share access in small groups), they will be able to participate.

The online forum could feature the same topic the circle of speakers is pursuing, or focus instead on a related question (for example, the circle of speakers might discuss whether or not Atticus protects his children adequately; meanwhile, the listeners might chat online about what this discussion suggests about parenting). Because the students in the digital conversation must connect to what the "live" speakers are saying as well as what is trending online, they have a range of opportunities to employ uptake.

Digital discussions both in and out of class are particularly beneficial for learners who need more support. One such student, Catherine, routinely struggled to contend with her peers' ideas. This was apparent during a discussion of William Golding's *Lord of the Flies*. With her knowledge of literature and history, Catherine shared interesting ideas in class, but she did not connect to what others were saying. In the excerpt below, Catherine's assertions bear little relationship to what Henry and Lindsay have said. While Henry asks a question about whether the boys' makeshift society functions, and Lindsay valuates that society, Catherine offers an apparently unrelated observation about the novel's historical setting.

Henry: Do you really think this society is disorganized? If you think about it, everyone is going toward the same goal. They want the meat, so they kill the pig; they want to kill something, so they kill Simon [student laughter]—no, they *did* want to kill something, they had bloodlust, so they wanted to kill Simon. And then they also wanted fire, and they all wanted fire, right? But if you look at it, they achieve every one of those goals. Would you call that disorganized? It's effective.

Lindsay: Well, their overall goal is to get off the island. So if they're killing other people, soon they're all going to be dead, and that's not very effective.

Catherine: Let's consider something that was around the era, World War II. Let's bring up a dictator, Joseph Stalin. In his reign, he used fear to get people in control. Whenever someone didn't do what he wanted to do, he got that person killed. Whenever that person wasn't likeable to him, he got that person killed. Whenever a person was there, he got that person killed too. So, people were constantly in fear.

The difference between Lindsay's and Catherine's uptake skills is significant; Catherine will need focused practice in order to improve. Given the constraints of a traditional classroom discussion environment, this might take several weeks. However, through a combination of in-class and online conversations, Catherine made notable growth in a much shorter time frame.

A few days later, Catherine participated in an online chat about whether Jack or Ralph was a more effective leader. Applying her teacher's coaching about uptake, Catherine's response here is intimately tied to Jennifer's question, suggesting she is more closely listening to what others are saying.

Jennifer: If . . . Ralph seems like a more sensible leader who thinks more logically than Jack, why do the boys choose Jack over him?

Catherine: Ralph doesn't supply the boys with food unlike Jack who does. The boys care about staying alive more than doing some "civilized" things.

In a second online exchange, Catherine goes beyond simply answering a question. Instead, she analyzes Nancy's assertion before posing a related question of her own. This question then propels the conversation forward and promotes the participation of others.

Nancy: Jack is preparing them for if they aren't going to get rescued, while Ralph is kind of relying on someone to rescue them.

Catherine: But which aspect is more important, being rescued (follow Ralph) or surviving (follow Jack)?

Phil: Being rescued is likely of more importance, but it would be unreasonable to simply light a fire and dwindle around all day waiting for someone to come save them. They need to be rescued, but until then they also need to survive.

In the excerpt, Catherine attends to the heart of Nancy's assertion, and in doing so, she also challenges Phil's thinking, inviting him to further develop the argument about Ralph and Jack, a move that should stretch and improve the reasoning of all the students involved in this exchange.

Catherine's online conversations yielded remarkable growth that ultimately translated to her "live" speaking and listening as well. Soon thereafter, Catherine participated in a debate about whether or not Ferdinand and Miranda, of Shakespeare's *Tempest*, are in love, from which the following is excerpted. Italics have been inserted to emphasize how Catherine incorporates others' ideas into her own thinking.

Caleb: So, I'm saying, Ferdinand and Miranda, *they're in love*. And Cory's going to continue what I'm saying. This is a tag team thing.

Cory: So, Ferdinand, when he sees Miranda the *first time*, *he says*, "Most sure, the goddess on whom these airs attend . . . hear my prime request, which I do last pronounce is, O you wonder! if you be maid or so?" So basically, he's saying, right as he sees Miranda for *the first time*, he's saying that Miranda is like a goddess to him, and he's willing to do anything to get her.

Catherine: Talking about *first times*—I would like to say that *Miranda and Ferdinand are not in love*. In *that same scene*, when they have *that little flirty dialogue*, Miranda says, "One of my sex, no woman's face remember, save from my glass, mine own." Miranda has never seen anyone else except her father. Ferdinand's the first man she's ever seen. So she immediately falls in love with him as he's the first man she's ever seen. So that proves that Miranda doesn't understand *what love truly is*. So she naïvely falls in love with Ferdinand.

Catherine can still expand her boundaries—for example, she could address the evidence Cory used to support his claim about Ferdinand and Miranda before introducing new evidence herself. Still, as the italics indicate, she has begun to enter Burke's proverbial parlor, a place where she can enrich her thinking by connecting meaningfully with others' arguments, and she will be a better scholar for it.

## BUILDING CONFIDENCE IN CONTRIBUTIONS VIA ONLINE CHATS

The most meaningful discussions feature issues people care deeply about: topics such as love, friendships, happiness, and justice easily engage. At the same time, these topics involve a certain amount of risk, particularly for adolescents in the throes of identity formation. Online conversations can help in this regard, allowing students to ease themselves into the realm of open and honest sharing that translates into confident face-to-face conversations.

Whereas it can feel risky to speak in class—students may wonder if they are sharing too much, not enough, or in ways that are similar or different than others—in an online chat, participants can survey the comments made before deciding what they themselves would like to share. Whereas time can limit how and when students share in a typical class session, in an online chat, participants can evaluate several strands of conversation before selecting what they respond to, without worrying about time constraints. In sum, digital discussions provide meaningful supports for students becoming comfortable talking in class.

The value of such support is demonstrated in the journey of Paul and Robin, two sophomores, both hesitant to speak in class. In a democratic classroom community, full participation in discussions is important, but in the unit about outsiders studied in Paul's and Robin's class, hearing all voices became more important than ever. At the start of the unit, Paul's and Robin's class responded to a series of statements about outsiders versus community; during these small-group talks, Paul and Robin were both polite but reserved. After the small-group talks ended, the class had one week to participate in any three of several online chats extending the conversation.

The improvement in Paul's and Robin's contributions was immediate and dramatic. Paul made three substantive comments; in one, he connected the inquiry to what he was learning in science about evolution, an observation to which two classmates eagerly responded. Robin, meanwhile, became the first participant in three different digital discussions, bravely sharing personal details to illustrate his claims. In one contribution, Robin writes, "People can be influenced by other people and the situation they are in. There's a lot of things that can happen in which you as a person will change and no longer be that person you once were. Again living in an extremely rough neighborhood with drugs and violence, it's kinda hard to keep you[r] will and moral[e] intact when that's all you see." Although Robin's experience may not have been representative of some of his classmates' experiences, his willingness to share generated nine responses with specific uptake, demonstrating that Robin's insight was valued by many. At another point, Robin addresses a question about cultural expectations, writing,

> I agree and disagree [that cultural expectations prevent us from becoming what we want to be]. I disagree because yes it may be possible to go against cultural expectations that's at the cost of your family, for instance, I'm expected to go to church every Sunday and believe in God. I do, but if I wanted to I could tell my parents I don't believe in God, and they will be pretty upset with me because they've grown up always believing in God and going to church.

A student with a background very different from Robin's nonetheless detects common ground, and responds this way:

I strongly agree with [you]; although many may not realize it, cultural norms play an extremely prevalent role in society—all the way from stereotypes to the cultural expectations pressured by one's parents. For example, my parents arc [immigrants]. They envisioned one career path for me ever since I was young; if I'm not interested whatsoever, I still walk a fine line between making them proud and fulfilling their vision versus doing something that I love and have a passion for. My parents could've placed this expectation on me since I was young and thus not even let me believe that I have a say in the matter.

When discussion is handled well, all students will grow, but the swift change in Paul and Robin suggests that they felt safe and authorized by the digital environment. Given the right kind of opportunity to survey the conversational landscape, they were able to speak their minds. Most importantly, this change in Paul and Robin translated to the classroom.

The week following the online chats, they showed marked improvement in engagement and collaboration, both in small groups and in whole-class talks. While their skills had improved, they had taken their places as valuable members of their community.

## Online Spaces as Extensions of Classroom Conversation

Once students become comfortable talking in class, teachers might face a new challenge: students wishing the conversation could extend beyond the bell! This can be true of any discussion topic that fascinates and ignites debate, such as whether Montag's defiance in *Fahrenheit 451* is heroic or inexcusable—an attempt to define what true justice is. This can also be true at different stages in the learning process. For example, at the conclusion of a unit of study, when many teachers assign a culminating essay, students crave ongoing conversation as they try to shape what is formative into a final product.

To that end, digital spaces can help bridge the gap from exploratory to conclusive learning. Establishing a simple threaded discussion board can provide students a place to share ideas, pose questions, and offer advice as they move from tentative discussion language into the more formal rhetoric of academic prose.

In one such case, students were preparing to write final essays about *The Catcher in the Rye*. The final essay prompt asked whether Holden's situation had improved or worsened by the book's final pages. The teacher extended the conversation online, encouraging students to "test out" their ideas about Holden with each other before committing them to essay form. Below is a representative sample from that discussion space.

Mari: Holden's situation suggests that disillusionment makes someone *stronger* if they are able to move past it and use what they've learned to their advantage. . . . For example, Holden is especially irritated with Stradlater's perception of writing, saying, "He wanted you to think that the only reason *he* was lousy at writing . . . was because he stuck all the commas in the wrong place" (33). . . . Because Holden is going through disillusionment, he can see past this kind of laziness and evaluate the kind of person who uses this overconfident attitude toward their problematic work.

Gabe: I understand what you are trying to say with how Holden uses his disillusionment to strengthen him. I disagree with how you said how Holden is able to evaluate a person. Holden often calls everyone a "phony," all teachers, the headmaster, Sally, etc. Since Holden calls everyone a phony, it leads him to not be reliable because it's repetition of the same words and language. He thinks everyone is fake and that everyone has the same personality without even knowing them. . . . You said that Holden tends to avoid someone who is cruel, but he sticks around Stradlater and admires him when all Stradlater does is push him around.

Tom: I disagree when you say Holden is unable to use disillusionment to evaluate people. While I agree Holden does call other people "phonies" a lot, some of these are not at all baseless evaluations. For example, when calling old Spencer a phony, Holden provides evidence to back up his claim. Teachers are professionals and should act professionally, but unfortunately when Holden talks to old Spencer, "he [Spencer] started picking his nose. . . . I guess he thought it was alright because it was only me that was in that room" (5). The clear display of lack of respect and professionalism justifies Holden calling his teacher old Spencer a phony. Not only is this justification shown here; it's shown throughout the book.

Xavier: Tom's claim that Holden can in fact evaluate people is questionable at best. Tom claims that unprofessionalism gives him grounds to call him a phony. However, the word *phony* describes something that is false or fake, as in someone boasting a better image than they have. However, while Spencer is not necessarily a good teacher, he is not trying to show off. Tom also contradicts his own claim.

Each of the students featured in the excerpt above submitted thoughtful, carefully reasoned essays, made stronger by the critical feedback of their peers. By designating a digital space, the teacher communicated the value of the students' task and authorized them as the ones most capable to carry it out.

## Maintaining Interest and Increasing
## Participation with Digital Conversations

Learners have a right to classrooms that generate curiosity and honor student voices; structured, high-interest discussions afford these rights. Therefore, it is important throughout a unit of study to maintain an environment where every student is engaged with the material and confident with speaking and listening.

At the beginning of a unit, gateway discussion activities boast a high degree of student involvement; participants are eager to jump in and share their perspectives in conversations that draw on their prior knowledge and feature high-interest, controversy-laden topics. As the unit progresses, though, students can sometimes draw back from speaking in class—some may feel uncertain about the texts they are studying; others might worry whether their perspectives will be received by their peers. In these cases, online discussion, occurring simultaneously with "live" debates, seminars, and other discussion structures, is a useful tool to maintain engagement and help a greater percentage of students become and stay connected to what is happening in class.

In one freshman class, digital chats bolstered student confidence and encouraged greater student buy-in. These particular learners spoke eagerly whenever given the chance, but they had found Shakespeare's *Tempest* challenging, and so their characteristic enthusiasm was subdued. Despite the compelling nature of the debate topics (see textbox 10.2), when the first circle of student speakers gathered to discuss Prospero's parenting skills, much time passed before anyone said anything. Finally, Isaac offered an unusual assertion, that Prospero is not an exacting colonist but rather a kind father figure to island inhabitant Caliban:

> Caliban was somewhat brought into Prospero's life. He says, "For I am all the subjects that you have, which first was my own king, and here you sty me in this hard rock, whilst you keep me." So this is kind of saying that we know that Caliban showed Prospero this island, and as a father . . . as a father-figure, he kept Caliban as his own, and started to have him as a servant/slave.

In most settings, Isaac's peers would have challenged his interpretation—indentured servitude as an approved parenting style?—but silence persisted. At this point, the digital chatroom, visible both on students' individual devices and projected from the teacher's laptop, proved invaluable. Diego, a student in the circle of listeners, posted a question online: "Does a father figure beat his 'kids'?"

Comments erupted from the students in the speaking circle. At the same time, the digital chat filled with reactions from the students in the listening circle. During the remaining twelve minutes of discussion, the eight designated speakers shared at length, and the fourteen outer-circle listeners contributed at least one related comment or question to the simultaneous digital chat; the result was 100 percent class participation, robust involvement by any measurement, but more so given the rigor posed by the text.

The ignited atmosphere was due in large part to the presence of the digital chat. For speakers, it became a safe intermediary space where they could experiment with ideas before voicing them in class; at the same time, the give-and-take between the digital chat and the designated speakers encouraged the listeners to chime in more, as they valued the impact they could make on the content of the discussion.

### Textbox 10.2. *The Tempest* Debate Topics

1. True or False: Prospero is a good father.
2. True or False: Prospero is a good ruler.
3. True or False: In cases where one has been greatly wronged, it is best to seek revenge.
4. True or False: By the end of *The Tempest*, justice has prevailed.
5. True or False: Of all of the people on the island, Caliban has been the most wronged.
6. True or False: Miranda and Ferdinand are in love.

## Using Digital Discussion to Refine Inquiry Concepts and Practice Writing

It is not only skills, of course, that teachers are bound to improve; it's also students' capacity to participate in a democratic society. As teachers, it is essential that we provide students with opportunities to discuss issues that further conceptual understandings and are also relevant to students' lives.

In fact, one of our most important curricular mandates is to connect learning to students' lives. For us, using essential questions and inquiry-based units are some of the best ways to not only frame discussions around pertinent issues but also challenge and advance critical understandings of big ideas. As Jeff Wilhelm notes, "If we give students the chance to pursue powerful guiding questions and help them develop the conceptual and strategic expertise they need to do so, they will do better on tests, and much more important, they will do better in their future learning and lives" (2007, p. 14). In other words, not only will students be more invested in units that are framed by essential questions, but also this type of inquiry-based approach speaks to best practice and how to best prepare students for future life goals.

Because inquiry usually requires students to grapple with complicated concepts, it is necessary to provide students with plenty of opportunities to discuss and think about essential questions. Using digital platforms to support these types of conversations offers students the moments to practice writing and refine key concepts related to the inquiry. Students still need to have these face-to-face discussions, but using digital platforms to support these discussions can enhance the interaction students have.

While listening to a variety of interpretations from a face-to-face conversation, students can simultaneously exchange ideas digitally. This setup works best when one group of students is directed to participate verbally and another group is assigned the task of participating digitally. In this way, students participating digitally are able to process their own ideas at a slower pace and refine inquiry concepts through writing. Not only does this allow students to see the connection between discussion and writing, but also these ideas become public, and all students can reflect and build off of these digital comments. Furthermore, while traditional face-to-face dialogues allow for one voice to be heard at a time, digital discussions allow for multiple interpretations to be shared simultaneously.

In conjunction with *When the Emperor Was Divine*, students focused their readings and discussions with an inquiry into the nature of *marginalization*. More specifically, students grappled with essential questions such as, Why do societies marginalize? And what are the effects of marginalization on the individual and on society?

After reading about half of the book, students took "agree or disagree" positions on statements such as, "Genetics define what happens to us." Students used evidence from *When the Emperor Was Divine*, as well as secondary texts such as Steven Okazaki's 1990 documentary *Days of Waiting: The Life and Art of Estelle Ishigo* and Hisaye Yamamoto's 1950 short story "Wilshire Bus" to support their positions. Students discussed these concepts face-to-face but also used a Google-based digital platform to comment on the same concepts. The face-to-face discussion was happening at the center of the classroom, with the listeners and digital participants on the outside. During this discussion, the following face-to-face exchange took place.

Riley: I understand what you were saying—that Estelle Ishigo went against cultural expectations—but I think that cultural expectations prevent them [Japanese Americans] from being who they are. They are prevented from being Japanese because they are not accepted. On page 76 [from *When the Emperor Was Divine*], with all the rules they had, it said, "A man stopped him on the sidewalk in front of Woolworths and said 'Chink or Jap?' and the boy answered, 'Chink' and ran away as fast as he could. And only when he got to the barn did he turn around and shout 'Jap! Jap! I'm a Jap!'" He's basically not able to be himself comfortably because they're being discriminated against.

Jennifer: Also on page 31 from *When the Emperor Was Divine*, this is when the little boy said that when he grew up he wanted to be a jockey but then everyone discouraged him from doing that. One person said, "Eat lots. Grow up to be an American boy." And no one supported his dream of being a jockey. They wanted him to be more of an American because they are in America, so their expectations are to attach to this culture and not have the Japanese culture that they've had before.

In these comments, students are able to explore complex ideas such as identity and cultural expectations. These ideas are challenging, yet necessary, to understand in relation to the inquiry. While the exchange allowed students to discuss their ideas publicly, students that participated in a digital conversation benefitted from this discussion as well. While their peers continued the face-to-face dialogue, Hanna and Maggie, now online, were able to slow down their thoughts, share their interpretations, and build upon the ideas posed in the face-to-face dialogue.

Hanna: I agree with what Riley said about how people are limited by their culture. People can't be themselves because of their Japanese heritage, and they are discriminated against. In *When the Emperor Was Divine*, the text reads, "The man scrubbing pots and pans in the mess hall had once been the sales manager of an import-export company in San Francisco" (Otsuka, 2017, pp. 55–56). Since this man was forced to be in the internment camps just due to the fact that he was Japanese, he can't live his life as he wants to and do what he wants to do.

Maggie: Going back to what Riley said about how they can be discriminated against, on page 2 of "Wilshire Bus," it says, "Why don't you go back to China, where you can be coolies working in your bare feet out in the rice fields?" The Chinese couple wants to be like any other Americans, but the vision from someone who is discriminating against them is, "Oh, they should work in rice fields," and this is their type of culture that they live in.

Both of these students responded to the initial face-to-face comment by Riley, and even applied a new secondary text to the discussion. If the dialogue had been solely face-to-face, Hanna's and Maggie's comments would have been isolated to these students' thoughts or, at best, independent note-taking. However, with the use of a digital platform, there are more comments shared publicly; these comments are permanent, and students can reflect on these ideas at any point. The digital comments are being made at the same time the face-to-face dialogue continues, and this increases participation.

More beneficially, this process spotlights the relationship between writing and discussion. While students have the opportunity to partake in digital discussions, they are also able to practice writing. From that experience, students can see the interplay between what they say and what they write. Students witness the immediate transfer of ideas and are able to understand that just as discussion is a conversation, writing is a part of a conversation too. Lastly, this process allows teachers to emphasize that the moves a writer makes are similar to the moves speakers make, which is a lesson teachers should emphasize to students: in discussion and in writing, students need to pose a claim, support that claim with evidence, and clarify their reasoning in a public conversation.

To emphasize, the digital platform allowed students to practice writing, increase participation, and expose the relationship between discussion and writing. More importantly, concepts such as "cultural identity" or "marginalization" are useful to students not only in this unit but also in their lives. By negotiating these concepts in class, students are more aware of how these ideas should function in society and within their own lives.

## Preparing Students for Live Conversations in an Online Space

Students bring different backgrounds and knowledge to discussion. Consequently, certain students might be at an advantage or disadvantage to participate in certain conversations. Given these differences, digital discussions can be an effective tool to prepare students for face-to-face conversations.

We would almost always recommend giving students time to prepare thoughts and evidence before having a discussion. Traditionally, this is done individually, with a partner, or in a group setting, but with digital discussion boards, students are able to test out ideas and explore a variety of perspectives before the live classroom discussion begins. In a senior elective course, Political Thought, a team of two coteachers focus a class's inquiry on this essential question: What is the balance between an individual's responsibility to himself/herself versus a civic responsibility to society?

One of the issues the class investigates is affirmative action. Given that many students have varying levels of understanding of affirmative action, it was helpful to give students time to prepare comments in response to a set of focus questions. After investigating these questions, students made digital posts and examined their peers' responses. In response to one of the focus questions—How does affirmative action relate to diversity?—students had the following digital exchange.

Patrick: Affirmative action can promote a student body with more ethnic or racial diversity. In allowing for more underrepresented applicants to have an equal opportunity, more diverse people will be students on more college campuses.

Jeffrey: Affirmative action sets out to diversify organizations and institutions. It's been successful but is reaching a point in my opinion that it is no longer needed. I feel many places have implemented affirmative action programs successfully leading to diversity in employment and colleges across our country. At what point are we diverse enough?

Mira: Affirmative action puts race as the big factor in admissions and hiring procedures. It allows a tolerance toward other communities because it exposes people to a variety of cultures and ideas that are different from their own.

In this manner, students are generating ideas and necessary vocabulary to participate in a live discussion the following day. Furthermore, students can examine alternative and competing viewpoints, testing out ideas in a less risky, more "low-stakes" way. This risk paid off.

The following day, the students were already "warmed up" to have a discussion in response to the question, To what extent should universities, the workforce, and US Law support affirmative action policies? Not only did students further their understanding of this specific issue, but also they were able to advance their understanding of the essential question. By discussing affirmative action, students were considering whether or not society has the responsibility to make opportunities more accessible to groups of people that were marginalized in the past and are potentially still marginalized today.

## CONCLUDING THOUGHTS: USING DISCUSSION TO BUILD CLASSROOM COMMUNITIES

More important than any skill or learning experience we provide students is the opportunity for students to feel like valued members of a community. In the realm of learning targets, assessments, and curriculum planning, it is vital that we do not forget the human element of education. Although students most likely will not remember the plot of many of the novels they read, students will remember the feeling that they received from being a member of a classroom community.

To authorize student voices and to build communities, classrooms need discussion. We are convinced that technology and digital discussions can enhance face-to-face conversations but must not replace face-to-face conversations. Digital platforms give students more opportunities to participate, more chances to practice skills, and more occasions to engage with inquiry and class content, but just as we want to live in a world in which technology does not impede our ability to communicate with others, we also want to create classrooms that honor student voices. In doing so, we not only maximize student voice—and reduce teacher talk—but also build relationships and ideas together; in other words, we build a classroom community.

## REFERENCES

Burke, K. (1941). *The philosophy of literary form*. Berkeley: University of California Press.

Golding, W. (1954). *Lord of the flies*. New York: Penguin.

Graff, G., & Birkenstein, C. (2014). *They say/I say: The moves that matter in academic writing* (3rd ed.). New York: Norton.

Markham, J. (2005). Inquiry versus naïve relativism: James, Dewey, and teaching the ethics of pragmatism. In T. M. McCann, L. Johannessen, E. Kahn, P. Smagorinsky, & M. W. Smith (Eds.), *Reflective teaching, reflective learning*. Portsmouth, NH: Heinemann.

Nystrand, M. (1997). *Opening dialogue: Understanding the dynamics of language and learning in the English classroom*. New York: Teachers College Press.

Otsuka, J. (2017). *When the emperor was divine: A novel*. New York: Knopf.

Prensky, M. (2001). Digital natives, digital immigrants. *On the Horizon, 9*(5), 1–6.

Salinger, J. D. (1951). *The catcher in the rye*. Boston: Little, Brown.

Shakespeare, W. (1994). *The tempest*. New York: Simon & Schuster.

Twenge, J. (2017). *iGen: Why today's super-connected kids are growing up less rebellious, more tolerant, less happy—and completely unprepared for adulthood (and what this means for the rest of us)*. New York: Atria.

Wilhelm, J. (2007). *Engaging readers and writers with inquiry: Promoting deep understandings in language arts and the content areas with guiding questions*. New York: Scholastic.

*Chapter Eleven*

# Discussion, Deliberation, and Democracy

## Tamara Jaffe-Notier

By redefining whose voice is valued, we redefine our society and its values.
—Rebecca Solnit, *The Mother of All Questions* (2017, p. 24)

After an enlightening and challenging two-day equity workshop where students, teachers, and administrators worked side by side to raise questions about why students are excluded from the very curriculum decisions that most impact their academic lives and how a district could open up the process of curriculum development to include student voices, a student spoke up about what she had learned: "I learned that talking and listening is 'a thing.' A discussion is not just a wasteful activity. It changes people." She explained how school had conditioned her to think that solving math problems or writing an essay was "a real learning experience," but discussing ideas was "just talking." In this workshop, staff members and students shared life-changing moments through talking and listening.

Discussions nourish democracy when we're ready to hear voices that might contradict our own knowledge and experience. A class discussion that prepares students for active participation in democracy doesn't have the closure that teachers ordinarily design. Making classrooms a laboratory for democracy means letting go of the idea of control and embracing the role of moderator or facilitator.

Are we willing to experience messy, incomplete days of listening and speaking that require students and teachers to experience the discomfort of unanswered questions? This is the natural condition of democracy. Discussions can sharpen problem-solving skills, but more often they sharpen question-asking skills, untestable skills upon which democratic institutions depend.

This dynamic happens in the classroom when meaningful discussions make participants aware of the power of engagement through words. Exciting discussions empower democratic action and institutions in school and out. Dialogue is a form of action and a training ground for full participation in a democracy. As such, throughout this chapter "democratic" and "democracy" refer to a nonpartisan definition of shared social power that is the opposite of "autocratic" and "autocracy."

How can we understand the relationship between discussion and democracy? The free speech clause of the First Amendment implies a direct correlation, yet less than half of registered voters vote in congressional elections. Each year the "Democracy Index" published by the *Economist* reveals that the practice of democracy, as measured by "electoral process and pluralism; civil liberties; the functioning of government; political participation; and political culture," in the United States is slipping. In 2017 the US tied with Italy, in twenty-first place, making us a "flawed democracy" instead of a "full democracy."

Could an emphasis on good class discussions help form the citizens who will build our democracy? An active class discussion models the democratic pluralism that supports civil liberties and political participation. Where individuals value and protect an array of competing or conflicting views, democracies thrive. The values measured in the "Democracy Index" blossom in classrooms where discussions about our direct relationships to one another and to contemporary issues are nurtured.

Our culture demonstrates how discussions fuel democracy. A large-scale conversation about gun violence initiated by teenagers who survived the February 14, 2018, shooting at Marjory Stoneman Douglas High School exploded on the political landscape beyond the peramaters of discussions around Sandy Hook, Las Vegas, or any of the other recent mass shootings. Why?

Parkland student leaders are continuing a *discussion* that ranges back to the relationship between gun violence in affluent places like Columbine and Sandy Hook and gun violence in impoverished US neighborhoods and then forward into the future. Organizers of Black Lives Matter and March for Our Lives have been in conversation with each other and with the culture at large, asking our democracy, "How are we going to stop the gun violence targeting African Americans and young people?" This is our democracy in dialogue with itself, and this process can begin in vital class discussions.

Meaningful class discussions embody the daily political life of the classroom and develop the listening, thinking, and speaking skills young people need for full participation in a democracy. It is no surprise that students who have been trained in participating in discussions within their public schools are leading democratic movements in society. But moderating a discussion on an emotionally fraught issue like gun violence in schools or the role of institutional racism in keeping our society segregated is daunting.

How do teachers facilitate a classroom conversation when the stakes are high and fear about speaking or not speaking permeates many public places in our culture? What is the role of teachers in such discussions?

On the day after the murders of seventeen students and staff in Parkland, Florida, teachers and students across the US were at a loss for words. Each time an unarmed African American citizen is killed by law enforcement officers, teachers and students are at a loss for words. That's the place to begin difficult discussions: the direct acknowledgment of a problem. As members of a classroom community, teachers model an authentically democratic response to a crisis when they listen to and acknowledge serious problems in our society.

After a catastrophe, natural or manmade, students want and need to talk. When teachers break a classroom silence after a shooting, the most commonly expressed position early in the discussion is confusion mixed with frustration over a lack of feelings:

"Ms. Brown, it's hard to feel anything at all except mad because this happens all the time."

"I don't know why I don't feel sad or angry—it's hard for me to care."

"I feel like, oh well, there goes another one."

"Why is it okay for an eighteen-year-old to buy an automatic weapon when he's not even allowed to buy a beer?"

"Why didn't the cops know that kid was in his own grandma's yard?"

The discussion after a shooting may range from hopelessness to a suggestion that the US ought to repeal the Second Amendment, or that police officers shouldn't carry firearms.

A democratic discussion position in a postcatastrophe scenario allows students to compare, disagree, and decide the direction of the conversation. In such a discussion, students and teachers agree to accept nonclosure. A class discussion is not a place to solve the world's problems—it is a place to acknowledge the meaning of the work ahead. If students ask the teacher, "What do you think we should do, Ms. Brown?" a teacher can honestly reply, "I don't know. But we have to start by listening to each other." This chapter provides specific techniques and ideas about where and how to begin discussions based on listening and speaking skills required for full participation in a democracy.

## SERIOUS CONVERSATION: LAYING THE GROUNDWORK

Teachers plan ahead for fruitful dialogue. While good class discussions may arise spontaneously, they don't happen accidentally. Openness, preparation, and flexibility are hallmarks of the democratic classroom. Teachers must lay the environmental, behavioral, and academic foundations that create a context of trust and mutual vocabulary. What follows are physical and intellectual guidelines for providing such a setting for democratic classroom discussions.

### The Environmental Foundation

Teachers make time in their curriculum for discussions, and then they modify the physical space in a classroom to maximize personal interaction during a discussion. To create the physical structure for a classroom where the participation of every student is the foundation for discussions, students and teachers need to see one another's faces throughout the conversation.

A circle or a horseshoe of desks is a simple arrangement that works. With a double horseshoe of desks facing a whiteboard or blackboard at the front of the room, each face is visible to the others and each voice can be heard. If this configuration can't be maintained on a daily basis, move the desks into the discussion format when needed. The work of creating an egalitarian space for discussion seems small, but it shows students that the class is committed to the goal of discussion as an end in itself. The physical space teachers create for discussion communicates that all the voices in the room matter.

Discussion matters for listeners as well as speakers, and welcoming and acknowledging listeners within a class discussion are important too. On the morning after an unplanned discussion in an honors class on a current event affecting all students, a teacher received an email from a parent. The teacher dreaded opening the email because Edgar had a C in this class, and the teacher was afraid Edgar's parent was either complaining about wasting class time on social issues or asking why Edgar had a C.

But the email was a positive reflection on the impromptu class discussion, not a complaint about a grade. This parent wanted the teacher to know that the class discussion had been very important to her son. Edgar had said nothing during the discussion, but the measure of the class discussion's influence on Edgar, although not immediately detectable, was indeed valuable. To participate as an active listener, as this young man did, requires an attentive engagement very similar to that of speaking up.

Students are often not aware that they have the power to choose an intellectually, emotionally, and morally active stance in a class discussion; some have become accustomed to being passive recipients of knowledge. In discussion-friendly classrooms, teachers ask participants to consciously set the intention to *stay engaged*, *be as clear as possible*, and *accept* the *discomfort* of knowing that all questions won't be answered, nor will discussions cause pressing social problems to disappear. But these discussions are an important form of action. If tensions flare in a discussion, teachers redirect students toward the context of the positions:

> Does one position express a culturally dominant or nondominant point of view?
>
> What assumptions underlie each position?
>
> What is at stake in the discussion?

## The Foundation of Shared Vocabulary

It is difficult to acknowledge and value perspectives that contradict one's own view, yet functional democracies rely on civil dialogue between contrasting positions. Teachers who build and model a shared vocabulary for describing power relationships in society provide tools for students to disagree respectfully with one another.

Elemental shared vocabulary for understanding relationships between dominant and nondominant positions within general culture provides an entry point for great discussions by giving students tools for observing and understanding conflicting views. With a few new vocabulary words students can make room in a discussion for a variety of positions. Openness to contrasting ideas and new words that describe power relationships feeds democracy; teachers have to train students how to engage in democratic speaking and listening, because hearing and understanding conflicting views is uncomfortable for all participants.

Designing lessons that ask students to think about how freedoms are reflected in their lives, society, and literature provides the opportunity to learn about "dominant culture" and "nondominant culture." The forces supported by institutional power represent the dominant culture of a society. For example, if anyone wonders if the Christian religion is part of dominant or nondominant culture in the US, a teacher can ask, "Is public school in session on Christmas Day?" The strands of American society that wield less institutional power represent the nondominant culture. An individual may possess traits of both dominant and nondominant culture, and students easily identify this phenomenon. These vocabulary terms offer students words to describe and understand ideas and experiences accurately, from an array of perspectives.

A four-minute YouTube video titled "Hasta Mañana," wherein Michelle Valles, a Texan news anchor, speaks about her experience of saying "hasta mañana" at the end of the evening news in Austin, is an object lesson in dominant and nondominant cultural forces in conflict. In the video, Valles narrates her experience of what happened when she ended an English-language news broadcast with the Spanish phrase "hasta mañana." Why do some people like hearing a news anchor say "hasta mañana"? Why are some people angry about it? How does this story reflect a relationship between *dominant* and *nondominant* cultures in Texas? How does this story compare to our experiences? Expansive class discussions depend on students having easy access to vocabulary terms like dominant and nondominant.

In discussion-friendly classrooms, teachers have regular conversations with students about the meanings of many words and the assumptions behind words. This can be part of lessons on denotation and connotation or part of an explicit explanation of historical context. For example, why might a white teacher choose not to read the "n-word" out loud in *Huck Finn* or *Panther Baby*, especially if the same teacher is willing to read other swear words aloud? Is this self-censorship? Does skin color matter in this choice? Does the relationship between dominant and nondominant culture have an impact on this choice? How? Why?

When teachers want their classes to communicate openly about topics of social significance, including race and racism, they must model how to do it. An important element of honesty in this discussion is acknowledging how race and gender influence perspectives and experiences. When teachers publicly acknowledge these variables by owning their own perspectives, they demonstrate a way of paying attention to the real world:

> "As a black female teacher in a dominantly white school, I've been asked . . ."
> "As a white male teacher in our society, I often feel that . . ."

When teachers model an acknowledgment of subjective perceptions, their honesty paradoxically elevates objectivity as a goal in listening and speaking. Students recognize and respect this vulnerable stance on the part of the teacher, and self-awareness becomes a tangible feature of class discussions. In these democratic classrooms, students acknowledge that the influences of race, gender, religion, and other variables are important, and they pay more attention to their own perspectives *and* the perspectives of students who are like or unlike them.

In difficult discussions of sensitive issues of race and gender, or the relationship of religious beliefs to politics, students demonstrate their growing awareness of language that can express precise differences in experience and perspective:

> "As a Hispanic Catholic male, I sometimes feel . . ."
> "As a nonreligious Asian female, I feel . . ."

These clarifications demonstrate that importance isn't an objective force, like gravity, that imposes itself on education or society.

## The Foundation of Trust

A trusting relationship, fostered through honesty and openness between students and teachers, makes democratizing discussions possible. Teachers who model honesty and openness with students proceed in class knowing that students also do their best to model these traits.

In democratic classrooms and societies, *we* determine what is important through our choices. When the vocabulary and quality of classroom discussions reflect what matters to the participants, a reservoir of intrinsic motivation and trust opens, and shared knowledge of a wide array of real characteristics that shape contrasting experiences and ideas creates a democratic understanding.

When students' views come into conflict, they are able to understand, tolerate, and even respect positions that are shaped by experiences unlike their own. Understanding, respecting, and listening to the plurality of voices and viewpoints, cultivating the courage to share ideas publically, and honing critical-thinking and speaking skills are all explicit goals of good class discussions.

## PARTICIPATORY DEMOCRACY: HEARING EVERY VOICE

Achieving a maximum percentage of actively participating students is an important goal of the democratic classroom. This section suggests specific models for class discussions that increase the democratic quality of life in the classroom community. Naturally occurring discussions, like the one cited above that was followed by a parent call, might have active listeners who do not speak; the unknown direction of naturally occurring discussions requires an additional level of speaking courage.

Naturally occurring discussions are student directed, for the most part, and the teacher's role therein is not to change the subject but to increase participation by influencing the approachability of the questions. Planned class discussions are designed by teachers for the explicit goal of 100 percent participation, in addition to all the other goals of discussion. What follows are models for guiding both types of discussions.

### Naturally Occurring Discussions

Students like to talk in class, and they may arrive breathlessly discussing events of significance in their lives. It should be easy to begin discussions based on events students care about, right? Then why do these excited voices sometimes disappear when the teacher raises a question? Wait time aside, sometimes abstract questions that seem intrinsically interesting accidentally narrow class discussions rather than broaden them.

Another damper on a good spontaneous discussion occurs when teachers try too hard to control content. It is not easy for teachers to relinquish a degree of control over content in their classrooms, but naturally occurring democratic discussions rely on students generating and owning topics that are important to them. Facilitating maximum participation in impromptu discussions requires teachers to negotiate the cognitive and emotional subtleties of questions.

When classes suddenly fall silent, it is often because a question has leaped to a level of emotional or intellectual complexity that students are unprepared for. Fortunately, teachers working to elicit vibrant discussions can take advantage of Benjamin Bloom's lifetime of research on how students learn. Bloom's taxonomy of educational objectives describes a hierarchy of concrete to abstract understanding implicit in learning.

If teachers internalize a simple mental rubric based on a hierarchy of understanding, they can adjust the level of impromptu questions to meet the needs of the classroom conversation. A model for generating questions that facilitate naturally occurring class discussions can be as simple as 1–2–3:

1. Facts on the ground: What narratives surround the event or idea? Who is telling them?
2. Bridge questions: Are we hearing "sides of a story," or are we hearing "spin"?
3. Broader meanings: How do we understand the differences between perspectives and spin?

This question progression from "facts" to "meanings" requires that teachers practice constant in-the-moment assessment through close listening. Because teachers are the facilitators in the dance of class discussion, it is the teacher's job to create moves and questions that make naturally occurring discussions work. These moves—facts, bridges, and broader meanings—are based on the six stages of comprehension posited by Bloom's Taxonomy of Educational Objectives, condensed into three steps. Brief periods of silence are necessary in a class discussion, but if wait time turns into five minutes of fidgeting and staring into space, teachers can assess the current level of discussion and move back down this simple hierarchy, offering a question that gets discussion moving again.

Questions about facts or the structure of facts elicit many responses because almost every student is interested and capable of sharing his or her grasp of facts. In the cognitive domain of Bloom's taxonomy this is the easiest knowledge to access: remembering/comprehending. It's an excellent place for students to begin a discussion of a subject they care about.

Once classes are comfortable with the motion of good discussions, teachers can ask students to generate oral or written discussion questions at various levels, making the "facts, bridges, broader meanings" strategy as general or precise as needed to fit the topic. But be prepared for surprises. Teachers who use naturally occurring discussions to empower student voices and promote democratic deliberation in class need to have the courage to allow students to confront their own biases.

One teacher encountered the following events in an impromptu discussion after a school-wide Martin Luther King Jr. Day Assembly. The following narrative shows one hazard of an impromptu discussion and how the students in this classroom negotiated it.

Teacher: What did you notice in today's assembly?

*(Here there were three or four minutes of enthusiastic responses describing and commenting on the assembly. The teacher did not interrupt. Students listened to one another and answered each other's questions.)*

Sheryl: The choir was amazing! Those photos they showed in the background!

Derrik: Who took those pictures? Students took those pictures! Art classes put that slideshow together! Did you hear that poem in Spanish? Wasn't that cool? I don't even speak Spanish, but I loved the way those two girls wrote that poem together and acted it out. I totally got it. Who wrote the speech that that girl gave? She did!

Brian: I think the assembly today was racist against white people. There were no white people talking, and they showed some pictures from a march against Trump——

*(Silence. Some students looked at the teacher, some looked at the ground, and some interrupted Brian, who was not done speaking.)*

Teacher: We don't interrupt each other. Let Brian finish. Everybody has a right to speak here. Could you explain what you mean, Brian?

Brian: I'm just saying that I think there's racism against white people nowadays. The whole assembly was about brown people, and there was a poem just in Spanish so that nobody else could understand it, and then there were those "hate Trump" pictures.

*(Silence.)*

Claire: Yeah, on the overhead they had that quote about sticking to love, not hate,[1] but then they had those pictures hating on Trump. That's a contradiction.

*(Silence.)*

Teacher: What do those pictures show?

Sammy: I'm in art class, and those photos were put together by students. I didn't help make the slides, but they were all done by art students. Our teacher said we could help if we wanted. She let students decide what pictures to show.

Anita: Yeah, students were running the assembly, and students took those pictures. That makes it their choice about what to include. It's art. They have a right to include it. Isn't it protected by the First Amendment?

CeeJay: I liked the Spanish poems. I don't understand Spanish, but I think they show that Martin Luther King's ideas apply to everybody. Students wrote those poems—they're part of our school. They're Americans too.

*(The pace of the discussion has slowed considerably. Students, including Brian, are listening to each other.)*

Tony: Well, you heard what Mr. Johnson said, the Black Student Union isn't just for black students. It's open to all the students in the school, and they want to see all the cultures represented there. You should join the Black Student Union, Brian. Then you could help decide what's in the program. You could help plan the Martin Luther King Jr. assembly.

The teacher opened this naturally occurring discussion with a "facts on the ground" question about the assembly: "What did you notice in today's assembly?" Students jumped in to describe what they saw, heard, and felt. When Brian joined the conversation, he immediately moved it to what he felt were "broader meanings." The silence followed by dismissive, interrupting behavior indicated not only that some students were appalled by Brian's views but also that the jump to generalization had happened too fast for the class.

Fortunately, the teacher remained calm. When she required the class to treat Brian's contribution with respect, she also asked Brian to explain what he meant, posing a question at the "bridges" level, which brought the discussion back to a more accessible place for all the students. This move reminded students, including Brian, that their voices matter, and at the same time reaffirmed their teacher's expectation to be thoughtful and precise in how they speak to one another.

When the discussion moved back to an intermediate place between pure description and pure abstraction, students were relieved. They once again listened closely to one another and spoke accurately, bringing their own knowledge and experience to bear on the discussion. Claire's observation about the theme of the assembly created a large arena for students to enter with their own "facts on the ground" knowledge. The teacher posed another "bridges" question about the photo, but the students took the dialogue in a different direction that was more suited to their own needs.

The teacher was still thinking about how to frame bridge questions for this discussion in terms of lessons about white privilege from the previous semester, but she didn't need to ask any more questions. The students built the bridges for this discussion, moving from the facts of the event to the conclusions they drew from thinking critically about it. They were polite, and they responded to Brian's view with interpretations of their own. One student responded to the poems in Spanish by saying that she liked to hear Spanish, even though she didn't understand it, and she reached up for the broader meaning: "They're Americans too."

The final student who spoke, Tony, also went from "facts" to "bridges" to "broader meanings" on his own, and at this point the participants were ready. Tony referenced an introductory speech given by the advisor to the Black Student Union, and the conclusions Tony drew created a transition for the teacher to move toward that day's lesson about cultural conflicts and race relations in *Othello*.

This narrative demonstrates some risks and rewards of naturally occurring discussions and illustrates how the "facts bridge broader meanings" hierarchy can give teachers some modicum of regulatory intervention in any discussion. Spontaneous discussions take advantage of student passions, but not every student will speak in this voluntary model. For ensuring 100 percent participation in a class discussion, planned discussions are best.

## Planned Discussions

Structured class discussions that build critical-thinking and analytical skills, and elicit 100 percent participation, come in many forms.

### Paired Interviews

One good discussion strategy that follows an impromptu discussion has students interview one another in pairs on the topic of the previous class discussion. Students who have opinions and ideas that were not voiced in the impromptu discussion might find an increased comfort level in discussion with just one other classmate. They will also have had additional time to reflect on the topic.

To prepare for these interviews, each student needs to compose three questions to ask another classmate, about the subject they had just discussed in class. What aspects of the topic weren't addressed in class? What do students want to know? If teachers can collect student-generated questions at the end of the period of class discussion, these questions can become the basis for further exploration of the topic with planned, interview pairings.

The following day, teachers can begin class by posting a list of compiled student questions. Or if this was not possible, the questions might be generated at the beginning of class. For either case, the class can review their questions and identify which ones are "facts" that can be answered quickly. For example, when the teacher asked for additional questions after the MLK Jr. Day assembly discussion above, some students wanted to know more about the Spanish poem that was presented by two student poets. Since this class had several Spanish-speaking students, they were able to find out a little more about the poem. The teacher's invitation for students to share their knowledge will reactivate students' consciousness regarding their previous discussion.

After students have discussed the "facts on the ground" questions, they would move into pairs. Every pair would select three or four questions from those that remain to discuss with each other. For example, some students from the MLK assembly discussion wondered what their classmates thought about having some elements of a school assembly presented in a non-English language, a broader meaning question. Since these remaining questions, having been scaffolded in previous discussion, would be at the bridges and broader meaning levels, they would quite naturally lead to fruitful, higher-level engagement where everyone participates.

After completing their paired discussions, the whole class can reconvene with students identifying what questions in the interviews led to the best discussions and why. The teacher may also ask if there are any questions that might merit further discussion. With rehearsal time in their paired interviews, some quieter students may venture into this wider discussion arena when given the opportunity.

## Descriptive Discussions

Another simple, effective lesson for 100 percent class participation in a planned discussion is the descriptive discussion. This activity is based on the "Descriptive Reading of a Text" presented in teacher workshops at the Center for Studies in Jewish Education and Culture at the University of Cincinnati, and related to the descriptive stance, a foundational pedagogy for the Prospect School in Bennington, Vermont (1965–1990).

A descriptive discussion can begin with a small portion of any text, from any genre. The chosen text should not exceed one page. The goal of the descriptive discussion is to understand that in a class discussion, oral commentary on a text is as important as the text itself. When a student speaks, reflecting on his or her perception of the text, that student voice produces an oral text that adds a layer of meaning to the class dialogue.

Before the discussion, one student reads the chosen text aloud. The next student reads the first phrase, sentence, or line of the passage, and describes what she or he sees there. No one is allowed to read more than one sentence; the goal of the discussion is to pay close attention to every aspect of the way words are being used in the text, and to pay the same attention to the interpretations and explanations offered by the speakers. The oral descriptions can address any element of the text, including punctuation, word choice, connotations, allusions, and the context within which the text is understood. At the end of the description process, class discussion explodes when students comment on the weirdness and depth of this form.

---

**Textbox 11.1. Descriptive Discussion: Teacher Directions**

1. Arrange students in a circle so that everyone can see and hear each speaker.
2. One student volunteers to be the note-taker. The note-taker records as much of the discussion as possible and reads the notes aloud at the end of each round.
3. Read the chosen passage aloud before the discussion.
4. One student volunteers to read and speak first; then the discussion proceeds clockwise or counterclockwise, with every student making a contribution.
5. The first student reads aloud the first phrase or a complete sentence. One sentence is the maximum amount of text a student may read. A student may choose to read only one word or one phrase.
6. *The reader then* describes *what she or he has read. The student may paraphrase what was read, or comment on any aspect of it—for instance, punctuation marks, adjectives, and metaphors—the student chooses what she or he will pay attention to in the portion read.*
7. The second student may go back to the beginning of the sentence, if the student understands the phrase or sentence differently, *or* the student can choose to read and describe the next phrase or sentence.

---

8. The third student may go back to any portion that has been previously read and described, if the student understands the phrase or sentence differently, *or* the student can choose to read and describe the next phrase or sentence. The rest of the participants follow the same guidelines.

9. Each speaker is heard without interruption. A student has one "free pass" to not speak.

10. No readers/speakers may leap ahead in the text, but they may leap back. Any portion of the text that has already been read and described is available to the next reader.

11. The descriptions that have been given become an *oral text* open to further description and commentary by any of the following readers/speakers.

12. When each student in the circle has had a chance to read/describe, "round 1" is completed. Then the note-taker reads aloud the entire commentary from the first round, and the students proceed to round 2. When the entire passage has been described, the teacher may choose to continue a few more rounds, or move to open discussion.

13. At the end of the process and note-reading, the teacher opens the discussion up with questions such as, What did you notice when . . . or, What did you notice about . . . or, What did you think when . . .

## Textbox 11.2. Descriptive Discussion: Student Directions

1. Arrange chairs so that everyone can see and hear each other.

2. One volunteer reads aloud the first phrase of a sentence or a complete sentence. You may read *as little of the text as you choose*, but you *may not read more than one sentence.*

3. *After you read, you* describe *what you read. You may just "say it in your own words," or you may comment on any part of it—such as punctuation marks, adjectives, and metaphors—you choose what you will pay attention to in the part you read.*

4. The second reader may go back to the beginning of the sentence, if the reader understands the phrase or sentence differently, *or* the reader can choose to read and describe the next phrase or sentence.

5. The third reader may go back to any portion that has been previously read and described, if the reader understands the phrase or sentence differently, *or* the reader can choose to read and describe the next phrase or sentence. The rest of the participants follow the same guidelines.

6. *No one interrupts anyone else.* If you disagree with an interpretation, you wait until your turn and you go back to the same phrase. You also have one "free pass" to not speak.

7. You may not leap ahead in the text, but you may leap back. Any portion of the text that has already been read and described is available to the next reader.

8. The descriptions that have been given become an *oral text* open to further description and commentary by any of the following readers/speakers.

9. When each student in the circle has had a chance to read/describe, "round 1" is completed and "round 2" begins. We will go over the same text as often as we need to.

The descriptive discussion technique boosts the confidence of students in class discussion because their task is to describe what they see in a sentence or to respond to what their classmates have discovered in a sentence. It brings the community of learners together. They can unite in an interpretation and discussion of virtually any text, nonfiction or fiction, prose or poetry, and simple or complex.

Excerpts from *The Federalist Papers* and the Bill of Rights provide a bounty of democratic ideas that are in conflict with each other yet together create the blueprint for the democracy we have in the US and a fruitful descriptive discussion. Using a descriptive discussion of one of these founding documents would help students unpack key democratic concepts following an impromptu discussion concerning them.

But even *Hamlet* as the focus of a descriptive discussion allows students to raise questions about power, politics, and gender equity, when these issues are in the news. A descriptive discussion on the end of *Hamlet*, act 2, line 1, where Ophelia reports Hamlet entering her private sewing room, "with his doublet all unbraced; No hat upon his head; his stockings foul'd, Ungarter'd, and down-gyved to his ancle," brought about the following exchange a few days after the Women's March on Washington, of January 2017.

Erica *(reading)*: "He took me by the wrist and held me hard." That sounds like Hamlet really grabbed Ophelia in a scary way. He grabbed her hard and wouldn't let her go.

Sunil: I'm going to stick with the same line *(reads)*: "He took me by the wrist and held me hard." I agree with what Erica is saying, and I want to add that Ophelia is talking to her dad, and giving him a blow-by-blow description of this whole assault. Samantha already read the part where Hamlet's pants are down around his ankles. I'd have Hamlet arrested.

Davida: I'm going forward *(reads)*: "Then goes he to the length of all his arm." This says that Hamlet held Ophelia at arm's length, so I'm saying that it's not exactly a sexual assault.

Nate: I'll keep going forward too *(reads)*: "And, with his other hand thus o're his brow." Here Ophelia has to be showing her dad how Hamlet was standing, with one hand over his forehead, and one hand grabbing her and holding her really hard. It's definitely some kind of battery. He's not letting Ophelia go.

Thirty minutes into uninterrupted reading and commentary, with ten minutes left in the class period, the teacher stopped this descriptive discussion so that the note-taker could read back the transcript. After the reading of the transcript, students became very animated in discussing whether Hamlet's behavior in Ophelia's room constituted assault, battery, or none of the above, and the teacher had to agree to allow the class to resolve this question the next day.

Descriptive discussion takes at minimum one class period per short passage. A good general follow-up to the descriptive discussion is a small-group discussion limited to five questions on a printed list, where each student in the group leads the discussion by asking a question from the list. In the case of the *Hamlet* passage, some questions for small-group discussion might include the following:

• How does Polonius respond to Ophelia's narrative?
• What was the effect of this event on Ophelia?
• What words in her narrative suggest the impact it had on her?

When teachers seek active and thoughtful student participation as the primary goal of class discussions, powerful moments of insight and synthesis occur. It's also fun for students and teachers to come to class. Students might beg to continue a discussion about a Shakespeare play, and teachers will be anxious to hear their insights. Such a classroom rewards students for thoughtfully participating in class, even when circumstances may make it difficult for them to complete work outside of class.

## CONCLUDING THOUGHTS

Students who have experienced classes oriented toward deliberate discussion are equipped to take responsibility for their lives in a democracy because they have participated in democratic behavior at its best.

## NOTE

1. "I have decided to stick with love. . . . Hate is too great a burden to bear." From Martin Luther King Jr.'s *Where Do We Go from Here*: *Chaos or Community?* (New York: Harper & Row, 1967).

## REFERENCES

Bloom, B. S., Engelhart, M. D., Furst, E. J., Hill, W. H., & Krathwohl, D. R. (1956). *Taxonomy of educational objectives: The classification of educational goals.* Handbook I: Cognitive domain. New York: David McKay.

Economist Intelligence Unit. (2017). Democracy index 2017: Free speech under attack. A report by the economist intelligence unit, 2018. Retrieved from http://www.eiu.com.

Solnit, R. (2017). *The mother of all questions: Further feminisms.* London: Granta.

Valles, M. (2011, October 12). Hasta mañana (Michelle Valles HBO Latino). YouTube. Retrieved from https://www.youtube.com.

*Part IV*

# Including Everyone in Conversations

From its Latin and Old French origins, *conversation* comes from "to keep company with," and yet within the academic calendar and community there are countless constraints on the formation of a kept company of classroom conversation: bell schedules, holidays and vacations, testing, curricular goals and objectives to name a few. Along with these, the teachers and authors of chapters within this section contend with additional constraints embodied in their student populations, issues of a restricted environment, of reticent dispositions, or of simultaneously decoding two languages or negotiating two perceptions. Yet the teachers in these chapters share techniques that foster discussion within their student populations so that constraints dissolve and the company of classroom conversation is kept for all.

Chapter 12 illustrates the challenges of English language learners who negotiate two languages and cultures while formulating ideas for discussion and offers ideas that honor differences while incorporating inclusion. Chapter 13 explains how to identify and capitalize on the strengths of students with significant learning differences so that their challenges are recognized and supported in a manner that nurtures inclusion in discussion. Chapter 14 presents the formidable restraints of teaching in a prison setting. While acknowledging these restraints, the chapter describes strategies that surmount them, making authentic discussion possible. Finally, chapter 15 offers supports and strategies for the reticent speaker so that the classroom becomes a welcoming place for all.

All of these teacher-authors acknowledge the added risks and challenges their students encounter in speaking during discussions. To enable students to surmount those risks and challenges, teachers build communities of trust and respect with their own learner-developed rules of engagement. They get to know their students as individuals through one-on-one interactions and through a variety of surveys and inventories that encompass interests, interaction preferences, and learning styles. They vary types of discussion formats to incorporate movement, scripts supporting foundational knowledge, and the reset pause.

Of course, instructional strategies such as these can enhance any discussion-based classroom. For instance, in our fast-paced world, what classroom conversation might not benefit from a planned pause where students and teachers reflect upon what has been said and gather their thoughts for what to consider next? While Patricia Dalton points out that many teachers will do anything to be "saved from silence," a "reset for reflection" pause helps foster deliberation for all, not just the student with slow processing speed or the English learner (EL) student.

When Deborah Appleman writes "good teaching is good teaching," she is right. But the techniques and strategies outlined in this section gain further resonance through the intentionality of their implementation. Whether one or two EL students or differently abled learners populate a classroom or these students comprise an entire class, the teachers here intentionally consider and plan for inclusion. If discussion is a learning tool, then no student is left behind in these classrooms. All students have the opportunity and expectation of entering the classroom discourse at a time and level that honors and respects them.

*Chapter Twelve*

# Discussion with English Learners

*Both Possible and Powerful*

Barbara Alvarez and Shannon McMullen

Until the age of five, Barbara spoke only Spanish, in a linguistically and culturally insulated neighborhood in Mundelein, Illinois. The local community was filled with *tiendas Mexicanas y panaderias* (Mexican stores and bakeries). Barbara's family had little need for English in order for them to function comfortably in Mundelein. It was not until kindergarten that Barbara felt the desperate need and desire to learn English—and learn it quickly.

The first utterance Barbara learned in English was "Can I go to the bathroom?" Her parents taught her this "functional" English for obvious reasons, although she may have forgotten how to ask once or twice, ultimately leading to a call home for a change of pants. The first word Barbara learned at school was *car*. Barbara's eager young voice and exploding-with-knowledge energy from that day remains engraved into her parents' memories as they adore telling the story of the first word their "English teacher" daughter learned.

Barbara has some gratifying memories as an English language learner and some embarrassing ones too. Yet the most poignant memories left a sour taste—even after many years—ones that made her feel shame. One distinct memory recalls the first year Barbara was placed into an English-only environment.

Students in the Mundelein school had math homework just about every night in first grade. The teacher conveyed instructions, and Barbara judged that she fully understood what the class had to do. "You are going to measure all of your family members," instructed the first-grade, monolingual teacher. The teacher distributed a half sheet of paper to each student and asked them to measure siblings, parents, and grandparents. Barbara's father worked late, but her mom and grandma were always home with her after school. Barbara explained the math homework to her mom, and they got to work. Mom even let Barbara stay up uncommonly late to wait for Dad to get home so they could get his measurements too.

Barbara was excited for math the following day because, for once, she had completely understood what the students were supposed to do for the assignment . . . or so she thought. During class, the teacher was writing on the board all of the data the students had brought in. It was like a contest! All the students were excited to figure out which father was the tallest of them all.

When Barbara's turn came, she proudly handed her teacher the homework. The teacher took one look at it and scoffed, "Your dad can't be this tall. This is impossible! I've met him. You must have not understood the homework." She abruptly handed the assignment back. No explanation. No mercy. Pure shame. Barbara felt her cheeks begin to burn as she noticed all of the students looking in her direction. She hung her head as the rest of the class continued to burst with joy as dads' names were erased and replaced with others.

In that moment, Barbara hated her parents. She hated them for not speaking English perfectly, and she hated that they had taught her to speak stupid Spanish. She hated being Mexican and shopping at *tiendas Mexicanas* and eating *pan con leche o huevos y chorizo* for breakfast. This shame followed her for a very long time. In fact, it was not until her years in graduate school that she truly began to appreciate her culture and language and discover that—unfortunately, more often than not—students do not let go of that shame and instead let go of their language.

In the years between that moment in first grade until Barbara gained confidence and became comfortable in her own skin, she would often refuse to speak Spanish, even at home. She also experienced moments of paralyzing stress in the classroom, especially when she had to speak in front of others. She was afraid to speak unless she knew she had perfected the utterance; she had become hyper-aware of how accurate or inaccurate she was, which impeded her willingness to practice speaking "publicly" for quite some time.

As years passed, the feeling subsided and Barbara eventually learned to love standing and speaking in front of large groups. Yet despite all of the other troubles and tribulations, she will never forget the shame she felt for her native language that day in first grade. Barbara does not believe her teacher intentionally meant to cause her harm—but, more importantly, she does not believe her teacher was even *aware* that her mom had used *centimeters* to measure her family, which, from her perspective, was the obvious standard to use. The teacher took one look at Barbara's sheet, identified an obvious mistake, and blamed it on a student's lack of the dominant language, without investigating what had happened.

Many teachers are guilty of dismissing the mistakes or misunderstandings made by English learners (ELs) as consequences of the fact that English is not their first language. Some teachers misunderstand students' mistakes as evidence of their deficiencies, claiming that "they're not ready yet" or that "they just can't" accomplish a particular literacy task. These lines have become common refrains in relation to the topic of engaging ELs in authentic discussion.

Often, teachers who work in classrooms containing large EL populations avoid both designing and implementing learning activities that center on authentic discussion. Dismissing their awareness of the benefits authentic discussion offers, teachers instead assume their students are unable to generate contributions of quality. Yet this mindset is dangerous for teachers to hold and, ultimately, a danger to the students who inhabit their classrooms.

Barbara's first-grade experience served as a powerful motivator, propelling her toward not only fluency in English but also a career teaching in the field. However, for many EL students, the rigid, "can't-oriented" mindset teachers often hold about ELs' capacity to achieve a level of literacy equivalent to that of native speakers becomes an insurmountable obstacle to their growth. Worse yet, this obstacle typically impedes not only their growth as speakers of English but also their overall self-efficacy in the academic realm.

Of course, some level of accuracy is necessary for ELs to engage in authentic discussion: how can a meaningful conversation occur if students cannot understand one another? Teachers may forget that developing accuracy is only one component of language acquisition, and value "correctness" over other elements of language development, such as fluency.

Ultimately, teachers need to recognize that the overarching goal of authentic discussion is for students not to "present" their thoughts in a perfectly rehearsed manner but to practice crucial literacy skills in real time. Therefore, when teachers decline to offer ELs regular opportunities for students to engage in authentic discussion, and even do so with the intent of advancing students' progress, they ultimately inhibit it instead. When teachers shift their mindset about students and regularly incorporate the key principles explained below into their overall practice, ELs are able to flourish in and through discussion.

## PRINCIPLE ONE: CONSIDER CULTURE

All students are carriers of culture. When they enter any dedicated learning space, students bear their cultures as much as their own potential as learners. Whether students—and their teachers—possess conscious awareness of the fact or not, culture is the ultimate lens through which literacy learning and behavior in the classroom are filtered.

British scholar Edward Tylor, regarded as the founder of modern anthropology, defined culture as "that complex whole which includes knowledge, belief, art, morals, law, custom, and any other capabilities acquired by a [person] as a member of a particular society" (as cited in Moore, 2009, p. 5). Tylor's definition—first published in 1871 but still utilized by twenty-first-century anthropologists—serves as an important reminder for teachers.

Culture encompasses every aspect of life, and in shaping both collective and personal identity, culture determines the nature of human interactions. Since authentic discussions mandate meaningful interactions across an entire classroom community (both student to student and student to teacher), teachers interested in engaging English learners in authentic discussion must cultivate a keen understanding of their students' cultures. Accordingly, teachers should apply this understanding to *all* the learning activities they design, but especially those that are discussion centered.

Speaking in class is daunting for many types of students, but it often particularly and intensely intimidating for English learners; they may not understand the meaning of academic discourse that a teacher and other students use in the classroom and may also lack confidence in their own speaking abilities, fearing that humiliation or embarrassment might result when teachers and peers hear their voices. If students feel daunted by the prospect of talking in class already, these feelings will only be compounded if they perceive the overall classroom environment they inhabit as one that alienates their culture rather than welcoming and including it.

Barbara's first-grade teacher was probably well meaning when she dismissed the homework Barbara had done. From the teacher's perspective, Barbara had not met learning, and the teacher's intention was likely to clarify for her student, rather than shame her. Yet in the process, she likely lost track of culture and failed to consider the fact that since Barbara's parents immigrated to the United States from a different country, they were accustomed to different units of measure and transmitted this habitual understanding to their daughter. Barbara clearly understood the concept of measuring, but because of her cultural schema, the application of her understanding varied from that of her classmates. Consequently, the funds of knowledge she possessed— which could have been maneuvered as an asset in the classroom—produced a profound emotional disconnect between her and her teacher.

In any classroom community, points of cultural variance, whether between teacher and student or among students themselves, will likely occur, but these distinctions are especially common when English learners are present. English language arts (ELA) teachers committed to engaging students in authentic discussion must embrace and champion this diversity and honor its powerful potential to impact discussion.

When students are exposed to cultures that differ from their own and encouraged to respectfully navigate, explore, and understand these differences, the depth and complexity of classroom conversations will likely increase. After all, civil controversy is the foundation upon which successful authentic classroom discussions rest. The impact and success of these discussions will only be greater when teachers take care to design a curriculum that respects the cultures represented among their students.

## How Does a Teacher Consider Culture?

A brief note about language: like many ELA teachers, a deep reverence for language inspired both of our careers. When designing activities and interacting with students, we factor in the power of language and weigh their words carefully. It is likely unsurprising, then, that our choice of the word *consider* in the phrase "consider culture" is deliberate here.

To *consider* is to contemplate, survey, and scrutinize carefully. Competing theories abound about the function of culture in the ELA classroom. Geneva Gay (2010) suggests that teachers should develop a "culturally responsive" practice, or one that uses "the cultural knowledge, prior experiences, frames of reference, and performance styles of ethnically diverse students to make learning encounters more relevant to and effective for them" (p. 31).

Carol Lee (2007) suggests that this mindset should extend as much to pedagogy as it does to curricular topics; teachers should practice "cultural modeling" (p. 58) by determining the cultural "ways of knowing" their students exhibit and designing learning activities that provide students a lens of understanding based on these frameworks. In the ELA classroom, this approach involves invoking interpretive problems that stem from students' lives—problems that schools and other institutions often dismiss—and drawing connections to similar problems in canonical texts.

The initial process of considering culture is an investigative one. Teachers need to delve deeply into the process of knowing their students, and knowing who they are outside of the classroom as much as inside.

During her first year of teaching, Shannon worked at a suburban Chicago high school with a sizable Latinx population. Eager to develop relationships with her students at the beginning of the school year, she questioned them about their interests. She wanted to ensure that her students felt honored and empowered in her classroom, especially since as a white woman with parents of European descent, she recognized that her own cultural framework might differ from that of many of her students.

But even with these intentions, around October she began to notice a particular pattern of student behavior that concerned her: students were code-switching, and doing so routinely. As she stood in the hallway outside of her classroom door daily to greet students as they came and left, Shannon realized that the doorway became an important symbolic threshold: the second students crossed over it, their identities also shifted somewhat. Many became quiet, but the second they exited the room, they conducted lively conversations in Spanish. Shannon was eager to shift this dynamic; she wanted her students to feel that inside the classroom and out, their authentic selves were worthy and deeply valued. As an initial gesture, she shared with her students her own desire to learn Spanish and asked them to teach her. Then, she conducted a series of surveys with her students.

Like many teachers, Shannon thought she knew her students as people, but when she began to question them deliberately—and intentionally set aside instructional time to do so—she was able to design curriculum that genuinely engaged and empowered her students. Technology proved an asset in this situation. Initially, to encourage honesty and lower anxiety over participation, Shannon created an anonymous online survey that asked her students a series of open-ended questions (shown in textbox 12.1).

## Textbox 12.1. Survey with Open-Ended Questions

The questions Shannon included in her survey are listed below. Students were encouraged to answer as candidly as possible, responding in complete sentences.

- In your opinion, what is the greatest problem in our community today, and why?
- What is the most significant problem facing people in high school today, and why?
- What do you value most?
- What are you curious about outside of school?
- What would you like to change in the world?

By administering the survey using the online platform Google Forms, Shannon was able to put together a data set that she could both review alone and share with her students.

She administered this survey to all levels and classes of students. Shannon then reviewed the results carefully and used them to devise a list of topics students might want to discuss. Each class reviewed the topics as a large group and then voted on which topics would be most compelling to explore together.

The information gathered from surveying students revealed insight into the funds of knowledge (Moll & Gonzalez, 2004), or the schemas, ideas, values, and skills, students gain in their home/family lives away from the classroom. Once teachers firmly grasp their students' funds of knowledge, culture transforms into a powerful asset to both curriculum and resulting conversations.

Just as every student is a carrier of culture, every student wants to feel included. Curriculum that considers culture, then, creates a deeper pathway to engagement. When teachers embrace students' cultures and funds of knowledge and deliberately consider these as they design curriculum, students' levels of comfort and interest in classroom conversations will likely increase.

## A Practical Example of Considering Culture

The freshmen ELA curriculum at Shannon's school did not include literary works written by Latinx authors or any plot lines that focused on Latinx characters, so in addition to designing conceptual units of inquiry centered on problems and topics, she set out to incorporate and represent her students' culture through text selection.

During a unit featuring the inquiry question "What makes a hero?" one of the major learning goals stipulated that students would be able to describe Joseph Campbell's "hero cycle" and trace its appearance in canonical works such as Homer's *Odyssey*. In the survey Shannon had administered prior to teaching this unit, a common response from many students was that they cared deeply about their families and maintaining closeness with members of their family, even if they left home to go to college or take jobs. Based on this common interest, she selected Ann Jaramillo's *La Linea*, a novel that tells the story of an adolescent boy, Miguel, who must embark on an odyssey of his own: a solo journey across the California-Mexico border without documentation.

At the beginning of the unit, students constructed a class definition of heroes and then read both works. Afterward, in small groups, students discussed similarities between Miguel's and Odysseus's journeys, and explained how the hero cycle is evident in both texts. The small-group discussions prepared students for subsequent whole-class discussions. During one of these discussions, students deliberated over the question "Who is more of a hero, Miguel or Odysseus?" During this discussion, and throughout the unit, students who had previously refrained from speaking up participated regularly. Students—including ELs—were comfortable and motivated to participate. Pairing the *Odyssey* with a text that directly resonated with her students' experiences was a breakthrough for Shannon's classes. Because she considered culture and gave it a prominent role in course curriculum, the quality and complexity of discussion, along with student comfort levels, increased dramatically.

## Many Cultures, Many Voices

Compelling, complex problems are a major driving force behind teaching practices that value discussion, but text selection is an equally powerful catalyst in designing a curriculum that considers students' cultures carefully. Most classes will contain students from a variety of cultural, ethnic, and socioeconomic backgrounds. If a teacher is truly honoring this diversity, then the texts that students read should feature an array of experiences and voices that are as diverse as the students in the classroom.

Within the texts they read, students should be able to discover a mirror or point of resonance with their own experience (Fleming, Catapano, Thompson, & Carrillo, 2016). Selecting texts of this nature may involve disrupting the conventional canon of works typically taught in American ELA classrooms. Of course, some schools are committed to their students reading canonical texts, and in these environments, teachers might have to consider students' cultures primarily through the inquiry questions they choose to explore with their students.

Ideally, a teacher can consider students' cultures by carefully selecting texts and orchestrating students' experiences of these texts through a lens featuring a problem that appeals to them. But ultimately, the goal is to strive for inclusion and empowerment of all students. English learners sometimes experience school as a place that marginalizes them, making them feel compelled to conform to particular norms that in some cases, they are still attempting to understand. But when teachers consider culture as they design curriculum and also establish a unique, pluralistic classroom environment, these students are more likely to become agents of their learning, motivated to strengthen their language skills and contribute to classroom discussions.

## PRINCIPLE TWO: ENVIRONMENT MATTERS

Curriculum that considers students' cultures needs to be implemented in an environment that also supports classroom discussion as a primary mode of learning. When implemented regularly and facilitated effectively, authentic discussion has the power to transform a classroom into a dialogic community—one where students from diverse backgrounds offer equally divergent perspectives on problems and larger questions, deliberately engaging in the practices of discernment and meaning-making. Successful, productive members of twenty-first-century society—what all teachers want their students to become—are shrewd critical thinkers, capable of analyzing all of the media, images, and information they encounter on a minute-by-minute basis. Membership in a dialogic classroom community demands that students regularly practice these skills; to engage in discussion, they must evaluate both text and peer talk.

But a dialogic community such as this one is not established through regular discussion alone. Teachers need to consciously cultivate an environment that supports the practice of discussion itself. While compassion and empathy for others are traits that teachers typically possess, they might still lose sight of students' experiences in their own classrooms and in school at large. Even when teachers strive to establish classroom communities that are not anxiety inducing for students, an environment that supports discussion requires additional levels of consistency and comfort.

Engaging in authentic discussion often feels like a risk for students. They are expected to offer a perspective on a topic that is entirely their own, rather than prescribed from somewhere deep in the pages of a highlighted textbook or class notes. While authentic discussion often intimidates native speakers, it can be especially daunting for EL students, especially if the prior language instruction they received was recitation oriented. Authentic discussions demand that English learners perform two tasks while native speakers focus on just one; ELs must juggle voicing their thoughts *and* finding the language that accurately expresses these thoughts all at once.

Teachers, then, need to recognize the multiple levels of trust and confidence building that fashioning a dialogic classroom community stipulates. For discussions to take place successfully, students need to trust their peers as much as they do their teachers. Every time Shannon's students shift seats, she requires them to interview the new people with whom they are now in direct proximity. Often, she asks students to generate interview questions. This provides a powerful opportunity to build community, and for ELs, this exercise offers a low-risk opportunity for speaking practice. While these interactions are social in nature, they provide an important foundation for the authentic academic discussions students regularly engage in.

Though a trusting, low-risk community atmosphere is crucial for sustaining authentic discussion, equally important is instilling a deep sense of empowerment in students. All members of a dialogic classroom community need to believe that their ideas are worth listening to and that voicing those ideas is of necessity to the entire group. If students do not feel they have a stake in the classroom community, their fears about speaking in front of others may further dissuade them from doing so.

What does a dialogic classroom community look like? Its first major characteristics are equity and support. Teachers who desire to establish a community of this nature should strive, first and foremost, to minimize their own voices. Their role shifts from an authoritative one to a facilitating one, and their students should have the sense that they are also curious learners, invested in exploring complex problems with their students.

This also implies that teachers minimize their own voices during any classroom interaction. Students can easily grow accustomed to patterns from other instruction where they perceive the teacher as the only person in the room to whom they should speak. This is easily glimpsed through body language: even when the entire class has their desks arranged in a circle, students might continue to orient their bodies and their overall pattern of eye contact toward the teacher. As a result, any member of the class might feel excluded and may likely disengage from the discussion.

At the beginning of the school year, both of us work with our students to set behavior norms for discussion, and body language is always addressed, but students occasionally need reminders. Shannon will gently say to students, "Talk to everybody, not me," or make a silent "turn around" gesture with her hands as students speak to reorient their posture and mode of speaking toward the class at large. This gesture, while seemingly simple, is significant: it communicates to students that being evaluated by a teacher is not the purpose of discussion and that all members of the class community are important and worthy of participating in discussion.

A crucial factor in the success of classroom discussion is student ownership of both ideas and process. If teachers transmit the message—whether consciously or otherwise—that their voices are the ones that matter most in the classroom, then the dynamic of the classroom community may shift dramatically.

Just as an environment that supports classroom discussion must feel balanced and supportive, it must also be active and collaborative in nature. When some teachers hear the word "discussion," they might imagine a large-scale Socratic seminar, but small groups are an equally powerful opportunity for students to engage in discussion. Additionally, students build relationships with one another that can lower levels of discomfort and anxiety prior to large-scale discussions. One of Barbara's positive memories of her early education experience involves working in small reading groups with other students. Whenever her peers endorsed the ideas she had, Barbara felt confident enough to raise her hand during whole-class discussions.

Of course, the frequency and groupings of interactions are as significant as the work itself. Small-group interaction demands engagement from students. If a teacher orchestrates a group carefully, then students will be likely to engage at higher levels with subject material or a particular task. Teachers need to deliberately arrange student groupings before any learning in this mode can occur.

In a class containing a small number of English learners, these students might be even more reticent to speak, fearing that other students will judge their utterances as inadequate. To prevent these feelings, especially during a class's initial lessons together, Shannon will group English learners who speak the same native language together, perhaps pairing them with one or two stronger and particularly kind native speakers. This arrangement can provide a cultural and linguistic safety net.

Many teachers might discourage nonnative speakers from interacting with one another, worrying that students will not actually work toward mastery in English if they have the opportunity to potentially interact in their native language. Yet for English learners with lower levels of proficiency, conversing in their native language at limited intervals might provide an opportunity for students to process content at more nuanced levels first, so that when larger-scale class discussions occur, students can contribute and concentrate on refining expression in English.

If a teacher forbids English learners from ever speaking in their native language inside an English classroom, students may perceive the classroom environment as a place of constant evaluation. A classroom environment that promotes and sustains authentic discussion, however, must be perceived by students as a secure space of intellectual exploration. If student groups are engineered intentionally, they support richer opportunities for students to practice conversing with one another while affirming this perception.

Ultimately, a classroom environment where authentic discussion regularly occurs is one that privileges consistency: modes of student interaction, behavioral norms, and procedures for conversation are regularly repeated in the same manner. When English learners are provided with repeated opportunities to practice interacting with one another and expressing their ideas, they gradually gain confidence in these arenas.

## PRINCIPLE THREE: PREPARE TO PARTICIPATE

Often it is the case that teachers bombard students with a list of well-thought-out questions developed from the previous night's reading in an effort to engage them in authentic discussion. Of course, teachers prepare these questions carefully and meticulously, but all too often they result in a subpar discussion. If EL students are not given sufficient time to think about these questions prior to a discussion, lack of preparation might be at fault for the quality of their contributions.

Engaging with questions without preparing to answer them is especially difficult for ELs due to the limited think-time teachers provide for responses and the likelihood that students may be coming into contact with new lexical items. In the time it takes an EL student to decipher a question, the rest of the class may have exhausted it and is already moving on to the next question. In addition, teachers could be using discussion procedures that students from other cultures may be unfamiliar with. Dedicating class time to prepare for discussions in addition to checking in with students throughout the pre-discussion process may help eliminate the stress ELs feel and allow their thinking to shine through.

## Practice the Procedure

ELs may be accustomed to a different discussion procedure from their previous schooling, and some students may not be accustomed to any discussion procedure at all. Students may not have had the opportunity to attend school yet or their previous school may not have instructed them on the cultural norms for engaging in discussion. If a student comes from a culture that positions students as learners and teachers as experts from whom they must absorb knowledge, they may find it intimidating or even inappropriate to jump in to speak, despite their American English teachers encouraging this practice.

Shannon practices discussion procedures early in the school year by holding "mini-discussions" with students on noncurricular topics. Although the desirable outcome of this activity is a rigorous one, students find it particularly fun because Shannon allows them to vote on the topics they want to discuss. These topics range widely and often connect to pop culture, such as, "Is texting really a form of valid communication?"

The topic choices need to be substantive enough for students to sustain an authentic discussion yet simple enough that students do not have to worry about mastering new content. These mini-discussions provide an opportunity for students to focus on procedural moves of discussion and develop comfort and fluency with these norms, rather than worrying about content or the quality of their responses. Often, EL students will find academic language daunting, and front-loading the procedures of it with an uncomplicated, low-stakes topic enables them to focus on the procedure of discussion instead of the language.

Both Barbara and Shannon also involve students in setting discussion procedures and expectations. Allowing this process to be student driven helps all students think about how they should conduct themselves throughout a discussion. For EL students, this process holds immense benefits because it allows them to orient themselves with discussion procedures without feeling overwhelmed or thrown into the task. Barbara initiates the process with her students by asking a simple question: "What makes for a good conversation? Why?" As students offer the guidelines, Barbara summarizes students' suggestions and asks for their approval before adding it to the list of classroom discussion procedures.

Abby: Only one person should speak at a time.

Ryan: Yeah, don't interrupt each other.

Ms. Alvarez: Well, then, how do we communicate to another person that we would like to speak? How does that shift occur without it being interruptive?

Ryan: Well, you need to be looking at the person to get that information from them.

Ms. Alvarez: So we need to maintain eye contact with the speaker?

Avery: Yes, and listen carefully. I hate it when people misinterpret what I say.

Ms. Alvarez: In a conversation, the other person or people should be able to take what you said and accurately represent it. They can accomplish this by maintaining eye contact and listening carefully. Does that about sum up the two guidelines you both have outlined?

Avery: Yes.

Ryan: Yep.

Barbara finds that asking a student if their words have been accurately represented or summarized is powerful. By invoking this question, the speaker receives recognition and validation of ideas, while the listener practices another crucial literacy task: accurate listening. During this process, ELs are hearing the justifications for discussion procedures and familiarizing themselves with the elements a good discussion should contain.

Through initial class discussions, Shannon will continue to scaffold EL students' understanding of these procedures by occasionally assigning them the role of "coach." In this role, students observe the first few minutes of discussion and provide feedback to their peers on whether they are meeting the expectations for discussion the class has collectively set. This allows EL students to observe other students implementing discussion procedures, and also empowers them as expert participants in class discussion. While this role benefits students, it can potentially discourage them from the practice of speaking, so Shannon typically assigns this role only once.

While some teachers may be reluctant to give up control of their classrooms in this manner, teachers need to push through this discomfort. By writing their own procedures, students construct rather than observe a framework for what authentic discussion should be and are more likely to use those procedures as a result of this process.

## "Over"-Scaffold Preparation for Discussion

Barbara has found that the most successful discussions occur when students have spent just as much time—and in some cases more time—preparing for discussion than they do actually having one. Preparing a visual organizer that students can actually use and refer to during the discussion benefits all students. However, this preparation practice is vital for EL students because it gives them a visual to refer to in case they have not quite mastered academic language. In addition, it forces students to prepare adequately by requiring them to generate ideas, arguments, or insights they will use during the discussion itself. Barbara spans preparation time over the course of several days. This allows her to check in with students and ensure they are headed in the right direction every step of the way.

Barbara implemented this preparation practice during the Gothic literature unit in the English III American literature course she teaches. During the unit, students listened to the podcast *Serial*. Host Sarah Koenig tells the story of Hae Min Lee and Adnan Syed, two students enrolled in a Baltimore high school during the late nineties. A month after Lee's body was found in Leakin Park, Lee's ex-boyfriend, Syed, was arrested and charged with her murder (Koenig & Snyder, 2014). Over several episodes, Koenig uncovers far more than what the courts had at the time of Syed's original conviction.

To prepare her students to write a synthesis essay that answered the question "Is Adnan Syed guilty or not guilty?" Barbara designed a discussion activity that simulated Adnan's murder trial. During the simulation, students took on the various roles of the characters presented in the podcast and deliberated over whether Adnan was guilty or not guilty from each character's perspective.

Before they began listening to the podcast, Barbara assigned each of her students a character role so they could track their assigned characters especially closely throughout the twelve podcast episodes. The focus on a particular character also helps EL students to listen to the podcast purposefully, thereby organizing their thought processes about the podcast prior to the discussion.

The week of the discussion, Barbara's students complete the following tasks:

Monday: Barbara assigns students to write their initial character statement and directs students to find the two pieces of evidence that would best support their stance by looking through the podcast transcript or their own notes.

Tuesday: Students checked in their initial character statements and evidence and then moved on to create questions or challenges for other characters that threaten their credibility.

Wednesday: Students check in their questions or challenges for other characters and begin preparing for questions that other characters may ask them that threaten their credibility.

While this process takes time, it produces a worthwhile outcome; the discussion is well organized and all students participate. Most importantly, students engage in a prewriting activity that is both purposeful and fun. Because students are having fun and laughing, students are relaxed, lowering their affective filter; this is especially important for EL students in these types of discussion situations. Additionally, participating in this unit provided students with an opportunity to discuss a noncanonical, news-media text that featured figures EL students might identify with: two adolescents from immigrant families.

## PRINCIPLE FOUR: SET CLEAR OBJECTIVES AND ASSESSMENT PROCEDURES

In order for teachers to set clear objectives and assessment procedures for English learners, teachers must understand that acquiring a language demands proficiency in the four major literacy skill areas: listening, speaking, reading, and writing. Ideally, teachers create activities that provide opportunities for students for practice in all of these skill areas, and although authentic discussion positively influences all of these areas of language, authentic discussion provides ample opportunity for EL students to target their listening and speaking skills during discussion.

Consequently, teachers also need to be aware that speaking is likely one of the most intimidating literacy skills to develop because in any conversation, students have limited time to process the meaning of the utterances they hear and respond accordingly; Barbara still recalls the anxiety-inducing moments when teachers asked her to speak during reading group discussions. She explains that the stress came from being hyper-aware of both form and fluency, and that if she stumbled over her words too much, the teachers and students would assume that she just did not know. Often teachers perceive what students are capable of in the nonnative language as representative of the student's full knowledge of a given concept or topic of inquiry rather than realizing that students likely possess deeper levels of knowledge but cannot yet express these in English with fluency.

Second language acquisition teachers and researchers recognize that both fluency and accuracy are important components of language acquisition; however, fluency should be prioritized and encouraged during authentic discussion. Fluency refers to a learner's speed of communication, whereas accuracy refers to the correct pronunciation and use of sentence structures, or form of the language (Ortega, 2013, pp. 197–199).

Although both are important for developing listening and speaking literacy skills, during discussion the goal is the combination of communication and understanding of ideas. Krashen (1982) emphasizes that interaction in the target language. This can be accomplished through "natural communication" (p. 24) where speakers focus on the message they send rather than the pronunciation of their utterances.

In other words, teachers run the risk that if they address form—even only once—they may raise students' affective filters and prohibit students from naturally communicating in the classroom. Often, great ideas are hidden from teachers because they are preoccupied with flaws in students' linguistic form; to uncover these great ideas, teachers must shift their priorities.

Clear language goals need to be not only written but also explicitly communicated to students in words they can understand. It is important that both content and language objectives are communicated in student-friendly language—and this is not to suggest that objectives are simply written on the board every day in language that students can understand.

*Content Objective:*
Students will be able to select and evaluate the evidence presented in the
    *Serial* podcast to argue for Adnan's guilt or innocence.
*Language Objectives:*
I can orally present and cite evidence.
I can orally summarize evidence presented by other characters.
I can orally justify or challenge the value of that evidence by using a
    sentence frame.

So, what do these objectives mean to a student? Oftentimes, absolutely nothing. Barbara admits that when she first started teaching, she would have students read the objectives and move on. She noticed that as students worked through activities or discussions, the objective of the lesson would get lost in the process; she realized reading these objectives was a wasted process. The true communication of objectives happens through interaction with students at the beginning of a unit, lesson, or activity, such as in the following example.

Ms. Alvarez: Okay, ladies and gentlemen. Open up your English notebooks. We will be going over our goals for the *Serial* simulation discussion. Sebastian, can you please read our first goal for the day?

Sebastian: I can orally present and cite my evidence.

Ms. Alvarez: In your English notebook, I want you to write down what that goal means. Connor, what did you write? What does it mean that you can orally present and cite your evidence for today's activity?

Connor: It means that, when I give my evidence, I can say exactly which episode and which character presented it in *Serial* podcast.

Deciphering these "I can" statements and applying them to the activity that day is a worthwhile practice because it establishes, for that particular day, what the task demands of students. It provided ELs in particular with an opportunity to familiarize themselves with the academic language and repeated processes of discussion as well.

In Barbara's classroom, the process was initially modeled by her. After a few weeks, this process became a consistent routine for Barbara's students, and she noticed students were more engaged in activities and were consistently practicing the outlined objectives. When ELs understand the objectives, they are more likely to understand whether the task is one for practicing fluency or form. Equally important, when teachers communicate these "I can" statements with English learners, teachers are less likely to build an environment that heightens their affective filter too high, which will likely block any opportunity for learning.

Additionally, to further encourage fluency, teachers must praise EL students for their contributions during authentic discussion. Directing ELs to focus on fluency should be a regular priority of teachers. To engage in discussion meaningfully, students need regular opportunities to develop fluency. Especially during initial class meetings, teachers should encourage and praise any sort of talk from EL students. To deepen the quality of students' ideas and the fluency with which they express them, teachers should prompt students to elaborate even slightly. Prompting and praising EL students reinforces the message that their voices need to be heard in discussion and will encourage their comfort levels with the overall process. In Shannon's classroom, prior to a formal discussion, an exchange like the one below might occur:

Karina: Well, there's all that transition stuff; what about that stuff? If we don't use those transitions, is that going to mess up our grade?

Ms. McMullen: Just stay in the game. What I really care about are your ideas and the expression of your thoughts in a way that others can understand and respond to. That's the whole purpose of our discussion, to redefine and deepen our thinking about the problems we are exploring in the text that we read.

Karina: But what if I forget a transition?

Ms. McMullen: Then I will gently remind you or someone in the class will. Focus on presenting your ideas in a way that others will understand because you have a lot to offer.

Although Shannon wanted her student to master the use of academic transition language during discussion, she knew that with repeated practice opportunities, Karina would eventually acquire this skill. By initially prioritizing Karina's ideas over the manner in which they were expressed, she invited her student into the conversation and encouraged her to continue participating.

This gesture also scaffolded Karina's language learning, narrowing her focus to expressing her ideas with fluency. Teachers need to envision English learners' capacity for discussion as a long-term process. With regular, repeated chances for structured talk, students accumulate facility and fluency engaging in authentic discussions in the classroom.

## CONCLUDING THOUGHTS

The principles above challenge the assumptions that many teachers make about English learners: their process of acquiring language prohibits them from ever engaging in authentic, rigorous classroom discussions. Implementing these principles, however, actually supports the language development of EL students and also stands to benefit native speakers; scaffolded activities facilitate the growth of all students, and moreover, the perspectives ELs bring to the texts and problems students explore in the classroom can force native speakers to think in important new ways. All of the principles complement one another and therefore should not be isolated.

Authentic discussion is fundamental to literacy learning, and all students deserve the opportunity to develop the critical-thinking skills, confidence in self-expression, and sense of empowerment it stands to offer them. When teachers assume that English learners cannot participate in authentic discussion, they are actually short-changing their students. With curriculum that considers culture, a supportive environment, deliberate scaffolding, and clear objectives, students grow and express themselves powerfully.

## GENERAL GUIDELINES FOR IMPLEMENTING DISCUSSION WITH ENGLISH LEARNERS: HOW TO MAKE IT HAPPEN

1. Encourage and celebrate speaking of any kind from English learners, especially during initial class meetings.
2. Allow English learners to occasionally converse in their native language when preparing for discussion, especially when processing complex content.
3. If necessary, offer sentence stems to English learners during formal discussions; then gradually eliminate these as students become more comfortable conversing in academic language.
4. When assessing English learners in discussion, focus on the quality of the content they generate rather than the linguistic form with which it is expressed.
5. Use repeated procedures and formats during discussions to allow students regular opportunities to practice engaging in discussion and to gain confidence.

# REFERENCES

Erickson, F. (2010). Culture in society and in educational practices. In J. A. Banks & C. A. M. Banks (Eds.), *Multicultural education: Issues and perspectives* (7th ed., pp. 33–56). Hoboken, NJ: Wiley.

Fleming, J., Catapano, S., Thompson, C. M, & Carrillo, S. R. (2016). *More mirrors in the classroom: Using urban children's literature to increase literacy.* Lanham, MD: Rowman & Littlefield.

Gay, G. (2010). *Culturally responsive teaching: Theory, research, and practice.* New York: Teachers College Press.

Koenig, S., & Snyder, J. (producer). (2014, October 3). *Serial* (audio podcast). Retrieved from http://serialpodcast.org/season-one.

Krashen, S. D. (1982). *Principles and practice in second language acquisition.* Oxford, UK: Pergamon.

Lee, C. D. (2007). *Culture, literacy, and learning: Taking bloom in the midst of the whirlwind.* New York: Teachers College Press.

Moll, L. C., & Gonzalez, N. (2004). Engaging life: A funds-of-knowledge approach to multicultural education. In J. A. Banks & C. A. M. Banks (Eds.), *Handbook of research on multicultural education* (2nd ed., pp. 699–715). Hoboken, NJ: Jossey-Bass.

Moore, J. D. (2009). *Visions of culture: An introduction to anthropological theories and theorists* (3rd ed.). Lanham, MD: AltaMira.

Ortega, L. (2013). *Understanding second language acquisition.* New York: Routledge.

*Chapter Thirteen*

# Discussing Difference

*Engaging Students with Learning Differences in Authentic Discussion*

Claire Walter

Whether in a general education or a special education classroom, tackling the needs of neurodiverse learners is an increasingly prevalent demand for educators. At the beginning of the school year when teachers look at the varying needs in their classrooms, it can be both daunting and overwhelming to imagine classroom discussion that not only meets the needs of every student but also engages every student in a productive and meaningful way.

It is essential to approach discussion in a neurodiverse classroom from a perspective of possibility. Building discussion that embraces neurodiversity begins with the mindset of the teacher and a shift away from seeing students with learning disabilities in terms of the diagnosis written on their Individualized Education Programs (IEPs) and toward understanding the underlying processes that contribute to the diagnosis and embracing the specific strengths and challenges therein. While the challenges of teaching in a neurodiverse classroom are real, students with learning differences bring many assets such as building connections, sparking debate, and cultivating depth that are critical to building discussion and understanding in the English classroom.

The strategies and approaches set forth in this chapter could be used for any student or classroom. What is important to take away, however, is that these strategies can make a world of difference for students with unique learning styles and enable them to participate fully in discussion. While the framework for building authentic discussion presented throughout this book should be used for neurodiverse students, employing the mindsets and strategies laid forth in this chapter in tandem with this framework will further promote the success of students with learning differences in discussion within the English classroom.

This chapter includes a breakdown of some learning disabilities teachers are likely to encounter and a window into the neurodiverse learner's experience. Next, each section details how to approach classroom discussion from a strength-based mindset. Each section concludes with specific strategies to support students with the profile in discussion.

Specifically, this chapter focuses on students with a diagnosis of dyslexia or attention deficit hyperactivity disorder (ADHD). The chapter also includes a section on supporting students with slow processing speed, a feature of many different language- and attention-based learning disabilities. Finally, a lesson scaffolded and structured specifically for a neurodiverse classroom highlights approaches in action for supporting neurodiverse learners in authentic discussion.

## INSPIRING CONNECTIONS: STUDENTS WITH DYSLEXIA IN DISCUSSION

What is *dyslexia*? The *Diagnostic and Statistical Manual of Mental Disorders*, fifth edition (*DSM-5*) includes dyslexia within the diagnosis of specific learning disorder with impairment in reading. The *DSM-5* develops this in terms of impairment in "word reading accuracy, reading rate or fluency, and/or reading comprehension" (American Psychiatric Association, 2013, p. 67). To a general education teacher and a fluent reader, this definition is a starting place but fails to address the heart or the experience of the learner with dyslexia.

---

### Textbox 13.1. A Student's Insight: Dyslexia

I recall feeling some anxiety about introducing the "Reading Autobiography" assignment to a classroom of students with dyslexia. A student conference during brainstorming, however, showed me not only the importance of giving students with learning differences opportunities and space for exploring their unique learning styles but also how much I could tailor my teaching based on their descriptions of lived experience. As Candice struggled to put onto paper her experiences as a student with dyslexia, she shared details of struggling to decode basic words all the way through fourth grade. She also shared how even now when she encountered complex, unfamiliar, multisyllabic words, her pulse began racing and she felt trapped and cornered. I recall one point

---

at which Candice turned to me and asked, "Did you know, at my old school freshman year, I never talked? Every parent-teacher conference was the same, 'I wish Candice would say more in class.'" I expressed my disbelief, as Candice was a vocal participant in our class discussions. Upon further questioning on my part, Candice articulated struggles during ninth grade both with the fear of being asked to read something unfamiliar out loud and with the subsequent fear of misreading it in front of her peers. Candice also mentioned a very real issue with, upon getting to class and listening to discussion, discovering that her dyslexia had caused her to misread certain words that had in turn put her entirely off the mark and resulted in a plot-level story dramatically different from the one literally printed on the page.

Candice's reflections ultimately made for a powerful and moving Reading Autobiography. Our conversation, however, has existed in my memory long past the assignment and has provided valuable insights into how I work to engage students with dyslexia in discussion.

What does the experience of a student with dyslexia look like during classroom discussion? Typical teacher comments regarding students with dyslexia in discussion often sound like the following: "Student X is so quiet, I can barely get her to participate." At a more problematic level, when very bright students with dyslexia take honors classes that match their critical-thinking capabilities, teacher concerns can take the shape of, "Student X, I'm just not sure if he can read. I'm not sure if this student is capable of discussing at the level of this class."

Students with dyslexia, meanwhile, will often acknowledge verbally that they "hate to read" or privately self-identify as "bad at reading" on a student survey. These mindsets come from both the lived experience of the student and the deficit mindset a diagnostic label on an IEP can provide. Frequently, these mindsets can set students with dyslexia off on the wrong foot in their English classes.

Due to their very real challenges with reading, students with dyslexia often lack confidence in discussion. If the reading load to acquire the information needed for discussion is too long and inaccessible or if there is an added burden of finding and citing text-based evidence in discussion, students with dyslexia can be alienated or excluded. This helps explain why students with dyslexia often end up as silent bodies in the classroom, flying under the radar and not voicing their contributions and insights.

A comment typical of teachers attuned to working with students with dyslexia, however, can be, "Student X is totally into discussion and really listens to her peers." Often, students with dyslexia have advanced auditory processing skills that can act in a compensatory way to mitigate their difficulty with printed text. Thus, students with dyslexia will often speak later in discussion and can do a remarkable job of responding to and expanding their classmates' ideas. The quality of dyslexic students' ultimate contributions, moreover, will often dispel any misconceptions over their ability to deal with high-level material and isolate the root of the issue as an information input rather than comprehension issue.

Imagine approaching students with dyslexia from a strength-based mindset. Of the potential discussion responses possible in an English classroom, students with dyslexia will often gather multiple contributions from classmates and comment on, debate with, or connect to other, outside, ideas. *The Dyslexic Advantage*, by Brock and Fernette Eide (2012), identifies and categorizes areas in which the dyslexic brain is uniquely wired to excel, highlighting a line of reasoning for why students with dyslexia can be so strong in this area of discussion. Specifically, the Eides identify "interconnected reasoning" as an area of strength for students with dyslexia.

Interconnected reasoning involves "the ability to see how phenomena are related by 'likeness' (similarity) or 'togetherness' (correlation or cause and effect)" (Eide & Eide, 2012, p. 83). This skill of combining and connecting plays nicely in discussion as it allows students with dyslexia to circumvent the small-detail process of evidence identification and articulation, a particular area of challenge for them, and instead work on formulating and articulating big-picture connections.

Interconnected reasoning is ideally suited to discussion as it allows students to process information and evidence auditorily from their classmates and then to create relationships between the ideas to push discussion onward in new and interesting ways. Interconnected reasoning also involves "the ability to unite all kinds of information about a particular object of thought into a single global or big-picture view" (Eide & Eide, 2012, p. 84). Discussion in the English classroom often begins with close examination of evidence. Ultimately, however, that evidence must come together in a productive and cohesive way to bring meaning to the larger, big-picture inquiry questions.

From a strength-based model, students with dyslexia play a key role in building toward the bigger picture. The teacher's role, from this perspective, includes helping students with dyslexia clearly articulate and communicate their big-picture connections and helping other students to see these big-picture connections. This sample dialogue comes from a ninth-grade English class reading chapter 8 of William Golding's *Lord of the Flies* and discussing in small groups the significance of the pig hunt.

Jon (with dyslexia): That was so bloody. The detail was so specific. I could totally see the scene in my head.

Nick: I couldn't believe it when they talked about how it went "right up the ass." I was like, no way, they did not write that.

Abby: Ewww. Gross. Why did you say that? What are they going to do if they kill the mother pig? What will they eat?

Shauna: It's not just that they killed the mother. That was really stupid though. It's also how they killed her. That red blood streaking on the face. Crazy.

Jon (with dyslexia): Did anyone else notice the pink rocks? They are always talking about pink rocks. It's like the island is built on pink and the blood hunt. They are all over the island. There is blood everywhere and then there are rocks everywhere.

Nick: What? I guess . . .

Shauna: And wasn't Simon watching the bloody slaughter the whole time? Brutal.

When Jon comments about the pink rocks, the other students in his group either ignore him or cite confusion. The teacher's role, in this example, is to validate that there is a connection by supporting Jon to develop the full web of meaning that connects the pink rocks to the red blood. Unless supported to explore and articulate the big-picture and unifying ideas of color and geography, the value of Jon's connection will slip away. Below, the continuation of the conversation illustrates how the teacher can intervene to support Jon in clearly developing and sharing his ideas while building the small-group discussion.

Teacher: Wait. Let's pause here for a second. Shauna, you bring up the blood again. Let's take a closer look at what Jon was saying and how these things are connected. Jon, I am interested in what you brought up. What made you mention the rocks?

Jon (with dyslexia): I don't know. They just keep mentioning the rocks.

Teacher: You've noticed a key detail that not many readers focus on, especially with all that blood! Let's think about what is interesting in examining the two images together. Why is this interesting?

Jon (with dyslexia): I don't know . . . it was stupid. It probably doesn't matter.

Teacher: Definitely not. This is an interesting question that I want to know the answer to! What connects the rocks with the blood?

Nick: The color? They are both in the same color family.

Teacher: Great! Thanks, Nick. Now, Jon, let's go back to how you phrased it at first. You mentioned that the island is "built on" the pig hunt and the pink rocks. Let's explore that. What does that mean?

Jon (with dyslexia): Well, underneath them are the rocks. And all around them is the blood from the hunt. And if the rocks are like the blood that comes from the violence, then there is violence all around them.

Shauna: I kind of see what you mean. It's like there is no escape from the violence once they are on the island.

Teacher: Great, I love the development you two are working on. I think that idea of being "built on" is so interesting. What are some other associations we can make with the idea of being "built on"?

Abby: If something is built on something else, it's underneath.

Nick: Yeah, like a foundation, or what something is built on.

Jon (with dyslexia): Yeah, so then no wonder they become more and more savage. They can't get away from what is already there, underneath them.

Teacher: There you go, Jon. There was something there. That is such an interesting connection and one I've never really noticed before. In what way does the idea of foundation also connect with the pigs?

Jon (with dyslexia): Well, like Abby said, they are destroying their food source by killing the mother pig. Is that also kind of like a foundation?

Abby: Yes, like the foundation of what they need to eat! Aren't they also always talking about the rocks being jagged? Could that be like a knife?

Teacher: Sounds like you all have some interesting ideas to pursue here. Let's make sure that we share with the whole class at the end.

Jon's dyslexic brain, in a burst of interconnected reasoning, was ready to be pushed to develop the color connections between the red of the pig's blood and the pink of the rock versus the foundation of food the pigs provide on the island and the foundation of bedrock beneath the island itself. Big-picture thinking is a real area of strength for students with dyslexia, but unless they are specifically supported and pushed to recognize and develop the skills to articulate, their comments can get lost as students with dyslexia can become dismissive of their unique reading strengths and give up in discussion.

It is wildly fantastic to be a teacher of students with dyslexia when they make a connection that the teacher would never have seen or imagined but, after thinking, the teacher too can see is valid. At these moments, it is essential to push students with dyslexia to fully develop their ideas while, in turn, engaging other students with the interconnected reasoning. The fact that the dyslexic brain can be uniquely suited to weaving together the webs of meaning that make literary analysis so much fun and so meaningful means that once English teachers orient to this strength-based model, they have set themselves and their students with dyslexia up for incredible discussion. Here, then, is a summary of strategies to support students with dyslexia as they engage in discussion:

- Provide audio texts to lessen the strain of decoding off the page and electronic texts to allow students to use text-to-speech features so that students with dyslexia can thrive via the comprehensible input of material. Additionally, manage the length of readings for students with dyslexia by breaking down lengthy texts to help them absorb the material in order to participate fully in discussion.
- Provide discussion questions ahead of time, and develop specific annotation strategies with tabs, sticky notes, or colored highlighters to allow students with dyslexia to efficiently locate evidence before and during discussion.
- Provide verbal cues such as "four lines from the bottom of the page" when a student in the classroom offers a piece of text-based evidence to help students with dyslexia quickly find and locate the quotation.
- Validate big-picture thinking and encourage class-wide contributions to identify and contribute pieces of evidence that support this reasoning, if necessary.
- Encourage students with dyslexia to enter into discussion at the analysis level rather than small-detail or plot-level questions. Or allow them to use their answers to comprehension questions completed ahead of time.
- Embrace the potential in nontraditional answers students with dyslexia might give by encouraging them to develop the line of reasoning in the moment, or if the teacher is unsure about how to connect this idea in discussion, follow up with the student and have them help the teacher think through the connection for a great opener the following day.

SPARKING DEBATE: STUDENTS WITH ADHD IN DISCUSSION

What is *ADHD*? The *DSM-5* defines attention deficit hyperactivity disorder as "a persistent pattern of inattention and/or hyperactivity-impulsivity that interferes with functioning or development" (American Psychiatric Association, 2013, p. 59). While this definition is clear and straightforward, to a general education teacher and a person with typical attention patterns and control, it can be difficult to understand the lived experience of a learner with attention issues.

**Textbox 13.2. A Student's Insight: ADHD**

I recall one summer leading the college essay-writing boot-camp class and helping students craft their statements of disclosure to show rather than tell about their diagnoses. As we engaged in various simile and metaphor writing activities, a rising high school senior with diagnosed ADHD (inattentive type) had a breakthrough moment when he compared the experience of having ADHD to looking through a kitchen junk drawer to try and find the chip clip. What started as a clear and focused objective got immediately sidetracked when, fully intent on finding the chip clip, he sees the birthday candles and starts thinking about his last birthday. Then, before committing to birthday, he notices old coupons and starts wondering where his mom is. My student identified that he often gets so lost in his thoughts that it is sometimes impossible to return back to the original idea, just as one can leave a junk drawer with the birthday candles and never find the chip clip. The junk drawer comparison helped me conceptualize in a meaningful way the experiences of the student with attention issues and understand the underlying processes that contribute to strengths, challenges, and behaviors of a student with attention issues.

Consider how students with ADHD look during classroom discussion. Teachers of students with attention issues express frustration over a perceived lack of focus or motivation. Overwhelmed teachers frequently cite missed directions or management issues as chief areas of concern. Teachers receptive to distinguishing the surface behaviors as a very real product of the attention issues, however, often note that students with ADHD are incredibly receptive to feedback and strategies for engagement.

From a strength-based perspective, students with attention issues liven up the classroom and are vociferous participators. While many high school students will groan about having to get out of their desks and move, students with attention issues are always ready to connect an activity to movement to help them stay present.

"Four Corners" activities that have students move to different areas of the room to debate points; "Moving Partner Discussions" where students discuss a specific question with a partner for a designated amount of time before one partner stays and the other partner moves on to discuss with a new partner; and "Gallery Walks" where students move around the room to encounter a variety of sources relating to a topic are all excellent movement-based strategies to facilitate discussion. Also, since the rate at which their thoughts move and the level of distraction that accompanies their learning difference can be quite unsettling, students with attention issues often value the redirection and opportunity to reorient themselves to the topic at hand.

There are ways to approach discussion with students with ADHD from a strength-based perspective. Dr. Ned Hallowell (2015), at a presentation at the Wolcott School, gave the analogy that having ADHD is like having "a Ferrari engine for a brain with bicycle brakes." Students with attention issues are often uncharacteristically bright thinkers who are capable of making excellent inferences and deductions. The "bicycle brakes," however, can lead to a lack of inhibition in discussion and real issues with focus and preparation. This, however, is what makes students with ADHD such a delight; they are risk takers who engage in the moment.

The lack of inhibition allows students with ADHD to say aloud in discussion the controversial viewpoints or the nonconventional positions that other students may shy away from articulating for fear of deviating from social norms and conventions. The example discussion below, taken from an English III American literature classroom at the opening of F. Scott Fitzgerald's *Great Gatsby*, highlights just such a moment.

Teacher: What questions do you have about the opening section?

Eric *(raises hand)*: I'm confused about the beginning of the book. There doesn't seem to be a story.

Justine *(raises hand and makes eye contact with Eric)*: Yeah, that's true. The vocabulary is also really hard. The guy [the narrator, Nick] talks really strangely.

Teacher: Let's start there. Who is this "guy," and what can we tell about him thus far?

Neil (with ADHD) *(does not raise hand)*: He is gay. He is totally in love with this dude, Gatsby.

*(Students erupt with laughter.)*

This situation illustrates the kind of management issue that students with attention issues can bring to the classroom. Thus, the teacher's response in the situation is crucial.

First, it is important to refocus the conversation and group without shaming the student. Phrases like "Student X, love the enthusiasm, but let's raise a hand for that" help to keep the tone light while also providing redirection. This also opens the opportunity to embrace the fact that Neil has bypassed the safer response for Nick's characterization of "inclined to reserve all judgements" and gone for a less concrete and wilder inference that can spark further debate and discussion.

In this case, the teacher can either ask Neil to explain his reasoning or open the conversation to the class with uptake, building upon Neil's observation and situating and extending it by commenting, "Let's explore that. Is there any evidence to substantiate this claim?" Opening the line of discussion allows for Neil and his classmates to revisit the text and look closely at whether Nick's inclusion that "there was something gorgeous about him" really substantiates this conclusion.

Neil's comment, moreover, opens the door for future discussion and debate at the end of chapter 2 and Nick's sequence of unreliable narration with Mr. McKee. From a deficit perspective, this student's lack of inhibition led to a classroom disruption. From a strength-based perspective, this student's comment set up a new line of inquiry and, with the proper reining in, can get the whole class involved in authentic discussion and debate.

There are a few useful strategies to keep in mind to support students with attention issues as they engage in discussion:

- Use a discussion ball to kinesthetically engage students with attention issues and keep their focus on the topic of discussion.
- Display a timer for timed discussions that students with attention issues can clearly see to help them conceptualize time and maintain focus.
- Build in opportunities during class time for students with ADHD to get their ideas for discussion down on paper in the moment rather than as homework. Students with attention issues often struggle to manage time outside of class to prepare for discussion but also often need additional time to thoroughly think through something due to the increased distraction in their thoughts. While the quantity of discussion time may decrease, this strategy will help improve the quality.
- Provide frequent redirection of students by name with supportive prompts to reground them in the classroom space and help them reenter the conversation. A supportive prompt includes a quick summary by the teacher of the debate going on in the classroom and a follow-up question to elicit

engagement from the student with ADHD. A supportive prompt sounds like, "Student X, in looking at the debate we've been having thus far on y versus z, with one side arguing 'a' and the other side arguing 'b,' I'm wondering where you fall? What are your thoughts, Student X?"

- Encourage self-monitoring and awareness by identifying the specific visual cues of engagement (eye contact, nonverbal responses, focus on speaker, and upright body position) and specific verbal evidence of engagement (refraining from talking over others, responding to another's idea, beginning a discussion, providing a counter argument, and introducing a piece of evidence or supporting idea) and how others perceive the various behaviors.
- Promote demonstrated evidence of engagement in discussion in place of note-taking. Provide teacher copies of any classroom notes, and offer alternative assessments of students based on aforementioned attention criteria and contributions.
- Provide opportunities for authentic debate and discussion detailed elsewhere in this book, and value edgy contributions as debate catalysts from students with ADHD.
- Promote self-reflection with self-tracking procedures that help students with attention issues "pump the brake muscles" and keep their thoughts from speeding out of control. Provide students with a tally check sheet to track the number of times they need redirection or the number of times they feel themselves losing focus. Teachers should follow up with explicit discussions about the collected data and what students can do to self-advocate in the future.
- Include opportunities for movement within discussion.
- Keep a box of fidgets (squeeze balls) in an easily accessible place for individual students who struggle to "sit still." Students can use these to satisfy their craving for movement in a way that is not distracting to other students during traditional seated discussions.
- Have students with attention issues repeat the question for discussion to ensure listening comprehension before delving into discussion.

## CULTIVATING DEPTH: STUDENTS WITH SLOW PROCESSING SPEED IN DISCUSSION

What are some characteristics of students with "slow processing speed"? While not a diagnosis students receive, slow processing speed is a feature of many learning differences and an important category for English teachers to be aware of and strategize for in discussion.

**Textbox 13.3. A Student's Insight: Slow Processing Speed**

Shannon, a bright and cogent ninth-grade girl with below average processing speed as a significant component of her generalized reading
disorder, created a project in her art class to explain her learning difference. Participating in the critique panel gave me incredible insight into
her experience as a learner. The project included three layers of trans-
parencies with each containing different markings that, when aligned in
just the right way, revealed a comprehensible block of text. In discussing her work with me, Shannon explained that her art project was
designed to give viewers the experience of what it is like to slowly and
laboriously piece things together before the magical "click" of understanding occurs. She explained that for typical processors, the "click"
of understanding happens almost instantaneously. For Shannon, the
comprehension is possible but takes longer to bring all the pieces into
place. As her teacher having this conversation with her, I grasped how
frustrating discussion could potentially be for Shannon and others who
process as she does and how important it is to implement strategies for
including them in discussion.

Consider how students with slow processing speed appear in the classroom.
Teachers struggling to include students with slow processing speed in discussion highlight challenges with lack of participation and incomplete comprehension. At a particularly problematic end of the spectrum, students with
slow processing speed can present as disengaged, unmotivated, or incapable.
Teachers approaching students with slow processing from a strength-based
model, however, will note thoughtful, thorough, and careful effort.

It is important to note that processing speed is not related to cognitive
potential and critical-thinking capabilities. While slower, these students are
capable of demonstrating the same level of skill as their typically processing
peers. Thus, in discussion, students with slow processing speed can add a
wonderful recursive element to discussion when they bring the discussion
back to an earlier point that, when others have moved on, they have been
methodically working through in their brains.

Again, it is possible to approach discussion from a strength-based perspective. Discussion is a particularly challenging area to adapt to students
with processing speed issues because authentic discussion moves fluidly and
is driven largely by student input and analysis. Students with slow processing
speed can get lost in discussion, therefore, when the topic moves on before

they are ready. If they are still processing one thought, they may miss the subsequent comments and the general thread of conversation. Thus, students with slow processing speed can feel insecure about participating if they have received negative attention for "off topic" contributions in the past.

Alternatively, students with slow processing speed may also carry insecurities about their thinking speed compared to their peers and, as a result, can give up on a thought they are working with because they know it will take a greater amount of time to come to fruition. In classroom scenarios that prize quick wits and lightning-fast thinking, students with slow processing speed end up disengaged at every level from the conversation.

The following sample of a student discussion from a ninth-grade class reading chapter 4 of John Steinbeck's *Of Mice and Men* highlights some classic examples of processing speed issues while also providing opportunities for the teacher to productively and authentically engage the student. In the sample, students have spent five minutes brainstorming ideas in response to the question "Who is the loneliest person on the ranch?"

Miguel: I think it is Crooks. No one talks to him, and he is totally separate.

Dayo: I agree. He even says, "'cause I'm black" for why he can't go in the bunkhouse!

Lilya (slow processing): Where is that?

Miguel: Crooks is definitely alienated on account of his race. Racism was incredibly strong at the time.

Sara: Yeah, Crooks is lonely, but I'd like to argue for Curley's wife. She is also lonely.

Dayo: Absolutely not! She has Curley! Crooks is way lonelier.

*(Conversation continues between Miguel, Dayo, and Sara as to whether Curley's wife is actually "lonely.")*

Lilya (slow processing): I found the quote where Crooks says no one will talk to him because he is black. It's on page 68. He is definitely alienated from everyone except Lennie, who is there talking to him right then.

In this scenario, Lilya is still in the process of working through the ideas about Crooks, finding the quote, and processing what the evidence means. Finding this quote is a valuable and productive point; however, by the time Lilya enters it into the conversation, the heart of the debate centers on Curley's wife and her position. The following teacher response model offers an opportunity to help the student with slow processing speed catch up and reenter the conversation while also feeling validated for her contribution.

> Teacher: Thank you. That is an important quote to make sure that we explore. Lilya, you bring up a nice point about Crooks's alienation with that quote. Let's further explore that with relation to the other idea that has been brought up with Curley's wife. I'm going to ask you a few questions so that we can bring all of these ideas together. Ready?

> Lilya: Sure?

> Teacher: Based on the evidence you have located, Crooks is alienated on account of his race. How many other African Americans are there on the ranch?

> *(wait)*

> Lilya: None. He is the only one.

> Teacher: Great. Now, we have also been talking about Curley's wife. In what way is she also the "only one"?

> *(wait)*

> Lilya: She is the only woman on the ranch.

> Teacher: Great. Can you now put those two statements together to effectively summarize where we are in terms of this debate of loneliness?

> *(wait)*

> Lilya: I think so. Crooks is the only African American on the ranch, and Curley's wife is the only woman on the ranch. Both are outsiders for being "the only one." So really, they are the same and different in terms of loneliness.

> Teacher: Interesting. Now that we have the summation that brings us back to the two figures at the heart of the matter, let's open it back up. Who can comment on that idea of "same" and "different"? What other evidence do we have in support of how they are the same? Different?

The teacher's response in this is crucial as it redirects the conversation and folds in the comment from the student with slow processing speed in a way that productively engages and values her contribution. Moreover, the summary response through directed questioning helps students with slow processing speed catch up with the rest of the class and offers them a new opening point to reengage with discussion.

This process can also become a gateway to thoughtfulness for the class as a whole. Managing pacing with students with slow processing speed in mind slows down the conversation and pushes other students with typical processing speeds to refine and clarify their thinking. Having students with slow processing speed in discussion is an opportunity to slow down discussion, authentically allowing the teacher to embrace the value of recursive dialogue and returning to a topic. A few strategies can support students with slow processing speed as they engage in discussion:

- Engage students in self-directed, silent discussions on paper by handing out quotes or questions for students to respond to within a given amount of time. When time is up, offer students the opportunity to continue engaging with their quote or question for another round or get up and move to a new one. This gives students with slow processing speed the opportunity to self-select and move at their own pace. While they may not get to all the quotes or questions by the end, this modified plan gives them autonomy and allows them the time they need to engage fully.
- Include periodic teacher-directed summary of the discussion with guided follow-up questions to help a student with slow processing speed to reenter the conversation.
- Make "Let's pause to think about that" a regular part of class discussion. Building in added wait time for students with slow processing speed to catch up in their thoughts helps them and pushes others to think more deliberately and deeply.
- Provide questions ahead of time to students with slow processing speed. This allows students to preview and plan their ideas for class discussion and feel ready and prepared to contribute.
- Engage in extensive prereading activities to activate students' schema around the discussion topic and help them acquire and process new information.
- Set goals for students with slow processing speed to build their confidence by being the first to participate in conversation or having a response already planned.
- Break down the skills of verbal contribution versus listening and summarizing into discreet parts to allow students with slow processing to focus on building these thinking muscles independently rather than feeling overwhelmed by trying to do it all at once.

## SAMPLE LESSON OVERVIEW

The following lesson was developed to facilitate sustained dialogue and discussion among students with a variety of learning differences. At this point, students have read through act 3, scene 1, of Shakespeare's *Romeo and Juliet*. Students complete the first activity, "Understanding All Sides," during day 1 and then prepare and practice their roles for homework. Students are given the role practicing as homework in order to prepare for discussion. The conflict resolution discussion activity occurs on day 2 as students use the prework to mediate a discussion between characters. The template and form in figure 13.1 is adaptable to any characters in conflict.

Name: _____

**Let's Settle This...**

**Part I: Understanding All Sides**

In a conflict, it is important to understand from where each side is coming. It is also important to speak in a non judgemental way using "I Statements." Use the chart below to identify *from the perspective of each character listed at the top of the row* how he feels and sees the situation.

| What is the conflict? | | |
|---|---|---|
| **Romeo** | **Questions** | **Tybalt** |
| I am upset about... | What am I upset about? | I am upset about... |
| I feel angry/upset with the behavior of .... because.... | What behaviors am I upset with and why? | I feel angry/upset with the behavior of .... because.... |
| I am so upset and frustrated because.... | Why am I so upset about this (what are the underlying causes)? | I am so upset and frustrated because.... |
| I have done .... | What actions have I taken already in this situation? | I have done .... |
| I have / have not had any consequences since.... | Have I had any consequences for my actions? What are they? | I have / have not had any consequences since.... |
| I would like to see ..... happen in this situation because..... | What do I want to happen in this situation? | I would like to see ..... happen in this situation because..... |

**Figure 13.1.   Understanding All Sides**

The character conflict resolution lesson works well for facilitating student-directed discussion and effectively scaffolds for students with learning differences. Initially, all students complete all sections of "Understanding All

Sides" in order to build an understanding of characterization and foundational understanding for the whole scenario. This preparation is an essential building block for supporting discussion the following day as it ensures comprehension by pushing students to review the events of the story, sets a foundation for making inferences by giving students scaffolded questions, and builds a reference point by giving students a script of notes to use in discussion.

The conflict mediation on day 2 (figures 13.2–13.4) pushes students to problem solve, take on characterization, generate original ideas, and evaluate those ideas. With the structured script in place for day 2, students are prepared to take charge and fully engage with each other in discussion. The design of the lesson, moreover, creates opportunities for students with learning differences to engage with discussion roles that make the most of their learning strengths.

The conflict mediator is a great role for students with dyslexia as it allows them to auditorily process what their classmates are saying and apply their big-picture thinking skills. Because there is verbal reading involved for the conflict mediator with the second-day script, have students with dyslexia preview and practice the script for homework to build their confidence with reading aloud.

Making a student with dyslexia the conflict mediator provides an opportunity to prepare and practice reading aloud and also provides multiple opportunities to practice using auditory input to generate meaningful comprehension. As the script becomes increasingly big picture, students with dyslexia in the role of conflict mediator will be able to specifically develop strengths of reasoning and connection.

Students with ADHD and students whose learning difference includes a slower processing speed are well prepared to take on the character roles as they have a self-prepared script to support their independent tracking and engagement in the discussion. Thus, if they lose track of the discussion, they have the tools to independently correct and reorient themselves in discussion. Students with ADHD will also thrive in the "live-action role play" aspect of the character and will bring the added enthusiasm and energy necessary to make this discussion activity really work in the classroom.

Name: _____

## Let's Settle This...

**Part II: Meeting with a Conflict Mediator**
Use the script below to conduct a mediation meeting between Romeo and Tybalt. The goal is to apply conflict resolution skills to help them think through their issues and reach a conclusion.

| Roles | |
|---|---|
| **Conflict Mediator** | |
| **Mediation Recorder** | |
| **Romeo** | |
| **Tybalt** | |

### Process for Conflict Resolution

1. Establish ground rules by asking individuals to treat each other with respect and to make an effort to listen and understand.

2. Allow each individual to describe the conflict, including what they want to happen. Direct individuals to use "I" and take ownership rather then "you" and create blame. Inform participants that they should focus their comments on specific behaviors and problems.

3. Have individuals restate what others have said to ensure listening and comprehension.

4. Summarize the conflict based on the information that participants provide and ask for participant feedback.

5. Brainstorm solutions and evaluate the outcome of these solutions.

1

**Figure 13.2.   Conflict Mediation**

## SCRIPT

MEDIATOR: Thank you for coming to this Human Resources meeting. First, I want to establish some ground rules. I am asking each party, Romeo and Tybalt, to make an effort to listen and understand the other's view. Romeo, do you agree?

ROMEO: (*answer*)

MEDIATOR: Tybalt, do you agree?

TYBALT: (*answer*)

MEDIATOR: I'm going to ask each of you to describe the conflict from your point of view. I'm asking that each of you use "I" statements. Romeo, what does this mean?

ROMEO: (*give an answer to the question*)

MEDIATOR: Thanks for sharing. "I statements" are when a person begins each statement with the word "I" to share their personal point of view rather than attacking. Tybalt, why is it important to use "I statements"?

TYBALT: (*give an answer to the question*)

MEDIATOR: Thank you, Tybalt. It is important to use "I statements" because it allows for everyone's view to be heard in a non confrontational way. Keeping confrontation out of this meeting is important to reaching a resolution that all parties agree with. Remember, focus on behaviors. Don't attack!

MEDIATOR: Romeo, I'm going to ask you to describe the conflict using "I statements." Tybalt, I want you to listen and restate what you hear Romeo saying.

ROMEO: (*use the "Understanding All Sides" sheet to explain Romeo's perspective*)

MEDIATOR: (comment on Romeo's response - did he follow the guidelines?) Thank you Romeo. Ok, Tybalt, what did you hear?

TYBALT: (*restate in your own words Romeo's perspective*)

MEDIATOR: (*comment on Tybalt's response and give feedback*). Tybalt, it's your turn to tell your side of the story using "I statements." Romeo, I want you to listen and restate what you hear Tybalt saying.

TYBALT: (*use the "Understanding All Sides" sheet to explain Tybalt's perspective*)

MEDIATOR: (*comment on Tybalt's response assessing whether Tybalt followed the guidelines*) Thank you Tybalt. Ok, Romeo, what did you hear?

2

**Figure 13.3.   Conflict Mediation**

ROMEO: *(restate in your own words Tybalt's perspective)*

MEDIATOR: *(summarize conflict based on Tybalt's and Romeo's comments)*.  Was this summary accurate, Tybalt and Romeo?

ROMEO: *(respond)*

TYBALT: *(respond)*

MEDIATOR: Thoughts and feelings often impact our decisions.  How did your thoughts and feeling impact your decisions and retelling of events?

ROMEO: *(respond)*

TYBALT: *(respond)*

MEDIATOR: *(comment on Romeo's and Tybalt's responses)*.  I understand that this is a very emotional situation for you both.  It's important to recognize and understand when our emotions are playing a major part in our decision making.

Now that we've talked about the conflict and our emotions, why don't we talk about some solutions?  It's important that we try and phrase all solutions in a positive manner rather than a punishing manner.  What do you think?

***Mediator facilitates further discussion to brainstorm solutions to the problem as the Mediation Recorder writes down possible solutions for the group***

| Possible Solutions | Why a good solution? | Why not a good solution? |
|---|---|---|
| Solution 1: | | |
| Solution 2: | | |
| Solution 3: | | |

MEDIATOR: Thank you both so much for coming to conflict resolution rather than fighting violently with each other.  Please shake hands.

3

**Figure 13.4.   Conflict Mediation**

## CONCLUDING THOUGHTS

Whether with one neurologically diverse learner in a general education curriculum or a whole classroom of diverse learners, it is important to take the strategies detailed in this chapter and tailor them to the needs of the classroom. No two students with the same diagnosis will present in exactly the same way. Thus, working with a neurodiverse population requires understanding each student's unique learning style before tailoring a plan for success. Reading student profiles is a start; however, engaging with students and discussing with them their experiences as learners are perhaps the most powerful tools in the teacher's arsenal for building authentic and meaningful discussion that includes and values the strengths of each member of the classroom.

## REFERENCES

American Psychiatric Association. (2013). *Diagnostic and statistical manual of mental disorders* (5th ed.; *DSM-5*). Arlington, VA: American Psychiatric Association.
Eide, B., & Eide, F. (2012). *The dyslexic advantage: Unlocking the hidden potential of the dyslexic brain.* New York: Penguin.
Hallowell, E. (2015). Using brain science to treat ADHD across the lifespan. Presentation at the James Tyree Center at Wolcott School. April 23, 2015, Chicago.

*Chapter Fourteen*

# "Talk Isn't Cheap in Here"

*Discussion in Prison Classrooms*

Deborah Appleman

Of all the tools in a teacher's toolkit, leading discussions is perhaps one of the most difficult, even in the most ideal of classroom circumstances. Discussion requires shifting the locus of authority. It transfers the role of dispenser of information and knowledge from the teacher to the students. The role of the teacher thus changes, as the old saying goes, from the sage on the stage to the guide on the side. The role and responsibilities of the students change as well, from observers to participants (Holden & Schmit, 2002).

Teaching and learning through discussion requires openness and flexibility, a willingness for things to not go exactly as planned and, thus, for coverage of material to be uncertain and timing to be up in the air. It requires a willingness to experience moments of awkward silence or moments of frank discourse that can cause discomfort or even hurt or anger. Discussion requires trust—trust between students and teachers and trust between students. In other words, in order for an authentic discussion to occur, a community of learners of mutual trust and respect, needs to exist.

## IMPEDIMENTS TO DISCUSSION IN THE CARCERAL CONTEXT

Given the need for authentic discussion to function in an atmosphere of mutual trust, it is difficult to imagine how to establish the conditions necessary for discussion in an environment as restrictive and forbidding as a high-security prison. Most correctional facilities have very strict rules that govern the interaction between students and teachers.

There are rules governing forms of address. Teachers are asked to use the term "Offender" as a direct address, rather than Mr. or Ms. or a first name. For example, James Smith is not to be addressed as Mr. Smith; he is to be called "Offender Smith." This rule frames every interaction around a student's criminal past and current status as an inmate.

Physical contact is limited to handshakes or fist bumps. While it's clearly obvious that certain kinds of physical contact should be banned between a teacher and her students in any context, even benign and often useful reassuring pats on the back or shoulder are prohibited.

In most facilities, any student-teacher interaction outside class is strictly forbidden—no office hours or individual conferences or meetings are possible; no quick before or after conversations can occur. Guards whisk the students away from the classroom and back to the cellblocks immediately (and sometimes even before) when class is over. Given these constraints, it seems nearly impossible to achieve the kind of trust-building and deep knowledge of individual students that teachers may need to encourage their students to participate productively in discussion.

In addition to limits on student-teacher interactions, there are limits to student-student interactions as well, thus making it nearly impossible for the prison classroom to become the community of learners required for productive discussion. There are often, for example, complicated dynamics among incarcerated students, of which the teacher may be completely unaware. Members of rival gangs, inmates who have been on opposite sides of a particular crime, individuals who belong to different groups, and cliques or gangs within the prison all combine to create a mix of wariness, reticence, and sometimes even fear.

Additionally, exposing one's ideas, thoughts, beliefs, and opinions—always a risk in any classroom—is particularly fraught in the prison context, considering how important it is for incarcerated students to present a strong, unwavering presence in the cellblocks. Finally, sometimes, just as hallway dynamics can spill into a secondary school classroom, the dynamics of a cellblock sometimes spill into a prison classroom and affect the atmosphere.

In addition to the limitations on the student-teacher and student-student dynamic, there are also elements of the carceral space that are antithetical to conducting free-flowing, authentic discussions. Guards, or corrections officers, as they are generally called, are usually visible, either in or just outside the classroom. Classroom processes are regularly disrupted by lockdowns, drills, and nightly "pill runs" to administer medication. Cameras are ubiquitous, and classroom proceedings are sometimes recorded. While the recording of a discussion of a literary text may not seem initially prohibitive, any possibility of making real-time connections between the literature the incarcerated students are reading and what they are experiencing in their lives is chilled by the possibility that someone in authority might be eavesdropping.

Given these formidable constraints, how can authentic productive discussions possibly take place in a prison classroom? Based on my ten years' experience teaching in a high-security prison, I offer the following suggestions in the remainder of this chapter.

## SETTING THE STAGE

Before productive discussions can take place, it can be useful to have a meta-discussion—a discussion about discussion—before the very first one is attempted. In the spirit of "saying the things that go without saying," the teacher can very explicitly introduce the expectation that some of the most important learning in the class will take place through discussion and will offer some reasons. As Brookfield and Preskill (2005) point out, there are many pedagogical reasons discussion can enhance learning. These include the following:

- helping students explore a diversity of perspectives
- increasing students' awareness of and tolerance for ambiguity or complexity
- helping students recognize and investigate their assumptions
- encouraging attentive respectful listening
- developing new appreciation for continuing differences
- increasing intellectual agility
- helping students become connected to a topic
- showing respect for students' voices and experiences
- helping students learn the processes and habits of democratic discourse
- affirming students as co-creators of knowledge
- developing the capacity of the clear communication of ideas and meaning
- developing habits of collaborative learning
- increasing breadth and making students more empathetic
- helping students develop skills of synthesis and integration
- leading students to transformation (p. 17)

After a general group discussion, it is often useful to discuss what makes a good discussion and to ask students to create ground rules, or a kind of social contract. These can be written on the board and the teacher then offers them the following week as a handout. Here is an example from a recent prison class:

**Reading Like a Writer: Class Rules for Discussion**
Only one person should speak at a time.
Try raising hands before you speak.
Look directly at whoever is talking.

Don't get up to sharpen pencils or go to the bathroom when someone is
talking.

What you say should be related in some way to what the person said
before you.

Don't dominate. (Hear that, Chris?)

Try to say at least one thing in every class. Make sure it's relevant, not
random.

Talk to your classmates, not just the teacher.

By drawing up such a "contract," the ground rules for discussion are student
based rather than teacher based, and students tend to feel more invested in the
quality of discussions.

In addition to this group exercise, it is also useful to have students complete an individual inventory on their own discussion styles. This provides
the teacher with useful information that can not only guide whole-class discussions and small-group formations but also often provides an opportunity
for students to self-reflect. Student self-reflection can be a useful move in
any classroom setting, but it's one that might be especially important in a
space where students often feel they cannot speak freely. As one student said,
"Talk isn't cheap in here. Our reputations, our safety—the overall nature of
the time we are serving and how we serve it—are shaped by what we do and
don't say . . . everywhere."

Textbox 14.1 provides an example of a self-inventory used in a recent
prison course.

---

### Textbox 14.1. Self-Inventory on Discussion

Do you consider yourself to be more of a talker or a listener?

What topics are you most passionate about discussing? (List at least
three.)

What topics are you uncomfortable discussing? Is there anything
that you consider to be "off limits"?

Are you comfortable being called on, even if your hand isn't raised?

Do you ever write out your comments before you offer them?

Are you comfortable with disagreement?

Do students have a right to never talk in discussion? Why or why
not?

Name two things your teacher can do that would help establish a
classroom environment that is conducive to discussion.

Name two things you can do that would help you participate regularly and productively.

## SPECIFIC TECHNIQUES

The balance of this chapter offers some techniques for facilitating discussion. Although the techniques were developed specifically to address some of the challenges of conducting discussion in the alternative space of the prison, they can easily be adapted (as I have) to more traditional educational settings, from secondary classrooms to college classrooms.

### "These Aren't My Words, But . . ."

The following activity can be used as an icebreaker. Sometimes just getting one's voice out into the classroom can encourage even the most reluctant students to participate more frequently. Yet students can be afraid to offer their own opinion for fear of being wrong, or worse, being ridiculed. This activity asks students to offer ideas and commentaries that are not their own.

Students are asked to respond to particular questions about a text or a topic. However, instead of verbal commenting, students are asked to write down their responses on large index cards. The teacher then collects the cards and redistributes them so that everyone has a response written by someone else in the class. Students then proceed with the discussion, offering the commentary or other responses that another in the class has written. Because everyone knows that what each student will be offering is not his own opinion, students are less hesitant to participate.

For example, in a recent prison class, students were discussing "One Today," the poem by Richard Blanco that was read at Barack Obama's 2013 inauguration. (https://www.poets.org). Students were asked to select one or two lines from the poem that were of particular resonance to them with one or two lines of explanation.

The teacher then read the poem aloud, asking students to join in when the lines indicated on their card were read. Then students were asked to volunteer why the selected lines had been chosen by the card writer as well as which lines had been selected by more than one class member. For example, the line "the 'I have a dream' we keep dreaming" was selected and read by six of the students, thus creating a kind of verbal highlight. The class discussed why particular lines in the poem seemed to evoke strong responses. As the discussion progressed, students broke out of the constraint of only offering the card writer's sentiments and began to offer their own. As a last step, students were asked to identify the lines of the poem that they had originally selected, and the poem was read aloud one last time. In a round robin, each student was asked to offer his own final thoughts on the poem.

## Human Barometer

Another discussion technique that has worked particularly well in the prison setting is what can be called the Human Barometer. In the activity, students are given some propositions, which are likely to provoke strong feelings. The propositions are stated simply and can be issues oriented or text based. Here are some examples, from a range of different classes, some based on contemporary issues and some text based:

- Adolescence is an invention.
- Race is a social construction.
- The second amendment is anachronistic.
- Prisons should be abolished.
- Gatsby never really loved Daisy.
- The "n-word" is necessary in *The Adventures of Huckleberry Finn* and its presence shouldn't prevent it from being taught.
- *The Bluest Eye* is too "triggering" to be read in classrooms.

The teacher then puts brightly colored signs on the floor with "strongly agree" and "strongly disagree" on either end of the room and "neutral" in the middle. Students are asked to line up according to the degree of their beliefs in relation to other members of the class, which they can only discern by discussing the nuances of their positions with one another. After everyone in the class has literally taken a position on the line, students can then discuss the reasons they are standing where they are. In a recent writing class in the prison, the following prompts were used for the human barometer as a prewriting activity for composing an editorial:

- Assisted suicide should be legalized in all fifty states.
- Marijuana should be legally possessed and sold in the US.
- Undocumented workers should be given a path to citizenship.
- All prisons in the US should be abolished.
- Postsecondary education should be free for anyone who wants it.

Textbox 14.2 provides a brief excerpt of a discussion in a prison classroom that used this discussion technique.

### Textbox 14.2. Reactions to a Proposition

The proposition "All prisons in the US should be abolished" was offered for the human barometer discussion. The class moved quickly on opposite ends of the spectrum with, perhaps surprisingly, few in the middle. There were eight guys on the "strongly agree" side and seven on the "strongly disagree" side. Only Lee stood, alone, in the neutral spot.

"What the hell is wrong with you all," Maurice called out to the classmates huddled on the position that prison should not be abolished. Maurice, who wrote impassioned editorials for the prison newspaper, was a fierce advocate for prisoners' rights and a voracious consumer of books like Michelle Alexander's *New Jim Crow*. "You are exhibiting slave mentality. You have been brainwashed by your captors."

"You're wrong," Ray exclaimed from the opposite side of the line, where he has firmly planted his feet on the sign that indicates strongly disagree. "Man, I would be dead by now if I hadn't been sent to prison. Someone would have killed me. Or I would have continued to do harm to myself and my community."

"Oh, is this the 'three hots and a cot' argument?" Ross, standing next to Maurice, replied.

"No, let's be real, now," exclaimed Ed, from Ray's side of the line. "Life wasn't working for us on the outside, and that's why we landed in here."

"But don't we deserve a second chance at life? Is this really living?" asked Fong.

"Maybe not," offered Richard. "Maybe this is the only life we deserve to have if we took away someone else's."

"Okay, but what about this whole Department of Corrections bull?" Maurice interjected. "We all know it's a department of punishment. Maybe the question shouldn't be "should prisons be abolished?" but "should prisons be changed?"

"Well, that would be a boring discussion," said LaVon. "Who doesn't agree with that proposition?"

In addition to sparking a lively discussion for the majority of the students in the class, the human barometer also moves the teacher largely out of the discussion, so that the dialogue really is among students. This exercise also helps nurture relativistic thinking (Perry, 1981) as students need to fine-tune their positionality. In addition to fostering critical thinking, this discussion technique also fosters critical listening.

## Rotating Pair or Speed-Talking Activity

Another technique that can be fruitfully used to facilitate discussion in the alternative setting of the prison is something called rotating pairs or speed talking. In some ways, speed talking is structured a bit like a speed-dating activity. Classroom chairs or desks are arranged in two lines so that students face each other. The students are given a set of questions. They are asked to discuss each question, one at a time, with the person facing them, for five minutes. However, after five minutes is over, students in one of the lines move to the next chair, so that new pairs are formed. In a fifty-minute period, for example, each student would have discussions with ten different people.

In a recent prison essay-writing class, this discussion activity was used to generate ideas for a specific essay, called "How To" inspired by the essay "How to Make a Slave" by Jerald Walker (2014). The students were given the following questions to discuss in their rotating pairs:

- How should we cope with fear of death?
- How can we get over the loss of a child or a beloved friend?
- How do we reconcile ourselves to the life we are now living?
- How do we forgive ourselves?
- How do we forgive others?
- How can we avoid getting drawn into a pointless argument?
- How do you cheer up a friend in despair?
- What should you do if you overhear someone being given bad advice?
- How should we deal with a bully?
- Where does meaningfulness reside?
- How can we be good to those we love?
- What is the best way to keep loving someone?
- Where should anger go?

Textbox 14.3 provides an account of some of the conversation that resulted from this activity.

### Textbox 14.3. Responses to "How To" Questions

Twenty-two men, in the Writing the Personal Essay class, rearranged their chairs from the normal classroom configuration of a circle to two rows of eleven chairs each. They are each given a handout with the questions listed above. The men sit, each across from another classmate, looking at each other somewhat awkwardly. Direct eye contact is broken by downward glances. A few nervous giggles erupt. The men gingerly begin discussing each question.

"I'm not afraid of death," says Marcus. "I am ready to die."

"Well, you may be ready to die, but I ain't ready for you to die. Why do you say such a thing?" asks Jeff.

Later on down the line, the same student, with a different partner, discusses the question "How do we forgive ourselves?"

"Oh, now I get it. I see the connection between these questions," shooting the teacher an inquisitive sideways glance. "Maybe I am ready to die because I can't forgive myself. What advice do you have for me about that?"

"Let it go, man; you are more than your crime. Remember what Willie (another member of the class) said: 'Everyone's better than the worst they've ever done.'"

Despite the seriousness of these exchanges, some laughter erupts down the line. Fong and Jon are discussing the question "How can we avoid getting drawn into a pointless argument?"

"I wish I had more than five minutes with you to discuss this, man," says Fong, "because pointless arguments are what you do. In here, in the cellblock, everywhere. Why don't you ever listen to reason?"

"Isn't reason in the eye of the beholder," retorts Jon. "I think I am always completely reasonable."

"You just made my point," says Fong. "Oh, good, I just heard the signal to switch partners . . . just in time! Get outa this chair!"

This discussion technique has several advantages and can be used in a variety of settings. The structure requires that every student participate. It prevents discussion from being dominated by a single individual. It keeps the discussion moving so that it doesn't get stuck. It provides safety because the topic is shared in a pair rather than to the whole class. It offers some opportunity to students to interact with other members of the class, including students with whom they might not voluntarily choose to discuss or pair. While the questions in the example discussed in textbox 14.3 were particularly personal, this activity can be used with much less personal topics as well as with text-based, interpretive questions.

## CONCLUDING THOUGHTS

The discussion strategies described in this chapter have worked particularly well in the unique context of the prison classroom. Yet they were created out of the wellspring of nearly four decades of regular classroom instruction in both traditional secondary and postsecondary classrooms. Each of the strategies described in this chapter—the card exchange, human barometer, and rotating pairs—can be successfully integrated into any classroom context. In fact, one of the most striking findings of prison teaching (Appleman, 2013) has been the realization that good teaching *is* good teaching and that the pedagogical skills that teachers have honed over years of experience are durable and portable, so strong in fact that they can move into even the darkest of spaces, the prison, and still be viable.

In some ways, authentic discussions may seem improbable in that dark space, a setting that operates, perhaps out of necessity, on conformity, fear, and control. Since discussion prizes opposite attributes of individuality, comfort, and spontaneity, the very nature of the carceral context can conspire to stifle discussion.

Yet many incarcerated students can be remarkably engaged and fearless in their quest to reshape and reframe their identity by fully participating in authentic discussion: trying out their own opinions and beliefs; listening, really listening, to the perspectives of others; and perhaps even modifying their own positions on particular topics. The free exchange of ideas and perspectives that characterizes an authentic discussion may be the only liberatory element in the lives of incarcerated students. As such, offering democratic learning through discussion can be the most significant learning activity in which these students engage, a true taste of liberal education. And for those who do reenter society, discussion can offer the kind of communication skills of listening and speaking as well as the intellectual flexibility and open-mindedness that may be key to their success on the outside.

## REFERENCES

Appleman, D. (2013). Teaching in the dark: The promise and pedagogy of creative writing in prison. *English Journal, 102*(4), 24–30.

Brookfield, S., & Preskill, S. (2005). *Discussion as a way of teaching: Tools and techniques for democratic classrooms* (2nd ed.). San Francisco: Jossey-Bass.

Holden, J., & Schmit, J. (2002). *Inquiry and the literary text: Constructing discussions in the English classroom*. Urbana, IL: National Council of Teachers of English.

Perry, W. G., Jr. (1981). Cognitive and ethical growth: The making of meaning. In Arthur W. Chickering et al., *The Modern American College* (pp. 76–116). San Francisco: Jossey-Bass.

Walker, J. (2014). How to make a slave. In J. J. Sullivan (Ed.), *The best American essays of 2014*. New York: Houghton Mifflin Harcourt.

*Chapter Fifteen*

# A Place for Reticent Speakers

## Patricia Dalton

Every teacher has experienced the feeling of powerlessness that occurs when students do not participate in class discussions. In the typical whole-class discussion, anywhere from one to possibly all of the students in a class may find themselves unwilling to participate. The following scenario is common.

Teacher: Okay, Arjun, yes. That's a strong summary of the first scene. So in the second scene of *Romeo and Juliet*, what does Paris ask Lord Capulet?

Marco *(hand raises slowly with a third of the class that has previously participated)*: He asked about marriage. He wants Juliet to get with him. He said no, kind of.

Teacher: Okay. So he wants to marry Juliet and asks her father's permission. Tell me more about Capulet's response.

Gaby *(hand raises with the same third of class)*: He said only if she wants to. She's really young—like *really young*—twelve or something, and he doesn't want her to be ruined, so he says for Paris to wait or to get Juliet to say yes and then Capulet will be okay with it, but not now.

Teacher: Great, exactly. And how does Capulet speak about Juliet? Let's go a little deeper. What does he compare her to? And maybe look at what he compares other women to as well.

*(Marco, Gaby, Arjun, and a few other students who have already participated raise their hands. The teacher allows for a short silence while students consider.)*

Teacher: Okay, I'd like to hear from someone I haven't yet heard from. *(All hands go down. No new students offer responses.)* No one else? *(The teacher again provides wait time of a few seconds. No new students offer responses.)* All right, Arjun. You had your hand up. What are your thoughts?

The teacher attempts to start with basic recall of a text previously read in class. Once students appear to be clear on a basic summary, the teacher then attempts to encourage students to process the next level of understanding. With the increasing level of difficulty, more and more students seem to become reticent to participate. Some students are reluctant from the start.

After initial attempts to motivate others to join the discussion, the teacher, possibly from a need to move the lesson along or from her own discomfort with silence, succumbs to the seemingly simpler solution, to allow a student who has no problem speaking in front of his peers, who shares consistently without issue, to save her from the silence, and in turn, a number of reticent speakers who have a great deal to share are not afforded the opportunity. In this scenario, both the verbal participants and their more reluctant peers lose out.

In every English language arts classroom, authentic student discussion is indispensable. True learning takes place when students are provided opportunities to grapple with challenging content, to consider what they currently know and how new information from the curriculum, their teacher, and their peers fits into that existing knowledge. It is, in essence, when students build off old schema with new schema.

One of the most effective ways to provide a vast amount of information with which students can construct schema is to allow for a substantial amount of classroom time for authentic discussion. Many students seem to have minimal issue with participating in whole-class discussion, for they freely speak their minds and appear to be comfortable interacting with their peers. However, the students who verbally participate the most often garner the most attention, and students who fail to verbally share often seem left out. We strive to include every student in our classroom discourse, but more often than not, we feel ill-equipped to do so.

## WHY THEY SHOULD AND WHY THEY DON'T

Why do certain students seldom contribute, and are their contributions truly necessary? Active student engagement results in greater retention of knowledge and a deeper, more extensive understanding of material. In essence, active learning enhances comprehension. Incorporating authentic discussions in the classroom has long been considered a best practice, and the benefits are many (Freire, 1970; McCann, Johannessen, Kahn, & Flanagan, 2006; McCann, Johannessen, Kahn, Smagorinsky, & Smith, 2005). Acknowledging this, the questions then become why is discussion so powerful, and what is to be gained if reluctant speakers begin to add more frequently to classroom discourse?

Sharing diversity of experiences is invaluable. What is true learning if not breaking down ignorances through opening our minds and hearts to the experiences of others? In a student's own words, "Everybody is different, and we all need to learn from each other in order to make us better people." Not only is discussion a tool for compassion, but also it allows for increased student interest and enjoyment, which leads to further student engagement.

When asked about the value of sharing in class, another student stated, "I feel like it makes a difference when I participate versus when I don't. First off, I'm not bored anymore. I often get into whatever we're talking about, and I want others to get into it too because I want to know what they think. I feel like I'm making a difference, helping out, and like I'm getting it on a different level." As this statement affirms, every student's thoughts have value, and every participant in the discussion profits with each distinct, individual voice that is shared.

Despite some students acknowledging the benefits of being involved in discussions, many still do not participate. Surveying students reveals that the primary cause of this lack of participation stems from a lack of comfort. Students report being either uncomfortable with the material or uncomfortable with individuals in class—both peers and the teacher. Regarding the material, students mention a lack of participation due to failure to complete their work in preparation for a discussion or a lack of understanding of the content. In addition, they more often report a lack of engagement with the content.

In other words, students report being bored. Regarding discomfort with peers and the teacher—the reason most often noted—students widely report a fear of judgment of some kind. Below are various responses directly from students:

- There are times when others, other kids or even the teacher, make it uncomfortable for me to be openly curious.
- If I say the wrong thing, I'll look like an idiot.
- I don't know how to say what I want to say. Like phrasing it or whatever.
- I feel stupid when I'm told I'm wrong.
- I don't want to look like a know-it-all.
- I fear I'm not right or don't know the material.
- I don't share if I feel my questions will be judged, or if there is some other form of hostility in my environment, then I keep myself from talking.

Consulting with students is an effective way to determine the cause of their reluctance to participate in discussion. Some teachers like to conduct a beginning-of-the-year survey or schedule individual one-on-one sessions with all of their students in order to learn as much as they can about them. Others prefer to wait until rapport is built and students have had an opportunity to adapt to a new school year. Regardless of how it is done, at some point, teachers must go to the source to discover the cause of an individual's lack of participation in discussions. They can then take steps to increase the chances of a student being intrinsically motivated to add to an authentic class discussion.

## THE POWER OF RELEVANCE

If a student does not engage due to a lack of work completion or understanding, speaking independently with the student can provide a simple yet significant solution, allowing for clarifying, reteaching, or providing for additional supports. If a student is not engaging due to boredom or lack of relevance, it is imperative for the teacher to create relevance. This benefits all students.

Connecting the core texts and units to students' lives goes a long way in encouraging participation. Asking about the way Lord Capulet refers to Juliet and women in general by only referring to literary elements is often not enough to inspire, but inquiring about the objectification of women and how that compares to treatment of women in modern-day society or in students' own lives often makes participation that much more enticing.

As a twelfth-grade student put it, "Don't force students. That's not creating genuine interest in what we're talking about. What will actually make students participate is if teachers teach things in a way that leaves a mark on their students' hearts and spirits. If they talk about something that is important to the students, it'll make them more involved and want to participate more." Open-ended questions that allow for exploration of significant human issues create greater student interest. If students understand that they cannot be wrong and that their experiences are unique and worthwhile to share, the fear of being wrong will dissipate.

## CULTIVATING CLASSROOM CULTURE

Creating an inclusive and comfortable classroom helps to alleviate student fears of being judged. This, however, is not a simple or speedy task; instead, it is a process that should begin the first week of school and continue throughout the year, with all participants working to build community and create a classroom culture of respect and support (Saphier, Haley-Speca, & Gower, 2008). Many teachers emphasize rapport building with students, but rapport building among students is equally important. Planning activities for peers to learn about each other, such as student-centered icebreakers, work well to begin this process.

Another invaluable activity is to create classroom norms in order to have set guidelines for appropriate classroom behavior. In contrast to "teacher rules," creating classroom norms allows students to have a say in how the class operates. The following activity was adapted from Tanya Misfeldt, an English teacher at Fremont High School in Sunnyvale, California.

To begin, ask students to individually create lists of what it looks like to be a respectful student and what it looks like to be a respectful teacher. Once completed, students share with three or four others in a small-group setting, comparing their thoughts in order to make a list of the top three or four characteristics of each on which they can agree. Students then put their top choices on sticky notes and place them on the board accordingly.

Once all groups have finished, the teacher shares the sticky notes verbally, asking students if they can agree to each characteristic of a respectful student. The same process occurs for the teacher traits. If anyone disagrees with a suggestion, a discussion ensues, with the sticky notes being either edited or discarded.

The final step is to create a classroom poster that allows both the students and the teacher to be held accountable throughout the remainder of the year. Discussion norms can be determined in a similar fashion or in some variation. Examples of discussion norms include these statements: value all comments and try to find worth in every thought; discuss, don't debate (unless the activity is a legitimate debate); and if not verbally sharing, take notes if needed or use appropriate body language (e.g., follow speakers with eyes, sit up straight, etc.).

Another simple shift in the classroom that can have a major impact on classroom culture is a mere change in desk arrangement. Arranging seats in a way that is conducive to discussion helps students internalize their own importance in the effectiveness of the class. If, for example, a classroom is set up in long rows, all desks facing the front where the instructor is the main focus, students would merely be reading the cues of the room when assuming that the teacher will be the one doing the majority of the talking.

Understandably, making this adjustment to a more collaborative seating arrangement may take some thought, for students must be able to see the board or projector screen; however, if a teacher desires all students to feel more comfortable with a discussion-based curriculum, having them face each other creates an environment in which they can engage in discussions more freely and more often.

Rapport-building activities for teacher and students, norm-setting activities for overall behavior and discussions, and adjusting desk arrangements all help to create a community mindset and a unique sense of each class's own culture. These suggestions allow for peer supportiveness, compassion, and encouragement, and they help prevent peer isolation and discrimination. If students jointly invest in creating a classroom culture and get to know each other in an authentic way, they will be more comfortable sharing authentically in discussions without fear of judgment. Students are accountable to their teacher as always, but over time they become accountable to their peers as well. Instead of students fearing judgment of their fellows, they begin to see through continuing experiences that the classroom is a safe and supportive environment.

In addition to the judgment of peers, student feedback concerning how teacher behavior prevents participation must also be addressed. If reticent speakers feel there is a right and a wrong answer, their chances of participating diminish greatly, especially if past teachers have reprimanded or simply dismissed them for "incorrect" answers. Teachers must work to earn the trust of students so that when they state that verbal responses will not be evaluative but will instead help build an overall class understanding of a subject, students will believe them.

Rapport building between a teacher and the students is essential. This process can begin with icebreakers. However, students have stated that a teacher's approachability is a key aspect of student comfort. Being friendly, kind, and respectful—with small acts such as making eye contact, smiling, and greeting students at the door or merely by name—can strongly influence student comfort.

Students also react positively to humor, positivity, and enthusiasm. In addition to actions such as playing music as students enter the classroom or sharing personal anecdotes or tidbits about one's life every so often, a teacher's handling of classroom norms is crucial. Validating all students' thoughts, being purposeful in responses to students, showing patience through wait time, assisting with phrasing of an answer if necessary, and from time to time allowing a struggling student to acquire assistance from a supportive peer all show reluctant speakers that sharing may still cause feelings of fear but is not as scary as they once thought, for there is support available if needed. They also see through a teacher's actions that she is just as accountable to the norms as the students; just as students are accountable to the teacher, the teacher must be accountable to them. A teacher's behavior must continually work to foster a mutual respect between teacher and student.

The process of increasing the comfort of reluctant speakers through relevance of content and culture building takes time, but many reticent speakers who fail to participate in all their classes state that these suggestions create the encouragement they require to take the risk to share, despite still having some anxiety. In the words of self-labeled reticent speakers, they greatly dislike participating but share in certain classes for the following reasons:

- It's expected. It's a "norm."
- The teacher allows for humor and adds little goofy things like Bitmojis to her PowerPoints, and it makes me feel more relaxed and friendly. She does these things that make me not want to disappoint her.
- The questions we're asked are more abstract (no right or wrong), and they are more fun to explore.
- My peers give me time and understanding I need to feel comfortable.
- Even if what I say may be worded wrong, the teacher will help to rephrase my answer to help it make more sense.
- What we read in class is very interesting so I feel like I have a lot to say.
- Before we have a discussion with the whole class, we're first separated into groups, which makes talking easier.
- The teacher makes me feel like my opinions are valid, and she welcomes students' input openly.
- I feel the environment is very welcoming and safe, and I respect my classmates.
- I care about the material—it's interesting. The topics apply to me and everyday life.
- I feel like I've gotten to know my classmates better throughout the year so now I'm less afraid to speak my mind and be vulnerable in front of them.

Gaining students' trust and having them trust each other admittedly takes time, sometimes more time than teachers are willing to allow. However, this investment eventually creates greater comfortability for all, and as the year progresses reluctant speakers tend to lose apprehension and join in when they have formed a strong class culture and have been provided a variety of authentic discussion-based activities with relevant content.

## TOOLS AND TASKS TO ENTICE THE RELUCTANT

Participation may look different for many students, especially the reluctant, so it is key to allow numerous opportunities to participate in a variety of ways. All reluctant speakers have varying levels of reluctance; therefore, a variety of tools or tasks can be provided, depending on a student's level of readiness. These options include but are not limited to the following:

- Provide sentence frames for academic discussion to aid students in phrasing their comments (see table 15.1).
- Instead of the teacher reflecting and summarizing student responses, allow reticent speakers to rephrase, which enables them to use thoughts of others as a starting point.

- Allow reluctant students to share personal experiences or prior knowledge, which may be a lower leverage commitment for them.
- Prior to the start of a discussion, let a student know ahead of time that you would like the student to participate in the discussion. A teacher can even guide the student to a specific question or assist the student in creating a comment he or she is comfortable sharing.
- Allow students to participate in the discussion through note-taking.
- Offer options to provide a specific question or comment instead of a higher-order skill such as analysis or synthesis (this could be determined in discussion norms).
- If students do not have an immediate answer, let them know you will come back to them after another comment or two so they can collect their thoughts.
- If students are not responding en masse, stop a moment and allow thirty seconds to a minute for students to turn and talk to a partner, discussing their possible responses; then resume the discussion.
- A few nonverbal options to garner participation from each and every student include polls with hands (simple yes or no answers) or using thumbs (the "thumb-o-meter") to show degrees of agreement (thumbs down is no, thumbs in the middle is maybe, and thumbs up is yes—or some variation).

Some may think that the above options do not show complete application of speaking or discussion skills. Although at times they may seem fairly low leverage, these tasks still require involvement and engagement in practicing skills. Teachers must meet students where they are, and allowing reluctant speakers an additional scaffold can be just the tool they require in order to enhance their current skills and gain the confidence to move them to the next level of engagement. Although students may not be verbal, studies show that their silence can be just as valuable, and when students do choose to verbally participate, their comments are all the more powerful (Schultz, 2009).

Another strategy teachers attempt with reticent speakers is cold-calling, or calling on students who have not volunteered to answer. Although some students who have admitted to disliking discussion have acknowledged that this method can be effective, cold-calling does come with many risks. A ninth-grade student stated, "I get nervous about when to jump in when we talk as a whole group. I know what I want to say, but I don't know how to transition in off of what another person said. It's just easier to be called on sometimes because then I can say what I want without the anxiety of jumping in or having to draw attention to myself by raising my hand."

With this student in particular, calling on him without prompting would be effective; however, a teacher would only discover this effectiveness for a particular student through a one-on-one discussion. Using this strategy with

**Table 15.1.   Sentence Frames for Discussion**

*Directions :* Use the broad skill categories on the left and the more specific italicized notes for each frame on the right to structure your thoughts academically in a class discussion.

| | |
|---|---|
| Making a connection | "This is similar to what _____ brought up earlier . . ." (summarize idea and state why that idea is important) <br> —*Connecting to another comment* <br> "What you have said reminds me of . . ." <br> —*Connecting to another source, text, student, etc.* <br> "I think that what you are saying can be seen in the text . . ." (find page and read quote + explain connection you see) <br> —*Connecting back to the text* |
| Extending an idea | *These frames are for extending or going deeper, based on another student's ideas.* <br> "Going off of what _____ has said . . ." <br> "To build on the idea that . . ." (summarize idea you just heard) <br> "In addition to what _____ just said, another example is . . ." <br> "So if what you are saying is correct, doesn't that mean that . . . ?" |
| Summarizing | *Summarizing helps to gather ideas so the group members can understand where they are in the discussion and transition into the next point.* <br> "What I am hearing from everyone is . . ." <br> "So what you are saying is . . ." |
| Clarifying | *Clarifying the point of another classmate can help you understand what is happening in the discussion. It can then help you to connect other ideas and dig more deeply into them.* <br> "(Student name), when you say that (summarize point you are confused about), what do you mean by that? What makes you think this?" |
| [Dis]agreeing with evidence | "I (dis)agree with the idea that (summarize idea) because . . ." <br> "My perspective is different in that . . . . I feel this way because . . ." <br> "While I agree with (student name) that (summarize idea), I also disagree because . . ." <br> "I respectfully disagree that (summarize idea) because . . .": |

Adapted from teacher Stephanie Fujii, Fremont High School, Sunnyvale, California

others may result in further reticence. Another student, an eighth grader, said that "when a teacher calls on me without me volunteering, it's like they're trying to catch me off guard or something, like they're looking for their next victim. I feel put on the spot, so even if I had an answer, I forget or I get really nervous."

Instead of being inclusive, which is most likely a teacher's intent, the student reads the method as somewhat accusatory, causing even further separation. Using methods such as providing prompts with relevance for students can be far more effective in leading to authentic student involvement, versus inauthentic, uninspired comments forced from an unwilling participant.

Online discussions are often mentioned as an alternate means of discourse. They can provide many advantages. Online discussions allow students to share worthwhile thoughts in an oftentimes far more comfortable format for reticent speakers. The reluctant can reflect and make comments in a safe manner without the anxiety often induced by the body language or facial expressions of peers in person.

Online discussions also allow apprehensive speakers to take additional time to craft a response with which they feel more confident. During oral interchanges in the classroom, time is often a deterrent to students' sharing, for by the time they feel ready, another more confident student has already chimed in. Furthermore, both during and after an online discussion, teachers are able to review each comment in order to assess understanding that otherwise may not be shared verbally by a reluctant speaker. Another benefit to moderating online discussions is the opportunity to have students explore appropriate online communication norms, which is quite pertinent to twenty-first-century students.

There are, however, a couple of cautions for teachers to keep in mind in using online discussions. First, discussions online should not replace in-class discussions completely but instead work as a scaffold to either prepare for, act as a continuation of, or offer a debrief for an in-class discussion. Second, teachers who have encouraged online discussions stress the need for diligence in moderating the exchanges. This process can be somewhat more time-consuming than typical class discourse, depending on the site used.

A simple internet search provides a plethora of discussion board and blog sites from which to choose. Many school district servers also provide the option for teachers to create their own web pages, which often include a function that allows for online discussion. A teacher could also create a separate social media account especially for this purpose.

## SMALL GROUPS AS A STEPPING-STONE

A major support for whole-class discussions is scaffolding them with smaller group discussions. Smaller class sizes often create a greater level of comfort for reluctant speakers, but for most teachers, this is not a reality. Small groups offer students a more comfortable setting in which to share their thoughts. Collaborative seating arrangements can facilitate small-group discussions more easily, enabling frequent application. Providing a clear task or specified questions or prompts for students to discuss is crucial within this small group. Confusion about the objectives or directions not only wastes precious classroom time but also can increase student anxiety.

Attempting to make questions as clear as possible, in addition to teacher movement around the room to each group during discussion time to clarify any confusion, will minimize the chance of losing instructional time and ease student anxiety. In addition, the inclusion of varying levels of questions is important. Students who doubt the value of their own responses often feel that their answers to higher-level questions are insufficient, causing them not to share; however, if questions of varying skill levels are provided, students can gain greater confidence with a skill such as summarizing, providing the efficacy to later apply the skills of synthesis, analysis, or argument.

One of the biggest benefits of small-group discussions is that they directly work against students' fears of being wrong or having an insufficient answer. When reticent speakers can verify their thinking with others, they feel validated. Later, during whole-class discussion, these students have already had two or three others offer feedback, allowing for more confidence to share their ideas at the whole-class level. Some teachers may be concerned with a possible lack of accountability at the small-group level, since a teacher cannot realistically observe the progress of each group throughout its entire discussion. Note-taking, an exit ticket, or some form of a written product can be incorporated into any small-group discussion activity, allowing a teacher to gauge individual student understanding and level of engagement.

There are several different ways to use small groups to increase the comfort level of reticent speakers. One variation is the graffiti wall. The graffiti wall begins with a teacher placing a prompt on the board. Students are given time to consider the prompt and complete a "quickwrite," or a brief written reflection of their thinking. Students discuss their responses in small groups for several minutes, and then each individual crafts a clear statement responding to the prompt, writing it on the board with their peers. After all students record their responses on the graffiti board, and time is provided for all to consider them, a whole-class discussion ensues. Here engagement occurs again on various levels: first, individually; second, in small groups; and third, at the whole group level. This type of scaffolded discussion allows reluctant speakers the time needed to consider their response and the validation of their thinking from peers in a less intimidating small-group setting.

## THE CONTINUUM

Another activity that incorporates a small-group format is the continuum. The continuum is used at the start of a unit of study and uses provocative statements to encourage student thinking about important themes in the unit.

Students are first asked to independently respond to a variety of statements by doing two tasks for each.

First, they are to mark on a continuum where they fall in agreement with the statement. Second, they are to explain the reason for their placement on the continuum in detail (see figure 15.1). Next, students share their responses with their small group. After all students have shared in the small group, they are encouraged to discuss their responses further, asking questions, adding thoughts, or offering feedback. After students have had ample time to discuss all the prompts in the comfort of their small groups, the teacher can then facilitate a whole-class discussion.

Prior to beginning the whole-group discussion, the teacher can either draw a continuum on the board or merely hang an *Agree* sign on one side of the room and a *Disagree* sign on the other. The teacher works as the facilitator, reading the first prompt as students then physically move to the location on the continuum that fits their response. As facilitator, the teacher can ask students representing different locations along the continuum to share their responses and probe with follow-up questions, if needed. However, students themselves are often able to continue this discussion organically with genuine vigor without much teacher assistance.

A significant advantage to this activity is that reticent students need not always add verbally to the discussion for the teacher to know they are engaged. Students can use the location of their bodies to show their thinking and engagement. An adaptation of the continuum is the four corners activity. Instead of placing themselves somewhere on the continuum, students move to a corner of the room that best suits their thinking: *Strongly Agree*, *Agree*, *Disagree*, and *Strongly Disagree*. With every prompt, students in each of the four separate corners can discuss their reasoning within the small-group setting before the whole-class discussion on the prompt.

Peers from a reticent student's group may also assist in encouraging her to join the conversation. For example, if Jonathan was in Emer's small group prior to the whole-class portion and she heard him share an intriguing thought at that time, during the whole-class exchange she can respectfully ask him to share. Emer may say something like, "That's a really interesting statement, Ram. When Jonathan was sharing in our group, he said something great that I think applies to what you said. Would you like to add that, Jonathan?"

As long as this norm is applied appropriately, it can allow peers to help each other become more involved. Throughout the discussion of each prompt, the teacher should encourage students to change their position on the continuum if they change their minds. This element of the activity demonstrates that learning is a process of making meaning over time and encourages students to adjust their understanding. Although the continuum activity works well at the start of a unit, it can be brought back at the end of a unit in a

---

### *Fahrenheit 451*: Continuum Prompts

**Most technology is useless.**

Strongly Agree                                                                                                    Strongly Disagree

I----------------------------------------------------------I----------------------------------------------------------I

Explain your response:

---

**Advancements in technology cause increased unhappiness.**

Strongly Agree                                                                                                    Strongly Disagree

I----------------------------------------------------------I----------------------------------------------------------I

Explain your response:

---

**Censorship is a necessary part of our society.**

Strongly Agree                                                                                                    Strongly Disagree

I----------------------------------------------------------I----------------------------------------------------------I

Explain your response:

---

**People should be able to say anything they'd like at any time.**

Strongly Agree                                                                                                    Strongly Disagree

I----------------------------------------------------------I----------------------------------------------------------I

Explain your response:

---

**Figure 15.1.**

discussion that revisits key themes and asks students if any of their original responses have changed.

Some teachers might assume that most students come into the classroom already knowing how to have meaningful dialogue with each other, but today's students increasingly admit to anxiety when it comes to discussions in the classroom. Teachers provide scaffolds to teach reading and writing, but speaking and listening may often be ignored—unless, of course, they are being assessed in the form of presentation. Providing scaffolds to support reticent speakers helps all students, for all benefit from total class involvement.

## A CONTINUUM OF SUPPORT AND ENCOURAGEMENT

Creating a classroom culture through norm setting for both class expectations and discussions sets up an atmosphere of trust in the classroom, which helps alleviate the key reason for reticence in discussion—fear of judgment from peers or the teacher. This process takes time, but once students feel more comfortable with each other, small-group discussions allow for a starting point for reluctant speakers to begin experimenting with verbalizing their thoughts in class. Once confidence is gained in these smaller groups, students will begin to test the waters in the larger group setting. The more opportunities reluctant speakers have to practice this skill of verbalizing their thinking, the more they, their peers, and their teacher will benefit from their now voiced, unique, and individual perspectives.

## REFERENCES

Freire, P. (1970). *Pedagogy of the oppressed.* (M. Bergman Ramos, Trans.). New York: Herder.

McCann, T. M., Johannessen, L. R., Kahn, E. A., & Flanagan, J. M. (2006). *Talking in class: Using discussion to enhance teaching and learning.* Urbana, IL: NCTE.

McCann, T., Johannessen, L. R., Kahn, E., Smagorinsky, P., & Smith, M. W. (Eds.). (2005). *Reflective teaching, reflective learning: How to develop critically engaged readers, writers, and speakers.* Portsmouth, NH: Heinemann.

Saphier, J., Haley-Speca, M., & Gower, R. (2008). *The skillful teacher: Building your teaching skills.* Acton, MA: RBT.

Schultz, K. (2009). *Rethinking classroom participation: Listening to silent voices.* New York: Teachers College Press.

# About the Editors and Contributors

**Andrew Bouque** teaches English at Adlai E. Stevenson High School in Lincolnshire, Illinois. He earned his BA in English from the University of Illinois, Urbana-Champaign, and an MA in English education from Northern Illinois University. In his nineteen years in public high schools, he has worked to build classroom communities for students to find, develop, and refine their spoken voices and craft arguments that matter. He lives in Genoa, Illinois, with his wife and two children.

**Dawn Forde** is a teacher at Adlai E. Stevenson High School and has been learning from her students for the past seventeen years. She has presented at local, state, and national conferences, primarily focusing on discussion and its effects on literacy and student engagement. She graduated with a BA from Loyola University of Chicago and an MA from the University of Illinois at Chicago. Forde lives in LaGrange, Illinois, with her husband, Mark, and her children, Niall, Tess, and Seamus.

**Elizabeth A. Kahn** taught English language arts for thirty-six years and served as English Department chair. She is currently teaching in the English teacher-education program at Northern Illinois University in DeKalb. She is coauthor of *Discussion Pathways to Literacy Learning* (2018), *The Dynamics of Writing Instruction* (2010), and *The Dynamics of Writing Instruction* series (2011–2012), *Writing About Literature* (1984 and 2009, updated edition), *Talking in Class: Using Discussion to Enhance Teaching and Learning* (2006), *Designing and Sequencing Prewriting Activities* (1982), and coeditor of *Reflective Teaching, Reflective Learning* (2005). She has authored or coauthored numerous journal articles and is a frequent presenter at National Council of Teachers of English (NCTE) and Illinois Association of Teachers of English (IATE) conferences. She has served as president of the IATE and on the NCTE Secondary Section Steering Committee and the executive committee of the Conference on English Education. She received a PhD in education from the University of Chicago and was a National Board Certified Teacher.

**Thomas M. McCann** is professor of English at Northern Illinois University, where he contributes to the teacher licensure program. He taught English in high schools for twenty-five years, including seven years working in an alternative high school. His books include *Transforming Talk into Text* and *Literacy and History in Action*. His coauthored books include *Talking in Class* (2006), *The Dynamics of Writing Instruction* (2010), and *Teaching Matters Most* (2012).

**Carolyn Calhoun Walter** supervises student teachers for Northern Illinois University. Previously, she taught English students for thirty years at both public and private high schools. During that time, she taught students of all ages and ability levels, but she reserves a special place in her heart for high school freshmen. Walter has enjoyed professional involvement by presenting at local, state, and national conferences and workshops for more than three decades and has coauthored the texts *Writing and Designing Pre-Writing Activities* and *Writing About Literature*, first and second editions, and *Discussion Pathways to Literacy Learning* (2018) as well as several articles. She earned her BA from the College of Wooster and her MAT from the University of Chicago.

\* \* \*

**Barbara Alvarez** is in her second year of teaching English at Huntley High School in Huntley, Illinois. In 2014, she earned her bachelor of arts from Northern Illinois University in secondary English education. In 2018, Alvarez earned a master of arts from Northern Illinois in teaching English to speakers of other languages as well as obtained a Spanish bilingual endorsement. Alvarez's interest for teaching English language learners stems from her own experience as an English learner and a desire to help a population of students who are often overlooked.

**Deborah Appleman** is the Hollis L. Caswell Professor of Educational Studies and director of the Summer Writing Program for High School Students at Carleton College. Appleman taught high school English for nine years before receiving her doctorate from the University of Minnesota. She has also been a visiting professor at Syracuse University and at the University of California–Berkeley. She is the author/coauthor of eleven books on adolescent literacy, including *Critical Encounters in High School English: Teaching Literary Theory to Adolescents*, winner of the Richard A. Meade Award; *Adolescent Literacy and the Teaching of Reading*; *Adolescent Literacies: A Handbook of Practice-Based Research* (editor); *Teaching Literature to Adolescents*, third edition; *Reading for Themselves: How to Transform Adolescents into Lifelong Readers through Out-of-Class Book Clubs*; *Uncommon Core*; *Reading Better, Reading Smarter*; and *Braided Lives: An Anthology of Multicultural American Writing*. Appleman's recent research has focused on teaching college-level writing and literature courses at a high-security correctional facility for men. She and her incarcerated students published an anthology of creative writing entitled *From the Inside Out: Letters to Young Men and Other Writing*.

**Julianna Cucci** has been teaching for twenty-two years in the suburbs of Chicago. Currently she serves as English teacher and academic literacy specialist at Maine South in Park Ridge, Illinois. She earned her BA in English and philosophy from the University of Wisconsin–Madison, an MAT from the University of Chicago, and a certificate in educational leadership from Roosevelt University. She views teaching and learning as a collaborative process, and her best ideas come in concert with others. She has copresented at state, regional, and national conferences for English language arts and reading.

**Patricia Dalton** has been an English teacher for eight years and currently teaches at Fremont High School in Sunnyvale, California. She is the PLC coleader for the ninth-grade English literature and writing team and the advisor for the Creative Writing Club. She lives in San Jose with her husband, John, and her husky, Loki Francis.

**Kimberly R. Gwizdala** is an English teacher and the forensics head coach at Glenbard West High School in Glen Ellyn, Illinois. She received her bachelor of arts degree in English from Northern Illinois University and her master of education degree in teacher leadership from Elmhurst College. She lives in Wheaton, Illinois, with her husband.

**Tamara Jaffe-Notier** has taught English in high schools for thirty-two years and still considers teaching the most interesting job in the world. At Niles West High School in Skokie, Illinois, she spent two memorable years teaching and developing curriculum in an interdisciplinary course called Collaborative Learning through Integrated Projects (CLIP). CLIP combined theater workshop, freshman English, and "people and cultures" (modern world history). The final assessment for CLIP one year included a Kabuki production of *Romeo and Juliet*. Jaffe-Notier has contributed an article to *Schools: Stud-*

*ies in Education* and an episode titled "A Lesson on Kindness" to the *Schooled* podcast.

**Shannon McMullen**'s passion for teaching was ignited in Bratislava, Slovakia. Working at a bilingual high school there, she learned important lessons about how English learners negotiate and learn English. Upon returning home from her "second" country, Shannon pursued secondary teacher certification and earned a master of arts in English from Northern Illinois University. She teaches at Glenbard North High School in Carol Stream, Illinois. Shannon also holds a bachelor of arts in English and history from the University of Illinois, Urbana-Champaign.

**Zanfina Rrahmani Muja** is an English teacher at Maine West High School in Des Plaines, Illinois. She has a BA from Loyola University, Chicago, and a reading endorsement from DePaul University, Chicago. Currently, she is a graduate student at Northwestern University. She has presented her research on empathy and reading comprehension at the National Council of Teachers of English (NCTE) annual convention.

**Mark Patton** is an English teacher at Adlai E. Stevenson High School in Lincolnshire, Illinois. He received an English degree from the University of Iowa and completed an MAT program at National Louis University, Evanston, Illinois. He is currently working on a principal endorsement program at Northeastern Illinois University. Patton also enjoys playing music and lives in Chicago with his wife, Katie.

**Nicole Boudreau Smith**, who has taught middle school, high school, and college-level English, teaches at Adlai E. Stevenson High School in Lincolnshire, Illinois. She considers the work she has undertaken to transform her method of instruction from teacher centered to student centered, empowering student voices instead of her own, to be the most important work of her career, and it is her goal to support other teachers to do the same. She lives in Evanston, Illinois, with her husband, Andrew.

**Claire Walter** is a founding faculty member and the English Department lead teacher of the Wolcott School, an independent college prep high school in Chicago for students with learning differences. Walter graduated summa cum laude from the University of Illinois, Urbana-Champaign, and received her master of arts in teaching from Johns Hopkins University. A regular presenter at the National Council of Teachers of English (NCTE) and the international Learning Disability Association (LDA) conferences, Walter is also a National Endowment for the Humanities scholarship recipient and a Golden Apple Teacher of Distinction.

**Lisa Whitmer** has been teaching English in secondary classrooms for the past thirty years. Working with students at Larkin High School in Elgin, Illinois, for the majority of her career has been a beautiful privilege. Teaching young adults to think critically never gets old. She obtained her undergraduate degree from Illinois State University and her masters of curriculum and instruction from Northern Illinois University. When not immersed in the classroom, she enjoys hiking through the woods and mountains with her husband, two children, and their dog, Ester.